The
Troubadour
Revival

The
Troubadour
Revival

a study of social change and traditionalism
in late medieval Spain

Roger Boase

Routledge & Kegan Paul
London, Henley and Boston

First published in 1978
by Routledge & Kegan Paul Ltd
39 Store Street,
London WC1E 7DD,
Broadway House,
Newtown Road,
Henley-on-Thames,
Oxon RG9 1EN and
9 Park Street,
Boston, Mass. 02108, USA
Set in Bembo 11pt 1pt leaded
and printed and bound in Great Britain at
The Camelot Press Ltd, Southampton
© Roger Boase 1978

British Library Cataloguing in Publication Data

Boase, Roger
The troubadour revival.
1. Spain—Social conditions
I. Title
301.29'46   HN583   78-40533
ISBN 0-7100-8956-2

To my teacher
A. D. Deyermond

Costumbre es en España entre los señores de estado que venidos a
la corte aunque no estén enamorados o que pasen de la mitad de la
edad, fingir que aman por servir y favorescer a alguna dama, y
gastar como quien son en fiestas y otras cosas que se ofrescen de
tales pasatiempos y amores, sin que les dé pena Cupido. (Gonzalo
Fernández de Oviedo y Valdés, *Batallas y quincuagenas*, MS. bat.
1, quinc. 1, diál. 28)

(It is a custom in Spain amongst men of quality, even if they are not
in love or have passed middle age, that they should, whilst attending
the court, feign love by serving and favouring a particular lady, and
that they should spend as much as befits their rank on festivities and
other things organised by way of pastimes and amorous intrigues,
without being troubled by Cupid.)

Si no se entiende bien el siglo XV, no se entiende bien nada de lo
que ha pasado después. (José Ortega y Gasset)

(If one does not have a correct understanding of the fifteenth century,
one cannot have a correct understanding of anything which has
happened since.)

Contents

Contents

List of plates

10   (i) Juana 'la Beltraneja' (1462–1530). Detail from a 'Genealogy of the Royal Houses of Spain and Portugal' (British Library, MS Add 12531, Table 10); (ii) Queen Isabella of Spain (r. 1474–1504). Painting; Spanish School (Windsor Castle. Reproduced by gracious permission of Her Majesty the Queen).

11   Queen Isabella with her daughters and a young man, presumably Philip the Fair, presenting her with a book. From Pedro Marcuello, 'Devocionario de la Reina Doña Juana la Loca' (Musée Condé, Chantilly, MS 604/1339, fol. 54ᵛ).

Preface

This book began life as part of a doctoral thesis submitted to London
University, and is a sequel to *The Origin and Meaning of Courtly Love*
(Manchester University Press, 1977). By this I mean that the latter was
intended as a prelude to my research on the culture of late medieval
Spain. As it happened, the prelude grew and developed into a work in
its own right, and during the course of my research I came to realise
that courtly love was very much more than a poetic convention: it was
a literary and sentimental ideology, a secular profession of faith, which,
from about the time of the First Crusade (1096–9) until the Protestant
Reformation, was the chief impulse behind the cultural achievements
and the style of life of the European aristocracy. It was my general
conclusion that this ideology was brought about by changes in the
social environment and by influences from the Arab world, and that
it was reinforced by behavioural codes that gave free expression to the
play instinct in man. I thus became interested in the more fundamental
cultural problems posed by the extraordinary abundance of amatory
verse composed in Spain during the fifteenth century. The uniform and
deliberately archaic character of much of this poetry and the evidence
of contemporary documents led me to believe that I was justified in
speaking of a 'troubadour revival', which occurred during the reign
of the Trastámaran dynasty (1369–1516), and to formulate the hypothesis that this cultural phenomenon was a response by the ruling
élite and their dependants to the decline of medieval values and
institutions. The subject of the present inquiry is therefore not
literature as such, but the crisis of the aristocracy as a factor determining
a revival of courtly and chivalric ideals and practices. Although this
work is chiefly concerned with Spain, it is hoped that it will indirectly
shed some light on contemporary events in other European countries.

I should like to mention those authors who have chiefly influenced my ideas and my theoretical approach. The first who springs to mind is Johan Huizinga, whose *The Waning of the Middle Ages* taught me the relevance of courtly and chivalric ideals as motives for action in everyday life as well as in diplomatic and military affairs. It is only to be regretted that he did not decide to incorporate Spain in his portrait of the period. Thorstein Veblen, in *The Theory of the Leisure Class*, drew my attention to the economic aspect of cultural history which Huizinga had underestimated, and persuaded me that the traditional liberal or civilised values of Western society are deeply impregnated by the mentality of the pre-capitalist élite. Max Weber helped me to differentiate between castes, estates and classes. His *Essays in Sociology* revealed that in Europe and elsewhere the court official was a key figure in the transition from a decentralised feudal or patrimonial society to a rational centralised bureaucracy. Arnold Toynbee placed Western society in its true perspective as one among several civilisations, some dead, some dormant and some still living, all subject to the same laws of change and decay. It was through reading a chapter of *A Study of History* that it occurred to me that the term 'archaism', defined as one of the ways in which a dominant minority tends to react to a situation of crisis, could be usefully applied to the aristocratic culture of fifteenth-century Spain.

There are a number of individuals to whom I owe a special debt of gratitude. I am particularly grateful to my father, Professor Alan Boase (whose intellectual abilities I could never hope to emulate), and my mother (whose life was cut short so tragically) for the encouragement which they have always given me; and to my academic supervisor, Professor Alan Deyermond, for the meticulous care with which he has corrected my imperfect typescripts. I wish to thank Professor Norman Cohn for finding time to read my work and for very generously supporting its publication; Miss Kathryn Stewart and Dr David McKie for the pains they took to assist me in the translation of Latin documents; Miss Margaret Johnston and Juan Masoliver for their comments on my translations; and Señorita María Dolores Mateu Ibars for checking my transcription of the Aragonese chancery documents quoted in Part III. Furthermore I would like to thank Professor Nicholas Round for giving me a long and detailed analysis of my work and Dr Angus Mackay for some useful last-minute suggestions. Peter Hopkins has shown great sympathy and patience; he is responsible for seeing this book into print. I am indebted to the staff members of the British Library, Senate House Library, London

Preface

Library, Westfield College Library, the Library of the Warburg
Institute and the Archivo de la Corona de Aragón for their
co-operativeness and willingness to oblige.

Her Majesty the Queen has given her gracious permission to
reproduce a picture in her collection at Windsor Castle.

I also wish to thank the following for allowing me to reproduce
miniatures, drawings and other works in their collections: the British
Library; the Victoria and Albert Museum; the Archivo de la Corona
de Aragón, Barcelona; the Landesbibliothek, Stuttgart; the Musée
Condé, Chantilly; and the Louvre.

I am grateful to the *Bulletin of Hispanic Studies* for allowing me to
reproduce the article on Urrea as an appendix. References to works
mentioned in the Bibliography are given in parentheses. Modern
editions of early texts are referred to by the author's name and
shortened title. Other works are referred to by the author's name and
the date of publication, e.g. Riquer, 1975. Foreign language quotations
are accompanied by English translations (except in the notes to the
final appendix). In Part III the original texts of documents that are
easily accessible have been omitted. Elsewhere this practice has been
adopted when quoting from modern critical works where the language
itself has no intrinsic importance. Accents and punctuation have been
supplied throughout.

R. B.
Easter 1977

xiii

Abbreviations

ACA	Archivo de la Corona de Aragón
BAE	Biblioteca de Autores Españoles
BARB	*Bulletin de l'Académie Royale de Belgique (Classe de Lettres)*
BBCat	*Bulletí de la Biblioteca de Catalunya*
BBMP	*Boletín de la Biblioteca Menéndez Pelayo*
BEHEH	Bibliothèque de l'École des Hautes Études Hispaniques (Bordeaux)
BH	*Bulletin Hispanique* (Bordeaux)
BHS	*Bulletin of Hispanic Studies*
BRAE	*Boletín de la Real Academia Española*
CC	Clásicos Castillanos
CCMe	*Cahiers de Civilisation Médiévale*
CFMA	Les Classiques Français du Moyen Âge
CH	Clásicos Hispánicos
CHA	*Cuadernos Hispanoamericanos* (Madrid)
CHE	*Cuadernos de Historia de España* (Buenos Aires)
CHM	Cuadernos de Historia Medieval (Valladolid)
CODOIN	*Colección de Documentos Inéditos para la Historia de España*, ed. Martín Fernández de Navarrete (112 vols, Madrid, 1842–95)
Col.Crón. Esp.	Colección de Crónicas Españolas
CSIC	Consejo Superior de Investigación Científica
CSSH	*Comparative Studies in Society and History* (The Hague)
CUP	Cambridge University Press
EETS	Early English Texts Society
EHT	Exeter Hispanic Texts
Fi	*Filología* (Buenos Aires)
FMLS	*Forum for Modern Language Studies*

Abbreviations

His	*Hispania*
HR	*Hispanic Review* (Philadelphia)
LCL	Loeb Classical Library
MAe	*Medium Aevum*
MLR	*Modern Language Review*
MUP	Manchester University Press
NBAE	Nueva Biblioteca de Autores Españoles
NRFH	*Nueva Revista de Filología Hispánica* (Mexico City)
OUP	Oxford University Press
PMLA	*Publications of the Modern Language Association of America*
PUF	Presses Universitaires de France
RAE	Real Academia Española
RAH	Real Academia de la Historia
RF	*Romanische Forschungen*
RFE	*Revista de Filología Española*
RFH	*Revista de Filología Hispánica*
RHM	*Revue d'Histoire Moderne*
RKP	Routledge & Kegan Paul
RLit	*Revista de Literatura*
RR	*Romantic Review*
SBE	Sociedad de Bibliófilos Españoles
SP	*Studies in Philology*
UCPMP	University of California Publications in Modern Philology
UISLL	University of Illinois Studies in Language and Literature
UNCSRLL	University of North Carolina Studies in Romance Languages and Literatures

Introduction

The late medieval period of European history was one of rapid socio-economic change, resulting in a moral and cultural crisis such as that which we are at present experiencing. It was a turning-point in history, witnessing the decline of a particular phase of civilisation to make way for a new order. I do not wish it to be inferred that in my opinion the post-medieval order was any better or any worse – an advance in one direction always has to be paid for, and one could argue that sometimes, as in the case of technological progress, the undeniable benefits are outweighed by the price. Nor do I wish to imply any moral judgment by the use of the term 'archaism' to describe the revival of medieval ideals and institutions at a time when these were rendered increasingly obsolescent by revolutionary changes in the nature of society. In *A Study of History* Arnold Toynbee shows that archaism or traditionalism is a characteristic response by the dominant social minority to a situation of crisis; it is 'one of those attempts at a forcible stoppage of change which result, in so far as they succeed, in the production of social enormities' (Toynbee, 1935-54, V, p. 384). 'Futurism' (i.e. messianism) takes root amidst the ranks of the proletariat or dispossessed and gains converts 'among the baffled and disillusioned devotees of an Archaism that has failed to bring salvation' (p. 398). Both patterns of thought and behaviour can be discerned in late medieval life, art and literature. The recurrence of revolutionary chiliasm as a consequence of oppression, insecurity and discontent has been studied by Norman Cohn[1] and others. Without making any claims for archaism as a universal law, I believe that it explains certain aspects of late medieval culture. The link between political conservatism and the desire to make art and literature conform to an ideal image of the past is mentioned by E. H. Gombrich:

From the time when Plato inveighed against change in music there is indeed a tendency of conservatism in language and in art to ally itself to restrictive governments. . . . Academies under royal tutelage were the outcome of this desire to arrest the flux of language and of art. (Gombrich, 1974, p. 932)

'The office of the leisure class in social evolution is', as Thorstein Veblen trenchantly puts it, 'to retard the movement and to conserve what is obsolescent' (Veblen, 1973, p. 137).

In the late Middle Ages cultural conservatism is perhaps nowhere more evident than in Spain. It is sometimes assumed that the cultural movement disseminated throughout the courts of Europe by the troubadours of southern France and Catalonia belonged only to the twelfth and thirteenth centuries. Guiraut Riquier (fl. 1254–92) is often considered the last of the troubadours; he is, for example, the last major poet represented in Martín de Riquer's magnificent anthology (Riquer, 1975). However, the court poetry of late medieval Spain was deliberately archaic and must therefore be seen within the perspective of the troubadour tradition. One could speak of a troubadour revival, associated with a general revival of courtly and chivalric idealism which spread from Aragon to Castile under the Trastámaran dynasty (1369–1516). Fidelity to the troubadour tradition is illustrated by the tendency to identify the terms lover and poet as though they were interchangeable; by the prominence given by poets to the subject of unrequited love; by the use of themes and forms that occur in early Provençal poetry; by the establishment of a poetic academy at Barcelona in 1393, modelled on the Consistori dels Sept Trobadors at Toulouse, which organised poetry competitions (the Floral Games) and commissioned the composition of rhyming dictionaries and treatises on Provençal grammar and versification;[2] by the continued use of the term 'trobador' (a word already found in a document from Palencia in the year 1197);[3] and finally by the social function which poetry fulfilled in the polite rituals of love and courtship. This cultural phenomenon was not exclusive to Spain. It was linked with an international court culture that flourished in Bohemia, Burgundy, France, England, Florence and other parts of Europe (Mathew, 1968). Yet few countries cultivated the Gay Science with such intensity as Spain where, despite close ties with Italy through the Spanish Neapolitan court of Alfonso V of Aragon and through trade and banking transactions with the Genoese, poets remained remarkably immune from contemporary Renaissance and humanist influences. The names of over 400 persons are listed by José Simón Díaz as having composed poetry in Spain during the fifteenth century (Simón Díaz, 1963–5, index), a figure that almost equals the number of European poets writing in Provençal from Guilhem IX (1071–1126) to Guiraut Riquier (d. *c.* 1292) (Frank, 1953–7, I, p. xvi, n. 1). Menéndez y Pelayo calculated, on the basis of a catalogue made by José Amador de los Ríos in 1863, that no fewer than 218 poets were composing in Castilian during the long reign of Juan II (r. 1419–54) (Menéndez y Pelayo, 1946, p. 31). These figures are astonishingly high. However, more recent bibliographical research suggests that, even making allowance for considerable overlaps and anomalies, there were at least 900 poets in fifteenth-century Spain.[4] The largest anthology, the *Cancionero general*, compiled over a period of twenty years by Hernando del Castillo, dedicated to a Valencian nobleman, the Count of Oliva, and published (soon after its completion) in 1511, contains 1,056 poems by about 170 poets[5] from many parts of the Iberian Peninsula; fifteen new names found their way into the 1514 edition, and more poetry was added to the 1535 and 1557 editions. One of the most striking features of this collection – a fair sample of the poetry that was being written in Spain in the latter half of the fifteenth century – is that almost all these poets, whether they were serious practitioners of their art or mere authors of occasional verse such as a motto displayed at a tournament, wrote about love, and they generally did so in a courtly manner. (Those who wish to know this proportion in terms of a percentage may consult the third volume of the *Bibliografía de los cancioneros castellanos del siglo XV y repertorio de sus géneros poéticos* by Jacqueline Steunou and Lothar Knapp.) This was the type of verse for which Spain became famous abroad. In 1538 Benoît de Court, in his Latin commentary on Marcial d'Auvergne's *Les Arrêts d'amours*, wrote as follows:[6]

Nulla enim gens frequentior, proclivior ad describendum amores, quam Hispanorum. Omnes enim illorum bibliothecae his libris refertae sunt, quos compitatim et per pergulas venales exponunt, scatent omnes villanicis amatoriis. In his enim exercent illorum idioma, quod Romansum vocant, ut ex eo plus honoris consequi arbitrentur, quam ex lingua Latina. Sic itaque sit ut pauci Latini apud eos sint.

(Truly no nation more frequently writes, or is more inclined to write, about love than the Spanish. Indeed all their libraries are crammed with books on the subject, which they display at the crossroads and at the cheap stalls; they all overflow with amorous villancicos. In these songs they use their own language which they call Romance, as they consider that more honour derives from it than from the Latin tongue. For this reason there are few Latin speakers among them.)

Pablo de Santa María's biographer, Cristóbal Santotís, records that Juan II enjoyed public recitations of Latin, as well as Spanish poetry (Santotís, 1591, fol. 41), but the nobility evidently did not share this enthusiasm. As Ian Michael says, they were 'indoctrinated with a belief that it was both socially improper and psychologically dangerous for those whose business was to defend the state with the sword to involve themselves seriously with letters, which were traditionally the business of priests'.[7] On the other hand the ability to improvise a love lyric in the vernacular had long been considered a sign of noble breeding. It is significant in this respect that over a third of the poets in the original list of contents of the *Cancionero general* can be classified as belonging to the upper nobility.[8]

Nineteenth-century literary historians, such as Boudet de Puymaigre and Menéndez y Pelayo, expressed their astonishment at the abundance of amatory verse which Spain was capable of producing during a century of civil war and popular unrest, aggravated by the rapaciousness of the aristocracy, economic paralysis and a number of disputed successions. This attitude is epitomised by the following quotation from P. J. Pidal's introduction to Eugenio de Ochoa's edition of the *Cancionero de Baena* (Madrid, 1851, pp. xlv–xlvi):

In these verses one looks in vain for the slightest reflection of life as it really was; and if other evidence did not exist, one might have been given to believe that that disturbed and turbulent age had been the fulfilment of a joyful and amorous Arcadia.

If, as it appears, court literature turned its back on life during the late Middle Ages, it surely had good cause to do so, and Huizinga has since taught us to appreciate that courtly and chivalric ideals, including the fiction of courtly love, informed manners and modes of conduct, transmuting disease, ugliness and the often despicable motives of war into a dream of heroism and love. It is therefore possible, as I have already suggested, that the troubadour revival and the prevalence of baronial anarchy were symptoms of the same sickness (if sickness is not too pejorative a term for the social and moral crisis experienced by the ruling classes at the close of the Middle Ages).

Apart from the virtual completion of the Reconquest (that is to say the reconquest of Spain from the Moors) in which Spanish knights had been engaged for over four centuries, the factors which undermined the nobility's *raison d'être* were by and large the same as those which throughout Europe presaged the modern capitalist era and the rise of the great nation states: the popular appeal for strong monarchical government; the growth of centralised bureaucracy; the king's reluctance to offer administrative posts to aristocrats; the absence of chivalry in the methods and motives of mechanised warfare; and the substitution of a monetary for a seigniorial economy. However, in Spain, contrary to the experience of most European countries, the number of persons entering the nobility (a non-productive class whose essential function was to wage war) increased rapidly throughout the fifteenth century, reaching an apex in the civil war period 1464–84 when the majority of poets in the *Cancionero general* were writing. This trend can be traced from the year 1369 when the pro-aristocratic faction brought the Trastámaran dynasty to power (see graph in Fig. 1, p. 160). The Trastámaran kings distributed lands and titles to those whom they believed would offer them military support, but in the long run this policy had the reverse effect: eventually this new aristocracy posed a threat to the maintenance of law and order and to the principle of monarchical government. Despite its wealth, strength and achievements abroad, the nobility must have sensed that it was becoming professionally redundant. It must also have been aware that through its lawlessness it had forfeited the moral authority which it had once exercised. Yet, instead of accommodating itself to the circumstances and applying its skills to the needs of the country, it retreated into an anachronistic world of make-believe, and cultivated literary conventions and chivalric practices associated with a utopian past.[9] It must be remembered that the attitudes of Spain's dominant minority – caste-consciousness, crusading idealism and scorn for trade and remunerative employment – had been shaped by centuries of antagonism and coexistence between Jews, Moslems and Christians. One does not have to agree with Américo Castro's historical methodology and existentialist terminology to concede that to some extent the tripartite ethnic-religious composition of the population of medieval Spain carried within it the seeds of its own destruction. The *hidalgo* mentality and religious prejudice paralysed the economy and ruled out any hope of racial harmony. Jews and Moors had excelled in many spheres including finance, tax administration, medicine, education, engineering, commerce and craftsmanship. When those who refused to be converted to Christianity were expelled from the country, Spanish Christians committed the regrettable error of despising these activities, endeavouring to fill the vacuum by 'the prestige of imperial power . . . in Europe and the New World' (Castro, 1971, p. 70). Jews who had been baptised, as many had been after the horrific pogroms of 1391, tended to adopt the values of their political masters. Spanish poets, many of whom were court officials, Jewish *conversos* and the lesser landless sons of noble families, relied on aristocratic patronage and modelled their style of life on that of the grandees.

There are, in addition, a number of subsidiary reasons why the expansion of the Spanish nobility should have resulted in an outburst of poetic activity and chivalric idealism. Those who had recently acquired lands and titles as a recompense for military or government service were anxious to demonstrate that they merited their new status. It was therefore natural that they should promote pageants, jousting matches, poetry debates and other pastimes that had long been considered the birthright of the aristocracy. Conspicuous expenditure on goods and services was in itself taken as proof of one's worth and generosity. Wives and daughters were relieved of domestic responsibilities, and were invested with 'that prerogative of leisure which was regarded as the chief mark of gentility' (Veblen, 1973, p. 53). Furthermore it is possible that a severe imbalance in the sex ratio in the upper social strata, produced by the great influx of men into the profession of knighthood, also contributed to the idealisation of women of noble birth (Moller, 1958–9). It was in the interests of the monarch to emulate in magnificence the courts of the magnates and to allure his noble subjects from the dangerous rural pastimes of conspiracy and rebellion; they in their turn wished to ingratiate themselves by writing or commissioning poems in praise of the ladies of the royal court. At a time when families were frequently divided in their political loyalties, the love lyric could serve as a means of reaffirming ties of kinship or fealty. Being essentially a patron–client relationship, courtly love may even have acted as a cohesive force against the very real threat of anarchy.

To understand the nature of this aristocratic culture, it is necessary to emphasise the close contacts which existed between Castile and her neighbours. Her non-European character has too often been exaggerated. In the late fourteenth century Castile became deeply enmeshed in European affairs through the intervention of foreign troops, trade, dynastic alliances, diplomatic relations and church politics. Many of the disasters, both natural and man-made, which afflicted Spain during this period were common to Europe: monetary inflation, anti-Semitic riots, popular discontent and outbreaks of plague. Even the measures taken to resolve these problems were markedly similar. For example, in 1351 the English Parliament and the Cortes of Castile simultaneously introduced a statutory wage freeze when the universal shortage of labour caused by the Black Death (1348–52) had compelled landlords to accede to demands for higher wages (a policy which, as in Europe during the present decade, failed to halt the wage-price spiral) (Cheyney, 1936, p. 328). In many parts of Europe in the last three decades of the fourteenth century, especially in courtly life and literature, there was a sudden shift in attitudes towards warfare, towards marriage and towards conventions governing the expression of emotion. The romantic idea, now largely taken for granted, that marriage should be based on love and free choice became widespread, and gentleness became the mark of a gentleman. These attitudes, expressed in the fine arts as well as in literature, were on the whole conservative, because they favoured ideals of courtesy and refinement that had long been advocated by the Provençal troubadours. They had in fact become an integral part of the aristocratic theory of society. In Spain the impetus for a definite troubadour revival came from the House of Barcelona, under whose patronage the movement had first flourished. (Provence and Roussillon had, after all, been principalities of the Aragonese Crown, and many of the early troubadours were actually Catalan or Aragonese by birth.) Aragonese culture was then assimilated by Castile, which became and has since remained (linguistically as well as politically) the dominant country in the Iberian Peninsula.

My general hypothesis may be summarised as follows: the troubadour revival in late medieval Spain was a conservative reaction to social crisis by those who belonged, or were affiliated, to a powerful, expanding and belligerent aristocracy; the crisis was produced by a discrepancy between social theory and social reality which could never be resolved, because the theory was based on the belief in a divinely pre-ordained system of social stratification in which change was inconceivable. The study falls into four parts. The first part analyses the aristocratic theory of medieval society with special reference to Spain. The second part places the troubadour revival in its historical perspective. The third part brings together some relevant documents. The fourth part consists of various appendices. Appendix 1 indicates the inflation of the titular nobility in fifteenth-century Spain by means of a table and a graph. Appendix 2 briefly mentions some of the messianic and apocalyptic prophecies coinciding with the troubadour revival. Appendix 3 discusses the life, literary works and poetics of Pedro Manuel Ximénez de Urrea, who was possibly the last of the Spanish troubadours.

Part I

The Aristocratic Theory of Society

At the close of the Middle Ages the dominant minority (comprising the nobility, the prelacy, the wealthier middle classes, and the court officials or civil servants) was reluctant to admit the need for readjustment when faced by the rapid development of a fluid monetary economy, the emancipation of rural labourers from vassalage, the decline of papal authority, the expansion of education and the rise of secular centralised government. Instead of coming to terms with these revolutionary changes, the privileged sought refuge in a theory of society that was further estranged from reality than it had ever been: the ideal of a united Christendom, conceived as a theocratic social hierarchy; the stratification of society into three occupational status groups (warriors, priests and labourers); the principle of corporative or conciliar government by the various branches of the body politic; the reciprocal obligations of feudalism; the quasi-sacramental institution of knighthood; and the metaphysical pretensions of Scholasticism. The theory rested on the premise that the established order is divinely pre-ordained and is therefore, from man's point of view, unchangeable. Anyone who advocated radical social reforms was liable to be branded a heretic. Orthodox Catholicism taught that every individual must uphold the honour of the station into which he was born, fulfilling his duties towards the community and towards the person to whom he had committed his services. Religion, warfare and agriculture remained the criteria by which, in theory, all human beings could be neatly categorised, which meant that the social and economic importance of the newly emerging bourgeoisie was inevitably overlooked. Chivalry remained the key whereby the chronicler sought to interpret historical events. Individual human relationships were still governed by notions of fealty and subservience, despite the fact that, with the growth of a non-seigniorial economy and the trend towards

11

centralised monarchy, the feudal contract (never firmly established in the Iberian Peninsula) ceased to exercise the same moral compulsion over the conscience of lords and vassals. Offices at court betrayed their origin in domestic household services, although they were fast developing into separate organs of government. Love based on the concept of patronage was still regarded as the knot uniting the estates of man and thus the remedy for social discord. In this part of the book three aspects of the medieval theory of society are discussed: the theory of the three estates; traditional forms of patronage; and the nature and functions of the royal court.

1

Theory of the Three Estates

During the Middle Ages the term 'estate' was frequently used indiscriminately to denote the moral and material conditions of men. One could thus speak of the estate of marriage, the estate of virginity, and even the estate (or state) of sin. However, in every instance the word had social implications, since to the medieval mind the circumstances of an individual were inseparable from his place in the social hierarchy. It can be rendered by the phrase 'station in life', but it also extends to those things, in particular land, which were considered indicative of status. In its more specific political sense, an estate may be defined as a form of association in which honour is the principle of solidarity, and in which, in the words of Max Weber, 'the material means of administration are autonomously controlled, wholly or partly, by the dependent administrative staff' (Weber, 1948, p. 81). In this sense the term is applicable not only to corporative bodies, such as guilds, universities and municipalities, each endowed with their own collective rights and prerogatives, but also to a feudal contract between two individuals, since a vassal was bound to administer his own fief and to equip himself for military service out of his own pocket. Fiefs, or lands held in feu, came to be known as 'estates' because they were a means of ensuring, at a time when money was scarce and unstable, that a person could provide for himself and thereby maintain his dignity and status.[1] The phrase 'real estate' is a legacy from an age when property, apart from personal effects, was almost invariably leasehold: men owned, not the land, but an 'estate' in the land, which was defined by the duties and privileges of the feudal contract. The importance of land as an index of social standing is illustrated by the following quotation from Caxton's *Sonnes of Aymon*: 'soo shall I gyve theym landes ynoughe for to mayntene theyr astate'.[2] It was of course not wealth or property as such which was a guarantee of status. An individual was eligible for membership of a status group by virtue of his birth, profession and education. Furthermore, even with the necessary qualifications, he was expected to abstain from activities which were stigmatised as demeaning, and he was encouraged to maintain standards of expenditure and modes of consumption commensurate with his status.[3] In fact, until very recently, it was status, rather than the 'market principle', which was the basis of social stratification.

The estates of man became a common literary topic, indeed a genre in its own right, when, as Ruth Mohl remarks, the Scholastic authors embarked on the encyclopaedic task of classifying the known universe:

While 'encyclopedias', 'treasures', 'bibles', and 'mirrors' catalogued the beasts and birds upon the earth, the fish in the waters under the earth, the hierarchies of angels in heaven above, the seven deadly sins, the Ten Commandments, the seven gifts of the Holy Spirit, the seven ages of the world, the four monarchies, plants, planets, stones, and anything else that submitted to classification, it was not likely that mankind would be omitted. (Mohl, 1933, p. 6)

It is no less significant that this genre should have developed at a time when men began to organise themselves into corporative bodies and political associations, that is to say into estates in the political sense defined above. Autonomous communes or *concejos* were established in many European towns from the middle of the eleventh century onwards. Government by representative assemblies came into existence in most parts of Europe between 1250, when the municipalities began to participate in the Cortes of Castile and Leon, and 1302, when the third estate first made its appearance in the French Estates-General (Cheyney, 1936, p. 329). In the late Middle Ages, when monarchical and papal authority were weak, this form of government acquired considerable prestige as the means whereby the nobility, the clergy and the municipalities could protect their traditional rights. This period likewise witnessed a flourishing revival of estates literature. It was an essentially conservative genre, harking back to an idyllic, but wholly fictitious, society in which class friction was non-existent and in which every man knew and accepted his place. The distinguishing traits of the genre are as follows: first, the author aimed to provide a comprehensive catalogue of the estates of mankind; second, he lamented the failure of the estates to fulfil their respective functions; third, he subscribed to the philosophy that the estates are a divine and immutable dispensation; fourth, he proposed remedies for the shortcomings of the different estates (Mohl, 1933, pp. 6–7; cf. Stéfano, 1966). Although Chaucer's intentions were less explicitly didactic, Jill Mann demonstrates that the portraits of the characters in the 'General Prologue' to *The Canterbury Tales* were based on this genre (Mann, 1973).

In both literature and politics it was customary to divide society into three occupational categories – *oratores*, *bellatores* (or *defensores*) and *laboratores* – according to a model of Indo-European origin. In ancient India there were three Aryan castes or 'colours' (Sanskrit *varṇa*): the *brāhmuṇa* (priests); the *kshatriya* or *rājanya* (kings, warriors and aristocrats); and the *vaiśya* (traders, merchants and townsmen).[4] Beneath the *vaiśya* were the non-Aryan *śūdra*, the untouchable caste, whose status was considerably lower than that of the slave class in ancient Greece and Rome. A similar tripartite division of society prevailed in the political assemblies of Europe (with the notable exception of Sweden and Aragon, which had four estates, the nobility or *bellatores* being split into an upper and a lower branch).[5] Within a Christian society there could be no place for an untouchable caste. Yet it should be emphasised that, according to the medieval theory of the three estates, the merchants and wealthy burgesses (who in some towns successfully defended their right to send representatives to these assemblies) shared the same estate as the serfs and farm labourers who formed the bulk of the population and whose condition was to all intents and purposes one of slavery. In theory, if not in practice, the structure of society had changed little since pre-feudal and pre-Christian times:[6]

> Throughout Gaul there are two classes of persons of definite account and dignity. As for the common folk, they are treated almost as slaves, venturing naught of themselves, never taken into counsel. The greater part of them, oppressed as they are either by debt, or by the heavy weight of tribute, or by the wrongdoing of the more powerful men commit themselves in slavery to the nobles, who have, in fact, the same rights over them as slaves. Of the two classes above-mentioned one consists of Druids, the other of knights.

The Druids, like the Christian clergy, were excused from military service, and claimed exemption from war taxes and other liabilities.

15

They also had important judicial powers. One of the worst penalties in ancient Gaul was to be forbidden to take part in religious ceremonies, in other words, to be excommunicated.[7] As in the Middle Ages, a warrior's status was proportionate to the number of his liegemen and dependants (Caesar, *The Gallic War*, VI, 15, p. 339).

The three estates were regarded as the essential and complementary components of every society, each deserving to be honoured for services performed on behalf of the community: the priest attends to the spiritual needs of the knight and the labourer, endeavouring to save their souls from eternal damnation; the knight protects the priest and the labourer from those who would do them harm; the labourer tills the land and ministers to the physical requirements of the priest and the knight. In the words of Don Juan Manuel, the classic exponent of the theory in Spain, 'todos los estados del mundo ... se ençierran en tres: al uno llaman defensores et al otro oradores et al otro labradores' (Manuel, *Lib. est.*, I, xcii, p. 192) (all the estates of the world ... are comprised in three: one they call the guardians, another the preachers, another the labourers). Alfonso de Cartagena, in a collection of laws concerning the nobility dedicated to Diego Gómez de Sandoval (c. 1430), still relies almost word for word on the Alphonsine law book known as *Las siete partidas* (compiled between 1256 and 1263):[8]

> Defensores es uno de los tres estados por que Dios quiso que mantuviese todo el mundo. Ca bien así como los que rruegan a Dios por el pueblo son llamados oradores. E otro sí los que labran la tierra y fazen en ella aquellas cosas por que los omes han de bevir et mantener se son dichos labradores.

> (The guardians [*defensores*] form one of the three estates by which God wished that all men should be sustained; similarly those who pray to God on behalf of the people are called preachers [*oratores*]; and those who till the soil and plant in it those things that are necessary for man's life and sustenance are called labourers [*laboratores*].)

Carlos, Prince of Viana, who translated Aristotle's *Ethics*, is no less conservative:

> es la ciudat o reyno de tres condiciones de gentes poblada, es a saber de sacerdotes que el divino servicio ministren, caballeros que la república defiendan, e otros artisanos e labradores que tracten

las cosas al sostenimiento de la cosa pública necesarias. (Yangüas y Miranda, 1840, I, p. 191)

(the city or kingdom is inhabited by three conditions of men, namely by priests who perform service to God, by knights who defend the commonwealth, and by craftsmen and labourers who deal with matters that are necessary for the support of the common weal.)

Francesc Eiximenis was probably the only late medieval hispanic author to have proposed the view that merchants formed an estate of their own which was vital to society both morally and economically.[9] Outmoded principles of social stratification remained firmly entrenched in chronicles, in codes of law, and in imaginative literature (perhaps more so in Spain than in the rest of Europe). In the newly emerging genre of biography, where one would expect to find man portrayed as a product of his own endeavours, character was still assessed within the context of two ideal social types: the knight and the noble prelate. Fernán Pérez de Guzmán, in his *Generaciones y semblanzas* (a work unflattering in its frankness), always considers it necessary in the case of a nobleman to judge the man's military qualities, and when, as sometimes happens, the person in question has not had any opportunity to engage in warfare, he conjectures how such a man would behave in the circumstances. Even ideals of sanctity were tinged with chivalric preconceptions: if a worthy prelate could not claim noble ancestry, then mitigating factors were discovered, such as the divine grace which inspired Pablo de Santa María and the prestige which his family enjoyed amongst his people, the Jews, or the vast erudition of Alfonso de Madrigal (El Tostado), the son of a family of labourers. The author of the *Crónica de don Álvaro de Luna* (probably Gonzalo Chacón) finds it necessary to demonstrate, at some length, his hero's nobility of birth and character. The author of the *Relación de los hechos de Miguel Lucas de Iranzo* carefully omits any reference to events which occurred before his protagonist had been ennobled by the king. The exclusion of certain well-known personages, such as Martínez de Toledo and Juan de Mena, from Fernando del Pulgar's *Claros varones de Castilla* (1486) could be attributed to similar motives. In all these works the moral supremacy of the knight is taken as axiomatic: the chief purpose of biographical history is to conserve the memory of honour gained through military exploit (Romero, 1944).

Political and social conservatism is still more evident in medieval treatises on chivalry, warfare, protocol and the education of princes, all of which tended to rely heavily on Aristotle's *Politics* and *Ethics*, which were indebted, in their turn, to Plato's *Republic*. Examples of the genre in fifteenth-century Spain include Juan Rodríguez del Padrón's *La cadira del honor* (*Obras*, pp. 131–73), Diego de Valera's *Espejo de verdadera nobleza* and *Exortación a la paz*,[10] and Rodrigo Sánchez de Arévalo's *Speculum vitae* and *Suma de la política*.[11] The authors of such works discovered in Greek philosophy a tripartite caste system, based on a totalitarian ethic, which endorsed those privileges and inequalities that existed in medieval society. They discovered a theory of social justice which maintained that the interest of the state, rather than the well-being of the individual, is the criterion of morality; that the ruling warrior caste possesses an hereditary moral supremacy; that the sovereignty of the rulers should be unchecked by the masses; that the workers or producing classes should be denied the rights of citizenship; that no social mobility, intermarriage or intermingling should be permitted between different castes; and that conflict between the castes or classes should be regarded as a sign of social degeneration. In Plato's ideal state there are three classes of men: the guardians or rulers, their armed auxiliaries and the workers. However, as Karl Popper points out, the guardians and their auxiliaries are members of a single caste, because 'the guardians are old and wise warriors who have been promoted from the ranks of the auxiliaries'. There are therefore 'only two castes, the military caste – the armed and educated rulers – and the unarmed and uneducated ruled, the human sheep' (Popper, 1966, I, p. 46). Plato and Aristotle show little sympathy for the condition of the unprivileged; their sole function is to provide for the material needs of the élite. The European aristocracy thus inherited from the Greek and Roman patriciate the tradition of *otium cum dignitate*, believing with Aristotle that 'leisure is necessary, both for growth in goodness and for the pursuit of political activities' (*Politics*, VII, ix, p. 301): 'And hit behoveth also that the comyn peple laboure the londes for to brynge fruytes and goods/ whereof the knyght and his beestes have theyr lyvyng/And that the knyght reste hym and be at seiourne after his noblesse' (Llull, *Ordre of Chivalry*, pp. 19–20). This system of social, political and economic inequality, from which only the dominant minority stood to gain, was further justified by belief in the providential character of the status quo. It was customary for medieval writers to back up their arguments with two analogies: that which exists between the Christian community and the human body, and that which exists between the terrestrial and the celestial hierarchy. The king is the head or the heart which governs the body; the knights are the limbs which defend it; the labourers are the feet which bear its weight. Court officials are symbolised, appropriately enough, by the stomach.[12] The image of the church or Christian society as a mystical body was expressed by St Paul in his Epistle to the Romans (xii, 4 and 5): 'For as we have many members in one body, and all members have not the same office: So, we being many, are one body in Christ, and every one members one of another.' Pagans, vagabonds, pirates, slaves and other social pariahs were scarcely considered true members of the mystical body of the human species.[13] Human (or perhaps one should say Christian) society was conceived as imperfectly mirroring the supernatural hierarchy of archangels, angels and saints assembled around the throne of God, the supreme overlord.[14] According to Gutierre Díez de Games, God has three chivalric orders: the first is the order of angels, many of whom supported Lucifer when he rebelled; the second is the order of martyrs who died for the Christian faith; the third is that of just kings and good knights who fight to defend the church and the kingdom. This third order will be rewarded with the celestial thrones vacated by Lucifer and the wicked angels (*Victorial*, pp. 38–9). The institution of knighthood and the military profession were sanctified by the concept of religious chivalry and by the belief, Islamic in origin, that those who die fighting unbelievers will be awarded eternal delights in Paradise.[15] Religious and secular attitudes thus became deeply interfused as in Islam (which makes no distinction between the two spheres). One could even speak of a feudalisation of religion: 'A man had to pray to God on both knees, to his lord on one knee' (Green, 1971, p. 187). The gesture of the hands in prayer was originally one of feudal submission: 'The ancient attitude of prayer, with hands outstretched, was replaced by the gesture of the joined hands, borrowed from "commendation", and this became throughout Catholic Christendom the characteristic praying posture' (Bloch, 1965, I, p. 233). Theologians and priests exhorted each man to uphold the honour of the status and the profession into which he had been born, without seeking to ascend or descend the social ladder:

Certa cosa és que nostre senyor Déu, creador del cel e de la terra e de tot quant fo, és e serà, feu diferència, e departiment e graus

en los cels, e encara en los inferns, hoc e en la terra. . . . Los
àngels no són tots de una o egual jerarquia, ans hi ha majors, e
mijans e menors. Los sancts del cel no han tots egual grau de
glòria; emperò tots e cascun se tenen per bé contents de lur grau;
los menors són obedients e reverents als majors, e tots a Déu.
(Eiximenis, *Doctrina*, p. 94)

(It is certain that our Lord God, creator of heaven and earth and of
all that was, is and shall be, made distinction, separation and degrees
in the heavens and also in the regions of hell, and likewise on
earth. . . . The angels are not all of one and the same rank, but are
high, medium or low. The saints of heaven do not possess the same
degree of bliss; however each and every one considers himself
content with his degree; the lower obey and revere the higher and
all obey and revere God.)

Jean Gerson preached that every man should be content with his lot:

The people should be content with its estate, and should suffer itself
to be led and conducted by the head and by the two sovereign
estates; or otherwise the order of the *corps mystique* of the commonwealth should be utterly perverted. (Green, 1971, p. 187)

The same sentiment was expressed by Hugh Latimer: 'Well, I woulde
al men woulde loke to their dutie, as God hath called them, and then
we shoulde have a florishyng christian common weale.'[16] In the words
of Plato, 'When each class in the city minds its own business, the
money-earning class as well as the auxiliaries and the guardians, then
this will be justice' (Popper, 1966, I, p. 90). An estate which failed to
comply with the norm, either by neglecting its predetermined
functions or by assuming the functions of another estate, committed an
offence against the will of God. Similarly an individual who strove to
enter an estate for which he had not been prepared by birth and
upbringing was accused not only of diminishing his honour and that
of his estate, but of contradicting the providential order. Victims of
injustice were taught to take comfort in the thought that, at the final
reckoning, each man would be rewarded or punished according to his
deserts. The idea of the perfectability of society was quite alien to the
medieval mind, and any attempt to seriously question the justice of the
established order was liable to be interpreted as a form of sacrilege
inviting anarchy. Even the reformer Wyclif condemned as heretical

those revolutionary doctrines which were being formulated at the time of the Peasant's Revolt of 1381, including the idea of the brother-hood of man and the theory that, through their un-Christian conduct, feudal lords had forfeited their right to command obedience:[17]

> But here þe fend moveþ summe men to seie þat Cristene men schullen not be servauntis or þrallis to heþene lordis, siþ þei ben false to God and lasse worþy þan Cristene men; neither to Cristene lordis, for þei ben breþeren in kynde, and Ihus Crist bou3te Cristene men on þe crois and made hem fre; but a3enst þis heresie Poul writiþ þus in Goddis lawe: 'What kynne servauntis ben under 300k of servage deme þei here lordis worþi alle manere honour or worschipe, þat þe name and techynge of þe Lord be not blasphemid'.... And þis is a feyned word of the Anticristis clerkis þat... servauntis and tenauntis may wiþdrawe here servyce and rentis fro here lordis þat lyven opynly a cursid lif.

It should be mentioned, in parenthesis, that there did exist a dynamic revolutionary anti-aristocratic model of society which was actually heretical, because it was established on theological historicist principles and denied the centrality of the dogma of the Redemption. There are a number of unexpected parallels between the ideas of Joachim da Fiore and conventional estates literature: a providential plan, a vision of love and a system of three estates (or *status* in Latin) referring, not to static social strata, but to historical epochs, linked chronologically with the three persons of the Trinity, Father, Son and Holy Ghost. These ideas also contain the seeds of Hegelian and Marxist thought, in particular the notion of a dialectical progression in history towards a communistic earthly paradise. The age of the Father was one of servile obedience; that of the Son is one of filial servitude; that of the Spirit will be one of freedom and love (Reeves, 1969, pp. 18–19). In the late Middle Ages men increasingly began to perceive cycles of retribution and redemption in history, and the oppressed classes were encouraged by demagogues to equate the ideal of evangelical poverty with the slogan *vox populi vox dei*.[18] It was a short step from the belief that the poor are God's special representatives to the idea that the populace is the divinely appointed catalyst in an inevitable historical process.

The preservation of status became a veritable obsession when the barriers between traditional status groups were eroding and no longer bore any semblance of reality. Thus Alexander Barclay, in his *Shyp of*

Folys (London, 1509, fol. 77), warned of the terrible consequences of promoting commoners, and denounced the folly of coveting another man's estate as one of the characteristic evils of his time:

> But it is great foly and also shame doutles
> For Carles to coveyt this wyse to clyme so hye
> And nat be pleasyd with theyr state and degre.

John Gower, over a century earlier, had used the tale of Icarus in *Confessio amantis* to illustrate this same vice, the moral being that 'in service/It grieveth forto go to hye' (*Complete Works*, II, bk IV, p. 329, ll. 1036–7). Shakespeare's attitude is proverbial: 'Take but degree away, untune that string,/And, hark, what discord follows' (*Troilus and Cressida*, I, iii, ll. 109–10). In Spain Juan Pacheco, Master of Santiago (who was himself a social upstart), saw the common people as a threat to his position and criticised them for dressing in a manner which did not befit their humble status:

> Tanta es la pompa y vanidad generalmente hoy de todos los
> labradores, y gente baja, y que tienen poco, en los traheres suyos,
> y de sus mugeres e hijos, que quieren ser iguales de los caballeros
> y dueñas, y personas de honra y estado: por lo qual sostener
> gastan sus patrimonios, y pierden sus haciendas, y viene grand
> pobreza, y grand menester, sacando paños fiados, y otras cosas, a
> más grandes precios de lo que valen. (Sempere y Guariños,
> 1788, I, pp. 183–4)

> (So great is the pomp and vanity of all labourers, common folk and
> people with few possessions nowadays that, in the way they and their
> wives and children dress, they wish to equal knights and ladies and
> persons of honour and substance. To fulfil this ambition they
> squander their inheritance and lose their savings, and by buying
> cloth on credit and other things at higher prices than they are worth
> they are brought to great poverty and want.)

These complaints, which were made in 1469 at a chapter of the Order of Santiago, were motivated not by a genuine concern that commoners would become impoverished through their extravagance, but by a growing sense of insecurity amongst the nobility. It is significant that in the following year the king authorised the local Hermandades to patrol the highways in order to protect travellers from the lawlessness of the Master of Santiago and his bands of armed knights.[19] The elaborate ceremonial which marked a person's initiation into a new order or estate was designed to check social mobility and to maintain the appearance of a rigid hierarchy, while at the same time permitting some fluidity. Sumptuary laws, which prescribed the modes of consumption appropriate to different degrees of men, covering such items as clothes, household possessions, wedding and funeral expenses and even food, naturally had to be modified to make allowance for changes in the wealth of the nation and in the type of goods available. Newly acquired wealth was not respectable unless it was accompanied by a title of honour which conferred upon its bearer the fiction of gentle birth. The clerical estate was open (at least theoretically) to all men, but the lack of a noble pedigree was an obstacle which had to be surmounted by the commoner who wished to gain access to the estate of knighthood. Furthermore, the squire and the novitiate priest had to undergo a period of apprenticeship, during which, according to the theory of education which prevailed during the Middle Ages, they imbibed the skills, manners and ethos of the station in life to which they aspired (see below, pp. 60–2).

It was generally agreed that strife was the chief cause of social decay: 'el principal impedimiento que corrompe toda çibdad o república es la división e intestina discordia de los çibdadanos e súbditos' (Sánchez de Arévalo, *Suma de la política*, p. 111). The opposite of discord is the love which should, in theory, bind together the social estates and link them with God. It is for this reason that the discussion of the shortcomings of the estates in the prologue of John Gower's *Confessio amantis* is not a mere digression. He evokes a golden age of chivalry when the temporal lords, the clergy and the commons lived in harmony and each man knew his place, and he suggests that this idyllic age was lost because men sinned through a lack of love:

> Now stant the crop under the rote,
> The world is changed overal,
> And thereof most in special
> That love is falle into discord . . .
> But now men tellen natheles
> That love is fro the world departed,
> So stant the pes unevene parted
> With hem that liven now adaies.
> (bk II, ll. 118–21, 168–71)

In the late fourteenth century, after years of warfare and class friction, men could not fail to agree with Gower's message. It is surely no coincidence that this was the first work of English literature which was translated into Castilian.[20] The same panacea for social ills was proposed by Sir John Cheke, tutor to Edward VI, in his *True Subject to the Rebell* (1549), at the time of the insurrection in Devon and Cornwall:

> For love is not the knot onely of the Commonwealth whereby divers parts be perfectly joyned together in one politique bodie, but also the strength and might of the same, gathering together into a small room with order, which scattered would else breed confusion and debate. (Mohl, 1933, pp. 52–3)

Ramon Llull had little to say concerning the erotic aspect of chivalry, which was as yet undeveloped, but he did assert, in his *Libre de l'orde de cavayleria* (*c.* 1275), that love, inspired by a lively sense of status, was the basis of social order:

> Thordre is not gyuen to a man for that he shold loue his ordre only/but he ouʒt to loue the other orders. For to loue one ordre/and to hate another/is nothynge to loue ordre/For god hath gyuen none ordre that is contrarye to other ordre. (*The Book of the Ordre*, pp. 26–7; cf. *Libre*, II, v, p. 17)

Nobility (defensores)

Military strength, landed estates, high office, ancient lineage and moral integrity or magnanimity are among the ideas conjured up by the word nobility. According to the *Siete partidas, gentileza* may be acquired by noble birth, wisdom, prowess in arms and fine manners (II, iii, 2). As a class, or, to be more precise, as a status group, the nobility claimed a monopoly of these attributes. The nobility can thus be broadly defined as the military, proprietary, office-holding, hereditary and exemplary estate; a person who was not a knight, nor a feudal landlord, nor a high official, nor a noble by birth, nor an honourable man could scarcely be called a nobleman. However, a nobleman did not necessarily possess all these qualifications, and theorists differ in their order of priorities. 'Nobility', wrote Aristotle, 'rests on excellence and inherited wealth' (*Politics*, IV, viii, 9). Dante cited

Juvenal's maxim 'Nobilitas animi sola est atque unica virtus' (*Satire*, VIII, l. 20) (Nobility of soul is the one and only virtue), and observed that men may be ennobled either by their own virtues or by those of their forebears.[21] In *De monarchia* he subscribed to the syllogism that 'since honour is the reward of virtue, and all precedence is honour, all precedence is a reward of virtue' (II, iii, 3), but in the *Convivio* he recognised that 'inheritances devolve by bequest or succession on the wicked more often than on the good'.[22] Unlawful gain does not fall to the good, because they reject it; lawful gain seldom comes to them, because they are not sufficiently concerned about material things. Dante therefore wrote: 'È gentilezza dovunqu'è vertute,/ma non vertute ov'ella' (IV, canz. ll. 101–2) (And nobility is found wherever there is virtue, but the reverse is not true). This growing stress on the moral and intellectual qualities associated with nobility was to become a characteristic feature of the Renaissance, but the aristocracy of the gentle heart, as Dante well knew, was an idea invented by twelfth-century troubadours: 'Nuz n'est villains se du cuer ne lui muet'[23] (No one is a villein unless it comes from his heart). Some of the early troubadours regarded nobility of birth as a potential honour, which had to be earned not only by deeds of prowess but by the social virtues of generosity, courtesy and refinement. These poets, most of them court officials or members of the lesser nobility (a social group without wealth, power or ancient ancestry), contended that the barons had no right to inherit noble status if they were not prepared to share their privileges with others. Thus Folquet de Romans urged the Emperor Frederick II, whom he addresses as *fre de rico* (*frein des riches* or 'bridle of the rich'), to strip the lords of their estates, arguing that their greed and tyranny should be considered a breach of contract (Köhler, 1964). A person who expected every castle to capitulate without a struggle and who refused to submit himself to love's precepts did not display true nobility of character. The honour which a lady could bestow upon her suitor was, in a sense, the spiritual equivalent of an unconditional gift of money from the king (which was indeed defined in Spain by the term *honor*) (*Siete part.*, IV, xxvi, 2; cf. below, p. 28).

According to Ramon Llull, the noble caste of knights was established to halt the world's decline from charity, peace and justice into anarchy. One man in every thousand (hence the supposed etymology of *miles*, Latin for soldier) was selected for his wisdom, justice and virtue and charged with the task of imposing order (*Lib. cav.*, I, i). This merito-cratic myth of origins was variously interpreted. On the one hand, there were those who continued to regard nobility as an hereditary honour and a moral predisposition, and they could buttress their arguments with quotations from Aristotle's *Politics*: 'The nobly born are citizens in a truer sense of the word than the low born. . . . Those who come from better ancestors are likely to be better men, for nobility is excellence of race' (III, xiii, 2–3). This was the opinion of Sánchez de Arévalo in his *Speculum vitae*:

> nous pouvons congnoistre clèrement que les princes ne pouent faire de leur seule volonté d'ung villain ung noble homme . . . villeinnie et deshonneur est des parens innobles (fol. c5^r)

> (we know full well that princes cannot of their own free will transform a commoner into a nobleman . . . villeiny and dishonour derive from ignoble kin.)

Royal jurists, on the other hand, tended to oppose the concept of hereditary nobility, because it weakened the monarch's authority. At a much later date one finds monarchists arguing that to bestow nobility on a commoner is to restore to him the status which he had once possessed before mankind degenerated into inequality:[24]

> es de saber, que lo natural, es la filiación, la sangre y el parentesco, y no la nobleza, que esta fue una calidad abstracta, dada por el Príncipe: y assí no es natural, ni cosa que se introduxo por propagación, ni se infundió con la sangre y sustancia de los padres.

> (in short, what is natural is a person's filiation, blood and kinship, not his nobility, for this was an abstract quality given by the monarch: and thus it is not something natural, being neither introduced through propagation nor infused with the blood and substance of the parents.)

Most fifteenth-century authors would have rejected such a theory. Rodríguez del Padrón, in *La cadira del honor*, does not accept the proposition that nobility rests solely on the monarch's will:

> la verdadera nobleza requiere quatro dignidades, es a saber: abtoridad del prínçipe o del prinçipado, claridad de linaje, buenas costumbres e antigua riqueza. (*Obras*, p. 139)

(true nobility requires four marks of distinction, namely the authority of the prince or principality, purity of lineage, good manners and inherited wealth.)

Diego de Valera cites a number of different definitions of nobility in *Espejo de verdadera nobleza*, including that of the Italian jurist Bartolus de Saxoferrato (1314–57): 'Nobleza es una calidad dada por el príncipe, por la qual alguno paresce ser más acepto allende los otros onestos plebeos' (Penna, *Prosistas*, pp. 92–3) (Nobility is a quality conferred by the ruler, whereby a person appears more acceptable than others who are respectable commoners). He had been told by French knights that in France a commoner who has followed the profession of a knight for seven years without reproach is considered a gentleman (*gentil onbre*). Yet, at the same time, he seems to have approved of Aristotle's anti-humanitarian doctrine that virtue and malice are what distinguish the free man from the slave and the nobleman from the commoner (p. 100). He later modifies this assertion by saying, with St Thomas Aquinas, that nobility is not in itself a virtue, but the sign (*señal*) of past, present or future virtue,[25] adding that it is a responsibility rather than an honour (p. 101). The most original feature of this treatise is its defence of the nobility of the Jewish race. Despite their divergences, social theorists (whether or not they were pro-monarchist) were committed to a system based on the concept of status.

Until the close of the Middle Ages the nobility was essentially a class of warriors. It was important (but not essential) for a nobleman to be knighted, because it gave him the right to fight on horseback, to wear a sword and armour, and, in return for his military duties, to enjoy certain privileges which will be discussed below. A knight did not necessarily have a fief, nor was he necessarily the heir to a title, although a knight who did not belong to the territorial hierarchy was unable to claim many of the benefits associated with the noble estate. In Spain the nobility was divided into three grades: *ricoshombres*, *hidalgos* and *caballeros*. The first were distinguished by their landed estates and high office; the second by their noble lineage; the third by their knighthood. The allegory depicted on the walls of Love's tent in the *Libro de Buen Amor* suggests a parallel between the progression from *caballero* to *ricohombre* and that of the seasons from spring to autumn.[26] As in Gower's *Confessio amantis*, the social estates seem to be linked with the idea of the ages of man, since the calendar year is an image of human life from youth to old age, exemplifying the process of growth, maturity and decay: 'Quod status hominis/Mensibus anni equiperatur.'[27] Great emphasis is placed on the proximity of the three partners in each social category and on the impossibility of their ever being able to touch one another, as though the cycle of the seasons and social aspirations were motivated, like the spheres in the Neoplatonic cosmos, by the frustrated desire for the Absolute.

Degrees of the nobility

Ricoshombres

The *ricoshombres*, who were generally called *grandes* in the fifteenth century, formed the highest category of the nobility. In Aragon and Navarre, according to a legal fiction of sixteenth-century historiography, it was decreed by the Fuero de Sobrarbe in AD 839 that a king had no right to call an assembly, administer justice, wage war or make peace without consulting twelve *ricoshombres* or twelve of the oldest and wisest men in the realm:

> fue de allí adelante de los nobles y principales barones, que se hallaron en la elección y en la defensa de la tierra: a los quales y a sus descendientes legítimos llamaron ricos hombres, a quien los reyes tenían respeto, que parecían ser sus yguales, con quien eran obligados a repartir las rentas de los lugares principales que se yvan ganando, y ellos a servir con sus cavalleros y vassallos, según la cantidad que montava lo que en cada ciudad o villa se señalava al rico hombre, que llamavan honor. (Zurita, *Anales*, I, bk I, v, fol. 9ᵛ)

> (Thenceforward the nobles and chief barons, who took part in the choice and defence of the land, and their legitimate offspring were called *ricoshombres*; such was the esteem bestowed upon them by the kings that they seemed their equals: the king was obliged to share with them the revenues of the main towns that were then being conquered, and they were obliged to serve him with their knights and vassals, in proportion to the quantity of income, known as *honor*, appointed to the *ricohombre* in each town or borough.)

It has been argued that the magnates acquired the title *ricoshombres* because monarchs had, since the earliest days of the Reconquest, adopted the practice of offering the largest share of conquered land

and booty to the bravest warriors (Chaytor, 1933, pp. 109–10). Whilst it is true that the *ricoshombres* undoubtedly owed their pre-eminence to their wealth (without which they would have been unable to fulfil their obligation to maintain a suitably equipped army), the adjective *ricos* originally meant 'ruling', not 'rich': '*Ricos* is from the same root as *Reich*, or the last syllable of bishopric, or the Latin word *regere*. *Ricos hombres* means men of the ruling class, not rich men' (Cheyney, 1936, p. 80 n.). Rodríguez del Padrón was aware of this etymology, because he mentions in connection with the *ricoshombres* the Germanic origin of the name Manrique (*Obras*, p. 133). Sebastián de Covarrubias shares the same view in his *Tesoro de la lengua castellana* (II, p. 162), although we also learn from him that some would derive the term *rico* from the Hebrew *rich*, meaning 'vanity'. Juan Manuel was careful to differentiate between *omnes ricos* and *ricosomnes*: the former are wealthy townsmen or merchants, where-as the latter are noblemen whose wealth permits them the privilege of having armed nobles amongst their vassals and of carrying their own banner (*Lib. est.*, I, lxxxix, p. 183). In the fifteenth century the term fell into disuse. In his *Doctrinal de cavalleros* (tít. v) Alfonso de Cartagena ascribed the term's decline from current usage to the proliferation of new titles (dukes, marquises and viscounts). The dignity was finally abolished in 1520, when the Emperor Charles V, who was totally averse to the aristocratic concept of the king as *primus inter pares*, made a definitive separation of the nobility into *Títulos* and *Grandes*, to be addressed as *primos* and *parientes* respectively. Henceforward the upper nobility was unable to assume any prerogatives until these had been approved and confirmed by the monarch, who was 'superior a los más Grandes' (Fernández de Béthencourt, 1897–1920, I, p. 25).

Luis Salazar y Castro distinguishes between three types of *ricoshombres* (Salazar, 1688, pp. 262–4). First of all, there were those who belonged to the ancient feudal nobility (*ricoshombres de sangre*): the Castros, Laras, Haros, Ponces, Guzmanes, Meneses and Girones. Second, there were those invested with the dignity of *rico-hombría* as a concomitant to their tenure of a royal domain (*ricoshombres de estado*). Third, there were those whose office at court automatically conferred upon them the status of *ricohombre* (*ricoshombres de dignidad*); these officials included the Majordomo (*mayordomo mayor*); the Chief Standard-Bearer (*alférez mayor*), Provincial Governors (*adelantados mayores*), Magistrates (*merinos mayores*), Chief Accountants (*contadores mayores*) and the Chief Notaries or Clerks (*notarios mayores*). In Aragon, where the nobility was represented by two separate juridical bodies or estates at the Cortes, a sharper division seems to have existed between the hereditary (or old) and the non-hereditary (or new) classes of *ricoshombres*: the *ricoshombres de natura* regarded themselves as the descendants of the early conquerors of Aragon, many of whom had held territory as the vassals of Charlemagne; the *ricoshombres de mesnada* were closely attached to the royal household (*mesnada*), and their families had generally served for several generations as royal officials and *mesnaderos* (Madramany, 1788, pp. 94–5). This second class of *ricoshombres* was officially established in Aragon by Jaime I (1213–76), much to the resentment of the old feudal aristocracy. According to Zurita, the practice of promoting favourites from the families of court retainers had long been current in Aragon:[28]

> era costumbre en los tiempos antiguos sublimar a aquel estado [de ricohombre] a los que eran caballeros que llamaba mesnaderos que de tal manera eran vasallos y de la Casa del Rey, ellos y sus padres y abuelos naturales de Aragón.

> (in the old days it was customary to promote to the estate of *ricohombre* those knights who were called *mesnaderos* [or palace retainers], since they and their native Aragonese parents and grand-parents were vassals and members of the royal household.)

In Castile there were also of course *ricoshombres* who owed their position to royal favouritism:

> Et ay otros [ricoshombres] que, seyendo cavalleros o infançones por privança que an de los rreys, tienen los rreys por bien de les dar vasallos et pendón, et llámanse rricos omnes (Manuel, *Lib. est.*, I, lxxxix, p. 183).

> (And there are others, who have become knights and *infanzones* through royal favour, whom kings see fit to offer vassals and a banner, and they call themselves *ricoshombres*.)

In Aragon the *ricohombre* could elect any one of his male offspring to succeed him, whereas in Castile the upper nobility adhered to the principle of primogeniture and established *mayorazgos* (landed estates entailed to the eldest son) (Madramany, 1788, p. 75). The landless sons of *ricoshombres* can be considered members of the second degree of nobility.

Infanzones and *hidalgos*
The second category of the nobility, that of the *infanzones* and *hidalgos*, comprised worthy landed knights, military commanders, and old families in court service holding fiefs from the Crown. The terms *infanzón* and *hidalgo* are not synonymous. Most knights were *hidalgos*, but only a few were *infanzones* or, as they were called in Aragon, *mesnaderos*. An *infanzón* was, according to Juan Manuel, a knight who had gained more wealth and honour than other knights in the service of his lord, and who had family estates (*solares çiertos*) and was able to marry his daughters into the lower echelons of the upper nobility (*Lib. est.*, I, xc, p. 184). In the *Siete partidas* the *infanzones* are equated with the Italian captains and vavasours (vassals of vassals, or *vassi domici*), who do not, despite their wealth and ancestry, have the right to exercise jurisdiction over their vassals, except when they are acting on the king's behalf as magistrates (*regidores*) or governors (*adelantados*) (II, i, 13). *Infanzones* were generally obliged to live in the countryside, because most towns refused to grant them permission to reside within their precincts. There were good reasons for mistrust: the houses of *infanzones* (known as *palacios*) were immune from trespassers and they could thus be used by criminals as places of asylum (Carmen Carlé, 1961, pp. 87–8); and in general the powers with which the *infanzones* were endowed were seen as a threat to municipal rights and prerogatives.[29]

The etymology of *hidalgo* is still a subject of some dispute. The *fijodalgo* is a 'son of wealth' or a 'son of honour' ('algo que quiere tanto dezir en lenguaie de España como bien', *Siete part.*, II, xxi, 2). Corominas maintains that, like *ricohombre*, the word originally meant 'una persona con bienes de fortuna' (a person with material wealth), whereas Menéndez Pidal would translate the term as 'hijo de persona de valer'[30] (son of a person of importance). The distinction is, however, largely an artificial one, because it is obvious that, both as regards the *ricohombre* and the *hidalgo*, wealth, honour, power and lineage were inextricably interlinked. The term *honor* was applied to gifts of money from the king, while *tierra* was the technical term for a regular fee paid to members of the nobility. The ambiguous term *algo* seems in fact to be a Castilian rendering of the Arabic *ni'mat*, meaning wealth, cattle, grace or favour. The construction *fijos d'algo* or *hijos de bien* is, as Américo Castro has shown, the counterpart of the Hebrew *benē tovim* and the Arabic *awlād ni'mati*: 'The "filial" manner of designating the condition or quality of a person is Semitic, that is to say, both Hebraic and Arabic' (Castro, 1971, p. 266). María de Carmen Carlé notes that the word *hidalgo* does not occur in juridical documents prior to 1187, although it is used several times in the *Cantar de Mio Cid*, which leads her to conjecture that it was initially a term of disparagement applied by *infanzones* of ancient ancestry to those who had recently joined their midst, and that it later gained currency as a blanket term for *infanzones* (Carmen Carlé, 1961, pp. 65–7). However, whatever the origins of the term, *hidalguía* came to mean 'nobleza que viene a los omes por linaje', a pedigree which made a person eligible for knighthood (*Lib. est.*, I, xc, p. 185). A person cannot claim to be an *hidalgo* or *infanzón* unless he can trace his noble ancestry back to his great-grandparents or further.[31] The early law books constantly recommend the appointment of *hidalgos* to positions of public responsibility, because, in their conduct and in their choice of a wife, they had a duty not only to themselves but to their forebears and to their descendants, and had, as a consequence, a greater sense of shame (*vergüenza*) than could be found in persons of humble origin (*Siete part.*, II, xxi, 2). Américo Castro, discussing a passage from the *Crónica de Alfonso XI* in which the king's knights, squires and *criados* are described as 'omnes de buenos corazones, et en quien avía vergüenza' (men of good heart, in whom there is a sense of shame), writes: 'The meaning of *vergüenza* here is really "honour, loyalty", an active and working virtue, not a feeling of restraint (modesty, embarrassment, or an inhibiting respect).'[32] *Vergüenza* is, however, defined in the *Siete partidas* as a sign of fear born of true love, a definition which surely implies all the qualities of restraint listed by Castro: 'Vergüenza, segúnt dixieron los sabios, es señal de temencia que nasce de verdadero amor' (II, xiii, 16).

Caballeros

Most noblemen were knights or aspired to knighthood. The *caballero* owed his name to the fact that he always fought on horseback, whereas the commoner generally fought on foot. Yet it was not the horse alone which made the knight, as Díez de Games points out: 'el que cabalga cavallo no por eso es cavallero; el que haze el hexercicio, éste es con berdad llamado cavallero' (*Victorial*, p. 40) (he who rides a horse does not, by doing so, become a knight; only he who practises knighthood can truly be called a knight). In Spain there was a 'peasant knighthood', whose members did not enjoy the full benefits of *hidalguía*, but who nevertheless considered themselves to be superior to commoners who practised commerce or manual labour. These peasant knights were not required to undergo any lengthy training, nor were they initiated into their profession by any elaborate ceremony. In fact there was nothing chivalrous about them apart from their horses, their military profession and their duty to avoid demeaning activities (Pescador, 1961). The squire, the companion in arms who tended the knight's horse, was of course also mounted.

In his *Discursos de la nobleza de España* Bernabé Moreno de Vargas distinguishes between three types of chivalry: 'La Cavallería . . . de Espuela Dorada', granted to *hidalgos* and merited by birth, deeds and services; chivalry conferred by royal letters patent without any actual ceremony; and the 'chivalry' ('cavalry' might be a more appropriate word) of *caballeros pardos*, horsemen who were exempt from taxation but without noble status, and *caballeros cuantiosos*, horsemen recruited from the third estate on a quota system on the basis of income, usually for a term of four years without any relief from taxation (fols 44–6). Members of the military orders, both lay and ecclesiastical, must be classed in the first of these catagories. The Orders of Alcántara, Calatrava and Santiago assumed the duties and laid claim to the privileges of both the noble and clerical estates, since candidates were required, on the one hand, to produce evidence of *hidalguía* and of proficiency in arms and, on the other, to take vows of chastity, celibacy and obedience resembling those taken by a person entering a monastic order (Merriman, 1918–34, I, p. 177).

Knighthood was in theory a society of equals, a fraternity, to which one gained access by undergoing an initiation ritual, which involved the girding on of the sword, the accolade (termed in French the *paumée* or *colée*), a blow with the flat of the hand (later of the sword) on the neck, cheek or shoulder, and the display of skill in the use of arms.[33] During the twelfth century, when it first became obligatory for couples to be married by an ecclesiastical ceremony, and when Hugh of St Victor and his successors formulated the doctrine of the seven sacraments, a determined, although not altogether successful, attempt was made by the church to sanctify the institution of knighthood: the prospective knight placed his sword on the altar and took it up again as a token of his dedication to the service of God; before taking it up, he solemnly swore to devote his energies to the protection of the king, the church and the community at large. These duties were expounded by Ramon Llull in his *Libre de l'orde de cavayleria*:

Ofici de Cavayler és mantenir e defendre la Santa Fe Catholique (ii, 2) . . . mantenir e defendre son Senyor Terrenal (ii, 8) . . . mantenir Vidues, orfens, hòmens despoderats (ii, 19) . . . haver Casteyl e Cavayl per guardar los camins (ii, 22).

(It is the profession of a knight to uphold and defend the holy Catholic faith . . . to uphold and defend his earthly lord . . . to support widows, orphans, the disinherited . . . to have a castle and horse to guard the highways.)

The publication of William Caxton's translation of this treatise (from the French version) over two centuries later indicates that the principles of chivalry were still judged to be valid (Ferguson, 1960, p. 13 *et passim*). It is nevertheless ironic that, instead of acting as a police force for the common good, the military orders in Spain became, as I have noted earlier, a threat to public safety.

Sánchez de Arévalo is confident, as an ecclesiastic, that the chivalric profession is capable of serving the interests of the monarchy and the church:

[El cavallero] jura ser fiel e leal a Dios e honrrar a la Santa Madre Yglesia e a sus perlados e a sus ministros, ca . . . no espere el rey ni el capitán alguno que le será fiel e leal el que a Dios es traydor . . . jura los cavalleros con toda fee e lealtad fazer todas las cosas que su rey o príncipe les mandaren . . . nunca dexar el campo ni fuyr vituperosamente, ni refusar la muerte por salud de su rey e de la república . . . amparar e defender a las viudas e huérfanos e personas miserables. (*Suma de la política*, p. 78)

(The knight swears to be true and loyal to God and to honour the holy mother church and her prelates and ministers, since . . . neither the king nor any captain expects a person who is a traitor to God to be true and loyal . . . knights swear in all faith and loyalty to do everything demanded of them by their king or prince . . . never to abandon the field of battle, nor to flee dishonourably, nor to refuse death for the salvation of the king and the commonwealth . . . to protect and defend widows and orphans and persons in distress.)

Furthermore he accepts the analogy between knighthood and the religious vocation: 'recibe orden como una estrecha religión'. Certain accessory practices, such as the purifying bath and the vigil of arms, were clearly designed to strengthen this analogy. The social and religious functions of chivalry were eloquently described by Afonso V of Portugal, in a speech which he is reported to have made in the mosque of Arzila in 1471, when he dubbed his son, Prince João, a knight:

> Sabed que esta [orden] es una virtud mezclada con poderío honroso según naturaleza muy nescessario para con el poner paz en la tierra, quando la cudicia, o la tirannía, con desseo de reynar, inquietan los reynos, las repúblicas y las personas particulares. . . . Demás de esto son obligados [los cavalleros] a morir por su ley, y por su tierra, son amparo de los desamparados, porque ansí como la orden sacerdotal fue ordenada por Dios para su culto divino, la de la cavallería fue instituyda por él para mantener justicia. y para defensa desu ley (Mármol, 1573, IV, fol. 117)

> (Know that this order [viz. the order of chivalry] is a virtue mingled with reputable power, which in the nature of things is very necessary to establish peace on earth, when kingdoms, republics and individuals are stirred by greed or tyranny, together with the ambition to rule. . . . In addition knights are obliged to die for their law and their land, and they offer a refuge to the unprotected; for just as the priestly order was ordained by God for his divine worship, so the chivalric order was instituted by him to uphold justice and to defend his law.)

It was thus that the chivalric ideology instilled high ideals of fidelity and public service, but at the same time justified war in the name of religion (in part, through the influence of the Islamic concept of *jihād*). It was a vocation which demanded a willingness to take risks and to make sacrifices. To judge by the comments made by Díez de Games in *Victorial* (p. 42), the knight looked at the bourgeois way of life with a mixture of envy and disdain:

> Ca los de los ofiçios comunes comen el pan folgando, visten ropas delicadas, manjares bien adovados, camas blandas, safumadas; hechándose seguros, levantándose sin miedo, fuelgan en buenas

35

posadas con sus mugeres e sus hijos, e servidos a su voluntad, engordan grandes cerviçes, fazen grandes barrigas, quiérense bien por hazerse bien e tenerse biçiosos. ¿Qué galardón o qué honrra merescen? No, ninguna.

(Members of the common professions eat bread at their leisure, wear fine clothes, have well-seasoned dishes and soft beds perfumed with incense; lying down in safety, getting up without fear, they take their ease in pleasant dwellings with their wives and children; and, waited on when it so pleases them, they develop fat necks, they grow large paunches; they are content to pretend to be good and to take their pleasure. What reward or honour do they merit? None whatsoever.)

Knights, in contrast, are depicted as men who lead a life of hardship, sleeping on hard beds and drinking from pools of rain-water.

Despite ecclesiastical pressure, the erotic element in this ideology was never eradicated, but on the contrary became more marked in the late Middle Ages. In the *Siete partidas* it is recommended that knights name the ladies whom they serve 'porque les creçiesen más los cora- zones et oviesen mayor verguença de errar' (II, xxi, 22) (that their hearts might be more encouraged, and that they might be more ashamed to fail in their duty). Jill Mann observes that 'an estates writer could say without impiety, "arma frequentare, decet hos ardenter amare"' (Mann, 1973, p. 116) (it befits those who love ardently to be familiar with arms). The Squire in Chaucer's *Canterbury Tales* is a 'lovyere and a lusty bachelor', whose deeds of valour are motivated by the 'hope to stonden in his lady grace' (*Works*, p. 18, ll. 80 and 88). Jacques de Lalaing (c. 1422–53) was told by his father that the greatest enterprises have been inspired by love:[34]

Sachés que peu de nobles hommes sont parvenus à la haute vertu de prouesses et à bonne renommée s'ils n'ont esté amoureux. . . . Pour ce, beau fils, il vous convient estre doux, courtois et gracieux.

(Know that few noble men have attained the great virtue of prowess and high renown without being in love. . . . For that reason, my dear son, you should be pleasant, courteous and gracious.)

The anonymous biographer of Jean Le Meingre, surnamed Boucicaut, makes the same point, although he insists that the lover's intentions must be good, the object of his affection must be virtuous and 'bien conditionné', and his conduct must bring no dishonour to himself or to the person he loves:

l'amoureux lien . . . n'empesche nie ne oste aux Chevaleureux de bonne volonté à poursuivre le noble exercise des armes, ainçois est ce qui plus faict és ieunes coeurs aviver et croistre le désir de l'honorable poursuite chevaleureuse. . . . Amour oste peur, et donne hardiesse, faict oublier toute peine, et prendre en gré tout le travail que on porte pour la chose aimée. (Le Meingre, 1620, p. 25)

(the bond of love . . . in no way prevents or disqualifies the sincerely chivalrous from pursuing the noble practice of arms; on the contrary, it is that which chiefly animates young hearts to undertake the honourable pursuit of chivalry . . . love removes fear and makes men bold, causing them to be oblivious of all sorrow and to take pleasure in all the suffering endured for the sake of the loved one.)

In *El Victorial*, the biography of Boucicaut's Castilian counterpart Pero Niño, it is stated that the queen and the ladies of the nobility consider themselves greatly honoured to be served by amorous knights (pp. 90–1):

E aún sabemos bien que tanto son loados los tales hombres en las casas de las reynas e de las señoras . . . porque saben que por su amor son ellos mejores, e se traen más guarnidos, e hazen por su amor grandes proezas e cavallerías, ansí en armas como en juegos, e se ponen a grandes abenturas, e búscanlas por su amor, e van en otros reynos con sus empresas d'ellas, buscando campos e lides, loando e ensalçando cada uno su amada e señora. E aún hazen d'ellas e por su amor graçiosas cantigas e savorosos dezires.

(And moreover it is well known that such men are highly praised in the households of queens and ladies . . . because the latter are aware that through their love they become better men and more handsomely attired, and that for love they do great exploits and acts of chivalry, both in arms and in play, and place themselves at great risk, and that for love's sake they seek adventure and travel to other realms with the particular emblems of their quest, seeking battlefields and contests, each praising and extolling his lady and

37

loved one. And also with these emblems and inspired by love they compose pleasing songs and delightful spoken compositions.)

The chronicler Froissart even believed that such conduct was appropriate to a king. In a passage in which he relates the thoughts of Edward III concerning the Countess of Salisbury, he suggests that the king's love would be beneficial both to himself and to his realm:

> et ossi se il estoit amoureux, c'estoit tout bon pour lui, pour son pays et pour tous chevaliers et escuiers, car il en seroit plus lies, plus gais et plus armerès, et en ordonneroit plus de joustes, plus de behours, de festes et de reviaux qu'il n'avoit fait en devant, et s'en seroit plus ables et plus vighereux en ses guerres, plus amis et plus privés à ses gens et plus durs à ses ennemis. (*Œuvres*, III, p. 467)

(and also if he were in love, it would be very much for his own good, for the good of his country and for that of all knights and squires, since through love he would become more cheerful, gay and amiable, and would organise more jousts, lance-combats, feasts and other revels than he had done previously, and through love he would become more able and vigorous in waging his wars, friendlier and more affable with his own people and harsher towards his foes.)

John Gower was one of the few medieval writers to protest against making the love of a woman the motive for military exploit.[35] On the whole it was taken for granted that the erotic aspect of chivalry had an ethical function which was compatible with the knight's other commitments – to God, to the king and to his feudal lord.

Privileges of the nobility

The nobility was the most privileged of the three estates because, as warriors, rulers and administrators, they had – so they would argue – more responsibilities than any other estate. These privileges can be broadly divided into honorific privileges, privileges of service and fiscal privileges.

Honorific privileges
Members of the nobility were to be shown precedence upon all occasions, except during Mass, when the prelates and clergy were

permitted to lead the way, and even then they sat in the best seats and were the first to receive Holy Communion. It was moreover customary in Spain for commoners to bow to nobles as they passed and to utter the words: 'omillamos nos'. According to the *Siete partidas*, only a knight or a person worthy of knighthood might share his table with the nobility (II, xxi, 23). In 1234 Jaime I of Aragon (1213–76) promulgated a similar decree that knights and non-knights should eat separately, adding the further stipulation that squires and other persons beneath the rank of knight were never to share the same table with a lady nor to wear scarlet stockings (Madramany, 1788, p. 165). This law, which was obviously intended as an incentive to squires to earn their spurs, proves, if any documentary evidence is required, that love service was not a mere literary convention.

It was both the duty and the privilege of the nobles to be clearly differentiated from other men by the superior quantity and quality of their possessions: their horses, saddles, tableware, jewellery and, above all, their attire (*Lib. est.*, I, lxii, p. 314). Sumptuary laws, issued in Spain from the twelfth century onwards, carefully prescribed what forms of consumption were permitted to the different degrees of men. These laws (which are a valuable source of information on foreign trade and the availability of luxury goods) were not motivated primarily by economic considerations but by the need to preserve distinctions of status. Sometimes, indeed, they could have an adverse effect upon the economy. The aim of these laws was still understood in the eighteenth century, when a *Pragmática*, drafted in 1723, declared that every man must dress 'según su clase, para que el vestir diga su profesión, y no se confundan los nobles con los plebeyos, ni los grandes con los medianos'[36] (according to his class, in order that his dress may indicate his profession, and in order to avoid any confusion between nobles and commoners, or between the grandees and those of lesser rank). It is stated, for example, in the sumptuary laws passed by Alfonso XI in 1348, that only a prince may wear gold fabric, and, again no doubt as an incentive to knighthood, that a squire may not wear furs or gold shoes until he has been knighted.[37] It is also specifically recommended in the *Siete partidas* (II, xxi, 18) that young noblemen wear gaily coloured clothes in order to strengthen their hearts and to avoid the appearance of melancholy:

Paños de colores señalados establescieron los antiguos que
troxiesen vestidos los caballeros noveles mientra que fuesen

mancebos, así como bermejos, o jaldes, o verdes o cárdenos porque
les diesen alegría: mas prietos o pardos o de otra color que les
feciese entristecer non tovieron por bien que los vestiesen. E esto
fizieron porque las vestiduras fuesen más apuestas, et ellos
andudiesen alegres et les cresciesen los corazones para seer más
esforzados.

(It was decreed by ancient authority that apprentice knights should,
as young men, wear cloth of approved colours, such as red or bright
yellow or green or purple to make them joyful; but it was not
considered right that they should wear black or dull brown or any
other colour that would make them sad. And this was done that they
might be more handsomely dressed, to make them merry, and to
make their hearts more valiant.)

The fashion for wearing black, which was to become the characteristic
colour of the Spanish courtier's dress in the sixteenth and seventeenth
centuries, seems to have been introduced by Álvaro de Luna and his
contemporaries.[38] Black came to be admired because the concept of
melancholy had itself undergone a change of meaning to denote
introspection and profundity of thought.[39]

A nobleman enjoyed certain privileges before the law. He could not
lawfully be imprisoned for debt, nor could his property be seized as an
indemnity. If arrested, he was confined to a separate prison. The
penalties which his crimes incurred differed from those incurred by a
commoner: he could be starved to death or beheaded, but he was
exempt from the degradation of death by the hangman. It was illegal,
except in the case of suspected treason, to extract information from him
by torture. More important still, he was entitled to the *riepto y desafío*,
that is the right to avenge an injury or an insult and to prove his valour
in a judicial duel before the king and twelve of his peers.[40] Doubts
were already being expressed in the thirteenth century as to whether
God's providence should be tested in this manner:

aquel que ha voluntad de se aventurar a esta prueba semeja que
quiere tentar a Dios nuestro señor, que es cosa que él defendió por
su palabra allí do dixo: 've a riedro Satanás, non tentarás a Dios
tu señor'. (*Siete part.*, III, xiv, 8)

(he who chooses to risk his life in this ordeal appears to wish to test
our Lord God, which is something that he expressly forbade when

he said: 'Get thee behind me Satan, thou shalt not tempt the Lord thy God.')

The practice none the less persisted until the sixteenth century.

There were, in addition, certain honorific privileges and seigniorial rights that were exclusive to the *ricoshombres*. These men shared with kings, princes and prelates the right to employ the title *Don* (from *Dominus*) before their name; they could display a standard and a cauldron to indicate their right to raise and to maintain at their own cost ('en acostamiento') a number of noble men-at-arms; they could possess numerous vassals, over whom they had the right to exercise civil and criminal jurisdiction; they had the right, indeed the duty, to participate in the Royal Council; they could remain seated and retain their hats in the royal presence; furthermore they had the right, either in person or by proxy, to renounce their allegiance to the king and suffer possible banishment from the kingdom.[41]

Privileges of service
Although key government posts, particularly those entailing powers of jurisdiction or involving financial matters, were usually given to commoners, the best military, administrative and domestic appointments were traditionally reserved for members of the nobility. Royal offices associated either with the king's person or with the management of exclusively aristocratic pursuits (such as hunting, falconry and cavalry warfare) were almost invariably held by noblemen. These included the chamberlain, the standard-bearer, the majordomo, the chief falconer and the king's cup-bearer. A list of such posts is given by Juan Manuel:

Vos devedes saber que los ofiçiales son de muchas guisas: ca uno[s] ay que por fuerça deven ser fijos dalgo et los omnes de mayor estado que son en casa de los sennores; así commo son mayordomos et alfere[çe]s e adelantados mayores, e mayorales que tienen la criança de los fijos de los sennores. (*Libro infinido*, p. 49)

(You must realise that there are many kinds of officials: for there are some persons in noble households who must of necessity be *hidalgos* and men of high estate, such as butlers, standard-bearers and governors of provinces, and stewards charged with looking after the children of the nobles.)

The king also disputed with the clergy the right to a certain share in the nominations to ecclesiastical benefices. In these appointments the king frequently decided in favour of the nobility (Colmeiro, 1873, pp. 457–63).

Fiscal privileges

The nobility was exempt from direct taxation. The burden of taxation fell upon the municipalities. This exemption is so well known that it would be superfluous to discuss it in more detail.

Duties of the nobility

In return for its many privileges the nobility had its duties. These may be summed up in two words: service and non-derogation. Theoretically ideals of service inspired all three estates. The services of the nobility were primarily military and administrative. Noblemen had to be prepared to fight on behalf of the king whenever summoned, and to assist him in the government of the realm. The *ricoshombres* were expected to put in an occasional appearance at court, if only to attend feasts and celebrations, and they felt slighted if the king gathered commoners or upstart nobles about his person. Towards the close of the Middle Ages political theorists began to view the relationship between privileges and duties in terms of a social contract: it was argued that the privileges of the nobility were only justified as a form of remuneration for public services, which were increasingly of an administrative, even bureaucratic, character (Kelso, 1929, pp. 36–63).

To uphold his rank, the nobleman had to avoid participating in activities which would bring his estate into disrepute, and to communicate nobility by means of procreation, and, if possible, to enhance it by earning titles and distinctions from the king. As Dante says, in an imaginary conversation with his noble ancestor, Cacciaguida, nobility is a mantle which becomes worn away with time if value is not added to it by daily effort (*Paradiso*, Canto XVI, ll. 7–9). The social imperative to marry women of superior rank is illustrated by the words of the Counts of Carrión, El Cid's sons-in-law (Díaz de Vivar, *Cid*, p. 192, ll. 3296–8):

De natura somos de condes de Carrión:
deviemos casar con fijas de rreyes o de emperadores,
ca non pertenecién fijas de ifançones.

(We are of the family of the Counts of Carrión and have a right to marry the daughters of kings and emperors, and the daughters of petty nobles are not our equals.)

The Chevalier de la Tour Landry, in a book of instruction which he wrote for his daughters, warns through the mediation of his wife against the dangers of losing status:

> Syre I wylle not/that they have or take any plesaunce of them that ben of lower estate or degree than they be of/that is to wete that no woman unwedded shalle not sette her love upon no man of lower or lasse degree than she is of/For yf she tooke hym/her parentes and Frendes shold hold her lassed and hyndered/These whiche loven suche folke done ageynste theyre worship and honoure. (La Tour Landry, *The Book*, pp. 168–9)

Knights are admonished by Ramon Llull to conserve the purity of their lineage:

> Demanar muyler de Cavayler, ni enclinar-la a malvestat, no és honor de Cavayler; ni muyler de Cavayler, qui ha fiyl de vilà, no honre Cavayler, e destrau la antiquitat de linatge de Cavayler; ni Cavayler, qui per deshonestat hage fiyl de vil fembre, no honre Paratge ni Cavayleria. (*Lib. cav.*, VII, vi, p. 71)

(To accost the wife of a knight or to incline her to wickedness does not contribute to a knight's honour; nor does the wife of a knight honour him by bearing the children of a commoner and destroying his ancient lineage; nor does the knight who illicitly begets a son by a common woman honour noble ancestry and chivalry.)

In the eyes of Sánchez de Arévalo, intermarriage between members of different social estates is no less scandalous than a Saracen prince who serves a Christian lord or vice versa (*Miroir*, 1477, fol. d2ᵛ). Despite these strictures, there was in fact little stigma attached to illegitimacy during the Middle Ages, especially in Spain where many members of the titled nobility were the bastard sons of royalty. According to Castilian law, the male child of a concubine (or *barragana*) whose father was an *hidalgo* retained his father's status upon the payment of a sum of money, even though he was not normally permitted to inherit land.[42]

More important than the choice of a wife were the customs governing the style of life considered appropriate to a gentleman:

> a Cavayler se cové beylement parlar e beylement vestir, e haver beyl armes, e tenir gran alberch, car totes estes coses són necessàries a honrar Cavayleria. (*Lib. cav.*, VI, xx, p. 66)

(it befits a knight to speak and to dress beautifully, to have beautiful arms and to have spacious lodgings, as all these things are necessary for the honour of chivalry.)

Giovanni da Legnano, identifying the Roman *miles* with the medieval knight, cites Justinian and Roman law to prove that soldiers 'ought to abstain from the cultivation of land, from the care of animals, from trade in commodities. They should not manage the business of other people; nor engage in civil duties' (Barber, 1974, p. 45). A French seventeenth-century treatise on the social estates is equally uncompromising on this point, and lists some of the posts which a nobleman should avoid:

> Les exercices dérogeans à la Noblesse sont ceux de Procureur postulant, Greffier, Notaire, Sergent, Clerc, marchand, et artisan de tous mestiers. . . . Ce qui s'entend quand on fait tous ces exercices pour le guain: car c'est proprement le gain, vil et sordide, qui déroge à la Noblesse, de laquelle le propre est de vivre de ses rentes, quoy que ce soit de ne point vendre sa peine et son labeur. (Loyseau, 1610, p. 62)

(The occupations which detract from nobility are those of public prosecutor, clerk of the court, notary, secretary, merchant and craftsman of all trades. . . . It must be understood that this occurs when one does any of these occupations for gain, because properly speaking base and sordid gain is what detracts from nobility, the proper business of which is to live off one's income, although one should not sell one's toil and labour.)

According to the *Siete partidas*, a person could be deprived of knighthood if he sold or mistreated his horse or arms, or if he pawned them at a tavern, lost them at dice, let a companion steal them or gave them to women of ill repute; if, second, he conferred knighthood on someone unworthy of the honour; if, third, he took part in commerce or 'algúnd vil menester de manos por ganar dineros' (some common manual job to earn money), unless he were a prisoner and compelled to do so; if, fourth, he fled from battle, abandoned his master or relinquished the fortress which he had been commanded to defend; and if, lastly, he did not endeavour to save his master from death or imprisonment (II, xxi, 25). In short, a knight had to respect the implements of his profession, defend the exclusiveness of his caste, refrain from gainful and profitable activities, and fulfil his personal and feudal obligations. The duty of non-derogation is also disclosed by the impediments to knighthood: extreme poverty, which would force a knight to beg or steal; a mental or physical handicap, which would be a liability in the military profession; the practice of commerce; and a legal conviction for treason (II, xxi, 12). These rules from the *Siete partidas* were recapitulated by Pedro IV of Aragon in his *Obra de Mossen Sent Jordi e de cavalleria* (Bofarull, *Colección*, VI, pp. 21–65). There is considerable literary evidence, for example in the dispute between *Elena y María* (Menéndez Pidal, 1914, pp. 59–60) and in the *Libro de Buen Amor* (Ruiz, *LBA*, sts 554–6, pp. 152–3), that knights were much given to gambling and frequently discredited their profession by pawning their horse and arms to pay debts. This is one of the criticisms levelled against the knight by María, the clerk's mistress:

Quando non tién que despender,
tórn[a]s[e] luego a ajogar ... (ll. 130–1)
joga el cavallero & el rroçín
& elas armas otro sý,
el mantón, el tabardo
e el bestido & el calçado.... (ll. 136–9)
Quando non tién que jogar
nin al a que tornar,
vay & la siella empeñar
alos francos dela cal. (ll. 142–5)

(When he has nothing to spend, he returns to gambling ... he gambles away his horse and nag and his arms as well, his cloak, tabard, clothing and footwear.... When he has nothing left to gamble and no one else to turn to, he pawns his saddle to the French brokers.)

He is even forced to pawn his spurs, and, having gambled away his clothes, he is driven to theft. The wise lover is advised by the Archpriest of Hita to shun the gambling tables: 'Desque los omnes están en juegos encendidos,/despójanse por dados, los dineros perdidos' (st. 555) (Once men are aroused by gambling, they strip off their clothes for the dice when their money has been lost). In Spain, until the accession of Ferdinand and Isabella, public attitudes to gambling seem to have been on the whole remarkably tolerant. To win through gambling was generally considered more honourable than to earn money through usury. Indeed the taboo against trade and commerce remained a constant feature of the *hidalgo* mentality which was to have such adverse consequences for the industrial development of Spain.[43]

Clergy (oratores)

The clerical estate can be defined as the body of ordained ministers of of the church, although it also comprised students and learned laymen or 'clerks' (a term already being used in this wider sense in the thirteenth century). Anyone, regardless of wealth and ancestry, could in theory enter this estate, provided that he possessed the necessary intellectual and moral qualifications and was prepared to accept the articles of the Christian faith. Just as 'chivalry' could refer either to the chivalric ideology or to the body of knights, so 'clergy' could mean either learning or the body of clerks. There was actually no general agreement as to whether knights or clerks should take precedence in the social order, and this uncertainty explains the vehemence of the *Elena y María* debate, in which the knight's mistress and the clerk's mistress each denigrate the estate of the other's lover and submit their argument to the court of King Oriol.

There was, especially towards the end of the Middle Ages, an enormous disparity in wealth, power and prestige between the upper and the lower orders of the clergy. Juan Manuel concedes that 'en la clerezía son muchos estados et muy departidos unos de otros' (*Lib. est.*, II, iii, p. 215) (in the clergy there are many estates and [they are] widely separated one from another). Gower, in his *Mirour de l'omme*, lists twelve degrees of clergy: pope, cardinals, bishops, archdeacons, officers, deacons, deans, curates, parish priests, chantry priests, students, members of monastic orders and mendicant friars (*Complete Works*, I, pp. 214–46). Enrique de Villena distinguishes between the *estado de perlado* (the prelacy) and the *estado de religioso* (the general clergy), subdividing the former into pope, cardinals, patriarchs, primates, archbishops, bishops, abbots, priors, masters of military orders, vicars, rectors, officers, ministers, convent superiors and stewards, and the latter into chaplains, friars, monks, nuns and members of religious guilds (*Doze trabajos*, p. 12).

The term 'prelate' (Latin *praelatus*, set above, from *praefero*, prefer), sometimes applied in the early Middle Ages to lay persons in prominent positions, came to refer to church dignitaries. Prelacy was defined by canonists as 'pre-eminence with jurisdiction', which meant episcopal jurisdiction, but the term was extended to all members of the upper clergy: cardinals, archbishops, bishops and abbots.[44] The prelates lived and behaved like the nobles, to whom they were generally related by ties of kinship: they derived large revenues from their ecclesiastical domains; they had numerous vassals over whom they exercised jurisdiction; they employed private armies to defend their interests; they attended political assemblies, frequented the royal palace and confirmed titles of honour conferred by the king. The whole ecclesiastical hierarchy was in fact contaminated by secular values and feudal practices:

> The bishop demanded homage from the dignitaries of his chapter or the abbots of his diocese; the canons who held the largest prebends required it from the less well-provided colleagues; and the parish priests had to do homage to the head of the religious community on which their parishes were dependent. (Bloch, 1965, II, p. 348)

Clerks even sought to appropriate the marks of respect accorded to overlords, as we learn from María, the clerk's mistress: 'Bien se tiene por villano/Quien le non besa la mano' (l. 173) (A person who does not kiss his hand he truly considers low-bred). This is precisely the gesture of submission with which the Emperor Love is received in the *Libro de Buen Amor* (st. 1246, p. 339).

The clergy possessed many of the privileges and immunities of the nobility, as well as certain privileges which were exclusive to their profession. Clerks shared with nobles immunity from torture, death by hanging and other demeaning penalties. In Castile they had a right to a sum of 1,500 sueldos for a blow received (Baeza, 1570, fols 136–55; Colmeiro, 1873, pp. 454–7). In addition to the privileges of *hidalguía*, they were protected by the church: a person who committed a grave offence against a clerk in holy orders was liable to excommunication; clerks had the right to be tried by an ecclesiastical tribunal, which was much less harsh to offenders than the civil courts; they were exempt from military service. Clerks and ecclesiastics were not permitted to undertake any work which entailed civil jurisdiction or which could be classified as servile or mercenary. They could not, for example, become majordomos, judges, prosecutors or servants. On the other hand, they could obtain certain posts at court: chaplains, tutors, teachers and secretaries. Furthermore, like the nobility, the clergy was exempt from direct taxation.[45] The clergy, united in the defence of its clerical 'liberties', thus formed, as R. W. Southern rightly observes, an invincible guild or trade union (Southern, 1970, p. 39).

Members of the clergy had a duty both to the community and to their estate. Juan Manuel lists three ways in which they should serve the community: first of all, they should be ready to take up arms against the Moors; second, they must combat the world, the flesh and the devil in their personal conduct; third, they must propagate Christianity by demonstrating, through rational argument, that Jews, Moslems and heathens are misguided in their beliefs (*Lib. est.*, II, iii, p. 181). This militancy reflects the peculiar conditions prevailing in the Iberian Peninsula.[46] In most European countries the clergy confined their evangelical zeal to prayer and teaching. To fulfil their vocation they were required to take a vow of celibacy and to imitate the life of Christ.

Clerks, no less than knights, were acutely aware of the honour of their estate. They were debarred from commerce and the mechanical arts, although they were not discouraged from cultivating their own land. Jean Bodin (1530–96), after quoting Aristotle on the proper activities of the nobility, adds that in ancient Greece holy men were forbidden to buy and sell. Even the *Vision of Piers the Ploughman*, in some respects a revolutionary work, contains the lines: 'Clerkes þat aren crounede of kynde understondyng/sholde noþer swynke ne swete' (Mohl, 1933, p. 297).

Third estate (laboratores)

The third estate can be defined negatively as that which was neither noble nor ecclesiastical. It comprised all those members of society who earned a livelihood from commerce, craftsmanship or manual labour. Enrique de Villena divided this estate into *ciudadanos* (wealthy townsmen not directly engaged in commerce), *mercaderes* (merchants), *menestrales* (artisans) and *labradores* (farm labourers) (*Doze trabajos*, pp. 12–13). Juan Manuel, like most of his contemporaries, regarded all these heterogeneous social groups as components of a single estate, that of the *labradores*:

> Sennor infante, commo quier que los ruanos et los mercadores non son labradores, pero porque [non] biven con los sennores nin defienden la tiera por armas . . . los estados de ruanos et de los mercadores ençiéranse en el estado de labradores. (*Lib. est.*, I, xciii, p. 193)

> (My lord, although townsmen and merchants are not labourers . . . their estates are comprised within the estate of the labourers, because they neither live with the nobles nor bear arms in defence of the land.)

Although the economy of Europe was predominantly agricultural, there were many people who resided within the precincts of the municipalities, and who were consequently free from territorial ties of dependence. There was thus in reality a sharp distinction between the rural seignorial sector and the semi-autonomous municipalities. The highest ranking members of the third estate were the rich burgesses who controlled municipal affairs. They claimed at the Cortes to represent the third estate, whereas in fact they ignored the interests of the vast majority. This urban patriciate infiltrated the territorial nobility and monopolised the royal bureaucracy. The magistrates who governed the popular assemblies were usually drawn in equal numbers from the ranks of the burgesses and from the body of knights. Since these urban classes were not accorded any social or juridical recognition as an estate distinct from the peasantry, it is scarcely surprising that when a bourgeois became rich or entered royal service he would mimic the aristocratic style of life, much to the indignation of impecunious knights. The impoverished peasant could expect little justice: 'si el cuytado es muy pobre e non tiene algún cabdal/Non le valdrán las partidas nin ningún decretal'[47] (if the plaintiff is very poor and has no property, no law book or papal decree will be of any use to him).

The general attitude of estates writers to commoners and lesser court officials is concisely expressed by Juan Manuel: 'parece mejor en los callar que en poner en tal libro como éste' (*Lib. est.*, I, xcviii,

p. 205) (it is better to say nothing about them than to mention them in a book such as this). The Burgundian chronicler Georges Chastellain is equally dismissive: 'Pour venir au tiers nombre ... il n'est gaires capable de hautes attributions, parce qu'il est au degré servile' (Stéfano, 1966, p. 130) (As regards the third estate ... it is hardly possible to attribute great qualities to it, because it is of a servile degree). According to Juan Manuel, the ignorance and stupidity of commoners makes them more prone to vice:

> muchos déstos son menguados de entendimiento, que con torpedat podrían caer en grandes yerros, non lo entendiendo; por ende son sus estados muy peligrosos para salvamiento de las almas. (*Lib. est.*, I, xcviii, p. 205)

> (many of them are deficient in understanding, so that through baseness they may be led astray without realising it; therefore their estates are very precarious for the salvation of souls.)

Enrique de Villena likewise maintains that members of the third estate are less intelligent and more given to idleness and lust (*Doze trabajos*, p. 71). This prejudice was by no means confined to literature. The deputies at the Cortes held at Palencia in 1431 believed that the municipalities would be discredited if representatives or *procuradores* were from the labouring classes:

> Otrosí suplicamos ala vuestra alteza que cada e quando le ploguiere mandar avuestras çibdades e villas que enbíen sus procuradores ... que non sean delos labradores nin sesmeros, nin del estado delos pecheros, por que mejor sea guardado el estado e onrra delos quelos enbían, e se puedan mejor conformar con los otros procuradores quando ovieron de tractar en sus ayuntamientos. (Colmeiro, *Cortes*, III, p. 101)

> (Moreover we beseech Your Highness, when it so pleases you to command your towns and boroughs to send their representatives ... that these men should not be selected from the labourers or district heads, nor from the tax-paying estate, that the estate and honour of those who send them may be the better safeguarded and that the representatives may be able to agree more easily when they have to discuss matters at their meetings.)

From an anthropological point of view the labourers were (and are) the feet of the body politic,[48] and they were despised as being morally inferior and, quite literally, of a more earthy complexion. Andreas Capellanus thus judges them unfit for love:[49]

> We say that it rarely happens that we find farmers serving in Love's court, but naturally, like a horse or a mule, they give themselves up to the work of Venus, as nature's urging teaches them to do. For a farmer hard labour and the uninterrupted solaces of plough and mattock are sufficient.

He adds that even if, as rarely happens, they are struck by Cupid's arrows, it would not be expedient to instruct them in the art of love lest they neglect their agricultural duties. Readers are advised, should they ever take a fancy to peasant women, 'to take what you seek and to embrace them by force' (p. 150). It was taken for granted that only a lady of gentle birth was worthy of true love or *fin'amors*. Dom Pedro, Constable of Portugal (1429–66), does not credit the lower classes with any knowledge of love:

> No amo ni punto: el amor popular,
> ni loo quien mucho: en el se confía,
> ca no sabe amar: ni sabe desamar;
> los más d[e] sus fechos: van torcida vía.
> Sin razón, sin causa: mantiene porfía,
> sin sazón, sin tiempo: se dexa daquella.
> Jamás discreción: no lieva por guía,
> nin honrra la virtud: nin se cura della.
>   (*Coplas*, fol. Bvi; *Canc. geral*, fol. 75^r)

> (I do not love plebeian love at all, nor do I praise someone who greatly relies on it, for the people do not know how to love or how to hate; most of their deeds go awry. Without rhyme or reason they continue a dispute; at an untimely moment they abandon it. They are never guided by discretion; they neither respect virtue nor care about it.)

In the sixteenth century, when a reaction set in against the over-sophistication of life at court, the shepherd became an ideal social type. Until then to love with courtesy and fidelity was very much a noble prerogative. The duty of commoners was to toil obediently from dawn to dusk without begrudging another man's estate:[50]

Theise folkes [the Comynaltie of this realme] maie not murmur nor grudge to live in labor and paine, and the most parte of their tyme with the sweat of theire face, nor let anie of them presume or counterfete the state of his better, nor let them in anie wise exceede in theire apparell or dyet, But to use them as their expence will surelie serve them.

2
Traditional Forms of Patronage

Patronage may be defined as a reciprocally beneficial and reciprocally binding relationship between individuals, or groups of individuals, of unequal status, based upon an exchange of protection for services rendered. In a feudal hierarchical society in which the state was impotent to safeguard a person's rights and interests, and in which the ruling classes saw it as their duty to defend the oppressed, most social relations could be so defined: kingship, feudalism, court tuition and service (*crianza*), patronage in knighthood, the tutelage of saints, and courtly love. Before the abstract concept of the state had emerged, political as well as individual relationships were conceived in terms of a contract between two parties: lord and vassal, patron and client, governor and governed. Mankind was perceived as a body, knit together by a web of individual contracts, branching out from the king at the apex of the social pyramid, and stretching down to the lowliest of his subjects. The contractual idea of patronage even extended into the supernatural sphere, the estates and degrees of men being regarded as 'the lower steps of the throne of the Eternal' (Huizinga, 1955, pp. 55–6). Estates, professions and guilds had a saint to protect their interests; individuals commended themselves to their celestial namesakes. In Wolfram von Eschenbach's *Parzival* the right of resistance inherent in the notion of patronage is applied to man's relationship with God, thereby provoking a grave spiritual crisis (Heer, 1974, p. 31).

Naturaleza is the word used in the *Siete partidas* to designate the indebtedness in which each man stands in relation to others. A *natural* is defined as a person who has an obligation to his fellow men as a consequence of any of the following factors: birth in the kingdom; vassalage; education (*crianza*); knighthood; marriage; inheritance; rescue from captivity, dishonour or death; conversion to Christianity; and ten years' residence in the land (IV, xxiv, 2). Furthermore, all men have a 'natural debt' to God for having created them and for judging them by their merit; to their parents for having begotten them and for having cared for them as children; and to their teachers for having educated them (IV, xxiv, 3). The natural debts which are most characteristically medieval involve the idea of reciprocity, as in the case of vassalage which is 'un grant debdo et muy fuerte que han aquellos que son vassallos con sus señores, Et otrosí los señores con ellos' (IV, xxv, prol.) (a large and very heavy debt which those who are vassals owe their lords, and which lords also owe their vassals). Five types of vassalage are listed: the sovereignty of the king (*merum imperium*); the dominion of lords over their vassals; that of the lord or benefactor of the *behetrías* (groups of tenants who selected their own protector); that of parents over their children; and mastery over serfs (IV, xxv, 2). Serfdom seems incongruous in this list: a serf had no legal or civil rights; his ownership was transmitted with the ownership of land. The word *siervo* may mean either a serf or a slave, and it was as an alternative to slavery that the institution of patronage first developed, the debt being, in this instance, that which existed between a slave and his ex-master.

In ancient Rome a *cliens*, from *cluere*, to hear, listen or obey, was a slave who had been freed on condition that he continued to fulfil certain duties on behalf of his master, in return for which he was permitted to retain the latter's family name or *gens*, which meant that, although excluded from burgess rights, he enjoyed a *de facto* freedom by virtue of his attachment to a patrician house. The ex-master was his *patronus* (patron, protector, advocate), from *pater*, father. He was a father figure, commanding the same respect that a child owed his father. The obligations were, however, by no means unilateral. Indeed, according to Dionysius and Plutarch, the duties of a patron to his client were no less sacred than those to his own children or his ward, and to neglect them was a capital offence. The patron was bound to provide his client with the necessaries of life, sometimes granting him a plot of land, comparable to the medieval fief. He was expected to represent his client in any transactions with third parties, and to be prepared to plead on his behalf in the court of law. The client, in his turn, had duties to fulfil, which varied according to the terms of the contract. They might, for example, include rendering pecuniary assistance to a patron in time of need. If any legal charge was brought against a patron or his client, neither might give evidence against the other. Patronage and clientage tended, like feudalism, to become hereditary.

Thus there evolved a client population whose status was midway between citizenship and servitude.[51]

The status of court officials in the Middle Ages was not unlike that of the Roman client population. In fact Roman laws concerning patronage appear to have left their mark on the system of patronage in knighthood and on the Spanish concept of *crianza*, regarded by some scholars as a Visigothic institution (Bloch, 1965, I, pp. 186–7). Like the Roman and Greek patriciate, the medieval nobility was able to preserve its privileged position in society by offering military protection in return for labour and by maintaining a monopoly of the military profession. Two separate meanings of the term *patronus* are present in the concept of the patron saint: a supernatural advocate or intercessor, and a tutelary god. God himself was a patron, offering protection and moral guidance to those who freely commended their souls to his care. Courtly love was essentially a patron–client relationship, in which a liege-lady (still addressed in early Provençal poetry by the masculine term *midons*) possessed most of the attributes of the *patronus*.

Kingship

No one in the medieval social hierarchy could claim immunity from patronage in one form or another. Kings and emperors were vassals of God, and it was assumed that they would receive a portion in heaven in return for their loyal services. A king's subjects were his vassals, either directly, as in the case of those nobles who resided in royal burghs or Crown lands, or else indirectly through a network of individual bonds, both feudal and non-feudal. In the *Fuero real* (IV, xxv, 5) it is stated that the king stands above the law, because he derives his power from God, not from man. This clause, which was intended to strengthen the king's legislative authority, not to make him exempt from the law, lent itself to an interpretation favouring absolutism. However, it was not repeated in the *Siete partidas* and subsequent law books. In medieval Spain the exercise of kingship was generally conceived as a duty rather than a right: the monarch was the custodian or trustee of his people's welfare. Juan I of Castile declared his adherence to this principle in his speech to the Cortes at Valladolid in 1385 (Colmeiro, *Cortes*, I, p. 348), and it remained very much the official doctrine until the accession of the Emperor Charles V. The relationship between the king and his subjects was ideally based, once again, on the notion of reciprocity. The king must keep his people in truth by upholding the Christian faith and by preserving it from infidels; he must protect his subjects from evil and oppression; and he must administer justice, distributing rewards and punishments in accordance with each man's status, character and merit ('por su linage, o por su bondat, o por su servicio') (*Siete part.*, II, x, 2). The people were, in their turn, called upon to serve the king, their sovereign lord, with fear and loyalty; to attend the royal court or council when summoned; to respond promptly to the call to arms; and to be prepared to assume responsibility for any property entrusted to them as fiefs (II, xiii, 16). The king must, in short, love, honour and protect his subjects; and they, like the bride in the marriage sacrament, must love, honour and obey him as their natural lord (II, x, 2 and 3).

In addition to his public obligations, namely to defend the realm, to maintain peace and to administer justice, a king was expected, as a patron, to set a shining example of moral rectitude by his personal conduct. His subjects might thus take him as their model or 'pattern', another word which is etymologically related to 'patron'. In the *Siete partidas* it would seem that, as in the Islamic *Sharīʿa* or religious law, there is no sharp differentiation between the laws governing public affairs and those governing a man's private words, thoughts and deeds.[52] Both were moral imperatives. The state of a man's soul is reflected in his outward appearance. Therefore speech, table manners, dress, deportment and posture are all considered subjects worthy to be comprised within the legislation of the realm:

> debe el rey ser muy apuesto, también en su andar como en estar en pie, otrosí en seyendo et en cavalgando, et otro tal quando comiere o bebiere . . . nin aún quando yoguiere en su lecho non debe yazer mucho encogido nin atravesado, como algunos que non saben do han a tener la cabeça, nin los pies. (II, v, 4)

> (the king should be very elegant, both in the way he walks and the way he stands, also in sitting and riding, and likewise when he eats or drinks . . . and even when he lies down in bed, he should not lie in a curled or an oblique position like some men who do not know where to put their head or their feet.)

Enrique IV, a far from exemplary king, did not forget what he had been taught as a child, namely that 'los reyes ... son como espejo en que los homes veen su semejança de apostura o de enatieza' (II, v, 4) (kings ... are like a mirror in which men see an image of their elegance or slovenliness). Thus, when his treasurer suggested that it was too costly to feed a bodyguard of 3,600 men, he, no doubt fearing for the safety of his person, replied:

> yo tengo de obrar como Rey, en quien, como en espejo, todos han de mirar e tomar doctrina; porque sabida cosa es que con los enxemplos del Rey se conforman los del regno. (Enríquez del Castillo, *Crónica*, xx, p. iii)

> (I must act like a king, on whom, as on a mirror, all men should meditate, and from whom they are expected to derive instruction; because it is a well-known fact that standards of conduct in the kingdom are modelled on those set by the king.)

The king not only assumed the role of protector and moral guide, but also that of an arbiter of taste and a *magister ludi*, setting the fashion and distributing prizes for literary and artistic merit. The extraordinary influence which the monarch **was** capable of exerting in the sphere of public conduct was perceived by Juan de Lucena:[53]

> Lo que los reyes hacen, bueno o malo, todos ensayamos de hacer. Si es bueno, por aplacer a nos mesmos; y si malo por aplacer a ellos. Jugaba el Rey, éramos todos tahures; studia la Reina, somos agora studiantes.

> (We all try to do what kings do, whether it be good or bad. If good, for our own pleasure; if bad, for theirs. The king used to gamble, we were all gamblers; the queen studies, we are now students.)

The royal court was traditionally a school of courtesy and a place of entertainment. In this courtly and chivalric environment the stress was on manners, cleanliness and sportsmanship, rather than on intellectual accomplishments.

Feudalism

Feudalism was a form of patronage based upon land tenure and solemnised by an act of homage, involving an exchange of military services for protection, which developed as a consequence of instability and decentralisation after the collapse of the Carolingian empire. The subordinate or vassal who had entered into this contract could not lawfully have his territory or fief taken from him unless he had committed a serious crime against his lord – killing his lord's brother, son or nephew, or dishonouring his wife, daughter or daughter-in-law – or had broken his pledge to provide services. In Spain the term *feudo* was also applied to a fee, known as a *feudo de Cámara*, which was paid annually to servants of the Crown and which might be annulled whenever it so pleased the king (*Siete part.*, IV, xxvi, 1). The practice of conferring 'money fiefs' was adopted by kings and grandees from the eleventh century onwards as an alternative to contracts based on land tenure. The advantage of this arrangement, from the lord's point of view, was that there was no risk of the 'fief' becoming hereditary; it 'kept the beneficiary in a much stricter subordination to the grantor' while at the same time relieving him of the necessity of having to provide food and lodging, as he would to a prebendary (Bloch, 1965, I, p. 174). The procedure changed little over the centuries. On a visit to Ferdinand the Catholic in 1512, the Florentine ambassador noted that court employees received a fixed wage according to their functions, lived in their own homes, and paid for their own keep.[54]

The Iberian Peninsula did not possess a network of feudal relationships such as that which existed in France, nor were ties of dependence so binding. In France the feudal bond was a lifetime undertaking, a contract which lasted in theory until the death of one of the parties. In Castile an oath of fealty could be broken after one year (*Siete part.*, IV, xxv, 7). The ceremony of homage whereby the contract was confirmed was none the less essentially the same throughout Europe. The subordinate, in a kneeling posture, joined hands as though in prayer and placed them in the hands of his superior to indicate an attitude of submissiveness and uttered the words: 'I am your man.' The vassal then took an oath of fealty, which was a unilateral commitment on his part to be loyal and true to his word, to offer good advice, and to defend his master from all those who would oppose him. Here is the relevant passage in the *Siete partidas*:

> fincando el vassallo los hinojos ante el señor, debe meter sus
> manos entre las del señor, et prometerle jurando et faciendol
> pleyto et homenaje quel le será siempre leal et verdadero, et quel
> dará buen consejo cada que él gelo demandare, et que nol

descubrirá sus poridades, et quel ayudará contra todos los homes del mundo a su poder . . . et complirá todas las posturas que puso con él por razón de aquel feudo. (IV, xxvi, 4)

(kneeling before his lord, the vassal must place his hands in his lord's hands, and he must promise, swearing and pledging fealty and homage, that he will always be loyal and true, and that he will offer him good counsel whenever required to do so, and that he will not disclose his secrets, and that he will assist him to the best of his ability against everyone in the world . . . and that he will fulfil all the conditions agreed upon by reason of feudal contract.)

The vassal was invested in his new status by the gift of a ring, a glove or a rod. This gift was sometimes accompanied by a kiss on the mouth or hands, symbolising accord and friendship. In the *Cantar de Mio Cid* the Cid, after capturing Valencia, pays homage to the king by falling to his knees and by seeking to kiss his feet. The king tells him to arise and to kiss his hands, not his feet. The Cid, still kneeling, kisses his hands; he then stands up and kisses his mouth: 'Inojos fitos las manos le besó,/Levós' en pie e en la bócal' saludó' (Díaz de Vivar, *Cid*, p. 128, ll. 2039–40). When Fadrique, Count of Luna, an illegitimate son of King Martin of Sicily, came to pay homage to Juan II of Castile in 1430, he behaved like the epic hero: 'E en llegando a veinte pasos del Rey, deçendió de la mula, e fue a pie, e vesole la mano e la boca' (Carrillo de Huete, *Crónica*, p. 26) (And when he was within twenty paces of the king, he dismounted from the mule and continued on foot, and kissed him on the hand and foot). Love is very often personified in medieval literature as a feudal lord demanding homage. A case in point is the naked embrace of Love and the old man at the end of Rodrigo Cota's *Diálogo entre el Amor y un viejo* (a small masterpiece deserving of wider recognition):

Vente amí muy dulce amor,
vente amí braços abiertos;
ves aquí tu servidor
hecho siervo de señor
sin tener tus dones ciertos.
    (*Canc. gen.*, fol 74ᵛ)

(Come to me sweet Love, come to me with open arms; here stands your servant, now your lordship's slave, possessing none of your undoubted gifts.)

(In Spain the kissing of hands was repeated on a number of occasions, including the ceremony of knighthood, as the native gesture of submission.)

Only a son or a nephew might inherit a fief. Persons who were disabled, blind or dumb and members of the clergy (unless they had special permission) were debarred from inheritance. On inheriting his father's fief, a son had a year and a day within which to renew the feudal contract by pleading homage to his lord (*Siete part.*, IV, xxvi, 6 and 10). Although a feudal lord was too grand to be required to take an oath, he had his obligations:

> Otrosí decimos que el señor debe amar, et honrar et guardar sus vasallos, et facerles bien et merced, et desviarles de daño et de deshonra. (IV, xxv, 6)

> (Moreover we say that the lord must love and honour and protect his vassals, and show them favour and goodwill, and turn them away from harm and dishonour.)

Court tuition and service

It was the practice in Spain, as in the rest of Europe, for a youth of good family to be sent by his parents to be educated in a noble, and preferably royal, household, where he would learn good manners, the rudiments of reading and writing, and the sports and military exercises befitting a gentle knight:

> fue en España siempre acostumbrado de los homes honrados de enviar a sus fijos a criar a los cortes de los reyes porque aprendiesen a seer corteses, et enseñados et quitos de villanía et de todo yerro. (*Siete part.*, II, ix, 27)

> (In Spain it has always been customary for honourable men to send their sons to be brought up in the courts of kings, so that they might learn to be courteous and educated, and free from villainy and all defects.)

In the words of Juan Manuel, 'los palacios delos sennores son escuela de los fijos dalgo' (*Lib. est.*, I, xci, p. 187) (the palaces of lords are a school for *hidalgos*). This type of education was termed *crianza*. A *criado* may be defined as a person brought up in a household other than that of his parents or natural guardians, who, in return for his board, lodging and upbringing, made himself useful to the lord or the mistress of the house. His position resembled that of the household warrior of a Visigothic chieftain. Regardless of his age and social standing, he retained, in relation to his benefactor, the status of *criado* (*Siete part.*, IV, xx, 2). The lord had no legal rights over the person or the property of his *criado*, but he was entitled to the respect which a father would receive from his child:

> debe honrar a aquel quel crió en todas cosas, et haberle reverencia bien así como si fuese su padre. (IV, xxi, 3)

> (he must honour in all things the person who brought him up, and show him respect just as if he were his own father.)

Like the Roman *cliens*, the *criado* was forbidden to bear witness against his master in a court of law. If he disobeyed this injunction, thereby causing his master loss of life, limb, honour or the greater part of his wealth, he was liable to be sentenced to death. It should be added that not all *criados* were young noblemen or potential knights. Some were court officials of humble origins who as children had been brought up within the environment of the court.

A knight's apprenticeship began at the age of seven, when he was made a page-boy to the women of the household. Although serious study was discouraged, the youth might gain some knowledge of books from the court chaplain or from the tutor of the lord's children. Pero Niño was only one and a half years old when his mother was appointed wet-nurse to the future Enrique III; by the age of ten he had a private tutor:

> fue dado a criar e a enseñar a un ome sabio e entendido, para que le enseñase a doctrinase en todas las buenas costumbres e maneras que pertenescen a Fidalgo bueno e noble. (Díez de Games, *Victorial*, p. 26)

> (he was sent to be trained and educated by a wise and prudent man

that he might be instructed in all the good customs and manners appropriate to a good and noble *hidalgo*.)

This elementary schooling ended when, after graduating to the rank of a squire at the age of fourteen, he concentrated on hunting and military activities.

Patronage in knighthood

On his initiation into knighthood a person received a second *padrino* or godfather. A deliberate parallel was thus drawn between Christian baptism and the metamorphosis of a squire into a knight:

> Et a este que le desciñe el espada llámanle padrino; ca bien así como los padrinos al baptismo ayudan a confirmar et a otorgar a su afijado como sea cristiano, otrosí el que es padrino del cavallero novel desciñiéndole el espada confirma et otorga la caballería que ha rescebida. (*Siete part.*, II, xxi, 15)

> (And the person who ungirds the knight's sword is called a *padrino* [godfather]; for just as at baptism godparents help to confirm and to authorise that their godchild shall be a Christian, so the *padrino* of the inexperienced knight, when he ungirds the sword, confirms and authorises the knighthood which the latter has received.)

Baptism symbolises a spiritual birth (I, iv, 7); therefore in theory a godfather fulfils the role of a spiritual father. In a society in which people are suspicious of government institutions and in which each man must find a friend to intercede on his behalf, whether it is in the law courts or in the pursuit of a job, this spiritual relationship has many practical advantages. Baptism can be an insurance policy, because it sanctifies a relationship which may eventually develop into a utilitarian friendship, bringing with it security and material benefits. It is probably for this reason that godparenthood has remained an important institution in Mediterranean countries.[55]

A knight was forbidden, on any account, to turn his sword against his *padrino*; he was bound to fight on the latter's behalf for a period of three, sometimes seven, years after the ceremony of knighthood (II, xxi, 16). The *padrino* acted as the knight's guardian until, at the age of twenty-five, he was old enough to command troops without supervision. This system of chivalrous patronage is again illustrated in the life of Pero Niño, Enrique III's foster-brother. In his case it was the husband of his wife's sister, Ruy López Dávalos, who became his *padrino*. The *padrino* could be the knight's own father. At all events he had to be a man of honour and a skilled knight.

Tutelage of saints

From earliest Christian times the saints took the place of the pagan tutelary deities. In this capacity they were *tutelares* or *patroni*.[56] Individuals, professions and countries had (still have, if one believes in their efficacy) their patron saints. Many Spaniards attach more importance to the feast of the saint after whom they have been named than to their own birthday. The relationship between a patron saint and his or her devotee is again conceived as one which entails reciprocal obligations. The client makes an oath, sometimes marked by an ex-voto, involving hardship and acts of self-mortification, such as the penance of walking barefoot or of bearing a cross in Holy Week, on condition that some favour is shown to himself or to a friend or close relative. Medieval knights frequently made ascetic vows of this kind in the name of a patron saint, the Virgin Mary or the lady to whom they had dedicated their services. It was to free himself from the self-inflicted penance of wearing a chain round his neck every Thursday that Suero de Quiñones organised his famous *paso honroso* (Rodríguez de Lena, *Libro*). It was widely believed that the human beloved could, like the patron saint, save the knight from harm:

> There was a very widespread belief in almost all barbaric chivalric societies that the loved one could, in some instances, supply her lover in peril with additional strength and an effectual form of protection. (Nelli and Lavaud, 1966, II, p. 253)

This belief was obviously current in the chivalry of the post-barbaric age. The Count of Foix claims, in a *cobla* addressed to Salvatge (*c.* 1285), that, provided his lady assures him of the protection of her beauty, he has nothing to fear from his enemies; he even has no need of armour.

The Arab epic hero 'Antar deflects the blows of the enemy by repeating the name of his beloved 'Abla.[57]

Just as the individual knight found courage in the memory of his lady, so armies were collectively inspired to fight valiantly by belief in a patron saint. Charlemagne in France, King Arthur in England and St James of Compostela in Spain gave the warriors of these respective countries a sense of solidarity and national pride which could not have been achieved by political leadership, because, politically, these countries were fragmented into kingdoms, counties and municipalities. It is no coincidence that the remains of King Arthur were 'discovered' at Glastonbury in 1191, shortly after the canonisation of Charlemagne by Frederick Barbarossa's anti-pope (Heer, 1974, p. 164). The cult of St James at Compostela grew up as a response to the threat of the Islamic troops, who fought in the name of the Prophet Muhammad.[58] Marianism was likewise a rival to courtly love: 'S'il a sa Vénus pour le protéger,' exclaimed Simon de Montfort, after intercepting a letter from Pedro II of Aragon to a young woman of Languedoc, 'nous, nous avons la Sainte Vierge!'[59] (If he has his Venus to protect him, we have the Holy Virgin!)

Courtly love

Courtly love has been described by some scholars as a morally and socially subversive doctrine. Reto Bezzola, for example, writes: 'Love as proclaimed by the troubadours and codified by Andrew the Chaplain ran counter to two of the pillars of feudal Christian society, namely class segregation and the sacred institution of marriage' (Bezzola, 1944–63, II, p. 385). This view is misleading, for it was neither democratic nor anti-conjugal. A poet would preferably serve a lady of high rank, whom he would endow with the superiority of a feudal overlord and the social perfection which every knight or squire strove to emulate. The pains of love service were, he would claim, ennobling; high social status made a woman seem inaccessible and therefore more desirable. It was generally taken for granted, as I have already indicated, that peasant women were not worthy of such deference and that commoners of either sex were unfit to enter Love's service. If a lady is married to another man, then marriage, like social status, is a constraint which fans the flames of desire. Marriage was never the avowed aim of love, because amongst most social groups a system of arranged marriages prevailed. In social, as opposed to psychological, terms these attitudes were far from being revolutionary. The following passage from Chrétien de Troyes' *Cligés* shows that courtly love was a complement to, not a substitute for, the feudal relationship:

> Vos qui d'Amors vos feites sage,
> Et les costumes et l'usage
> De sa cort maintenez a foi,
> N'onques ne faussastes sa loi,
> Que qu'il vos an doie cheoir,
> Dites se l'en puet nes veoir
> Rien qui por Amor abelisse,
> Que l'en n'an tressaille ou palisse . . .
> De peor doit sergenz tranbler,
> Quant ses sires l'apele ou mande;
> Et qui a Amor se comande
> Son mestre et son seignor an feit:
> S'est droiz qu'an remanbrance l'eit
> Et qu'il le serve et qu'il l'enort,
> S'il vialt bien entre de sa cort.
>
> (*Romans*, pp. 116–17; ll. 3819–26, 3840–6)

(Ye who are interested in the art of Love, who do faithfully maintain the customs and usage of his court, who never failed to obey his law, whatever the result might be, tell me if there is anything that pleases because of love without causing us to tremble and grow pale. . . . The servant ought to tremble with fear when his master calls or summons him. And whoever commits himself to Love owns him as his lord and master, and is bound to do him reverence and fear him much and honour him, if he wishes to be numbered in his court.)

Love in Juan Ruiz's *Libro de Buen Amor* demands the same attitude of submissiveness: the man who does not bend his knee and kiss his hand is judged to be a villein or commoner (p. 339, st. 1246). This art of love provided the European aristocracy with an outlet for fantasy, and inculcated an ideal of humble respect for women which tempered the arrogance of men who had been trained as warriors.

A woman of noble birth, invested with the sovereignty, real or imaginary, of a feudal overlord, was almost by definition a patron. To her admirer she performed the functions of a tutelary god, protecting him from the dangers of the battlefield, dispelling the fear of slanderers and acting as a spiritual guide. Moreover, she was often a literary patron, like Marie de Champagne or Isabella of Castile, capable of judging a poem's merit.

3
The Royal Court

The word 'court', from the Latin *cortem* or *cohortem*, originally denoted an enclosed space or a gathering of people. It then came to mean a judicial tribunal, no doubt because judges and officials sat within an enclosure, while the counsel, attorney and general public stood outside the 'bar'. In medieval Europe, before the separation of judicial, legislative and executive powers, these three functions of government were exercised by the king and his counsellors. The king would personally preside over judicial assemblies, giving ear once or twice a week to pleas from his subjects. The royal household thus came to be known as the 'court'. (The term was also applied to the household of any lord who exercised judicial authority over his dependants.) Some knowledge of the etymology of the word is displayed by Alfonso el Sabio's legislators:

> Corte es llamado el logar do es el rey, et sus vasallos et sus
> oficiales con él, que le han cotianamente de consejar et de servir, et
> los otros del regno que se llegan hi o por honra dél, o por alcanzar
> derecho . . . et tomó este nombre de una palabra de latín que
> dicen *cohors*, que muestra tanto como ayuntamiento de compañas,
> ca allí se allegan todos aquellos que han a honrar et guardar al rey
> et al regno. (*Siete part.*, II, ix, 27)

> (Court is the name of the place where the king is to be found, and
> with him his vassals and officials who must daily advise and serve
> him, and the other people of the kingdom who come either to pay
> their respects to the king or else to seek justice . . . and the name
> derives from a Latin word *cohors*, which can be roughly translated as
> a gathering of companies, for it is there that all those who have to
> honour and protect the king and the kingdom converge.)

67

(One metaphor for the court, that of the *hortus conclusus* or enclosed garden, is particularly appropriate if one considers the relation between the two concepts in Latin and English etymology. *Cohorte*, the etymon of Latin *corte*, appears to be a compound of *hort-* [as in *hortus*], while English 'yard' [the primitive meaning of 'court'] is itself etymologically related to 'garden'.) The Alphonsine law book goes on to suggest, quite erroneously, that a relationship exists between the Latin *Curia*, the papal court (originally the assembly of the tribes or divisions of the Roman people), and the verb *curar*, to cure, the court being the place where matters are remedied.

According to the above definition, the royal court was the centre of government, of justice and of patronage, where the king received counsel and homage from his ministers and vassals. Furthermore, it was a place of leisure and entertainment, and, as has already been shown, a school of courtesy and of chivalry. The aristocratic style of life tended towards an ideal of play, a virtue to which St Thomas Aquinas refers by the almost forgotten name of *eutropelia* (Rahner, 1965). It was in the interests of the king to attract the grandees to his court, because, as Lawrence Stone remarks, an alluring court was 'a stabilising political factor' (Stone, 1965, p. 476). Since it was the king's duty to reprove arrogance and to teach virtue by precept and personal example, the authors of the *Siete partidas* treat courtesy, the cardinal social virtue, as an extension of the court's judicial functions. Even in the late fifteenth century, when there were at least twelve universities in Spain, the royal courts of Castile and Aragon still retained their importance as educational institutions for the nobility. The archetypal court was the court of love. When Alfonso Álvarez de Villasandino speaks of abandoning the court of love, he is referring simultaneously to the royal court and to a state of mind:

Amor, poys que veio os boos fugyr
de vossa mesnada et de vossa corte,
si Deus enderesçe a ben miña sorte
que ora me veño de vos despedir. . . .
(*Canc. Baena*, I, no. 147, p. 274)

(Since, Love, I see good men fleeing from your household and your court, if God graciously directs my fate, I have now bidden you farewell.)

Legislation, homage, play and education were four spheres of activity with which the royal court was concerned. They were also four aspects of courtly love, linked with the functions of a patron as judge, protector (and object of worship), prize-giver and teacher.

The court official

Officials in the service of monarchs and aristocrats formed a distinct social class which could not be satisfactorily accommodated within the occupational categories of the three estates. Juan Manuel was uncertain whether they should be mentioned in connection with the 'nobles defensores' or with the 'labradores'. In fact he had obviously overlooked them whilst planning his work (*Lib. est.*, I, xciii). Some court officials were *criados* or *hombres de criazón*, men who had been educated in a royal or noble court from an early age. The majority sprang from the mercantile and artisan classes, whose status in the traditional picture of society was equally ill defined. In the *Siete partidas* the monarch is advised, on the authority of Aristotle's instructions to Alexander the Great, to select his officials from the middle classes, because such men have neither the boorishness and the ingratitude of the peasantry nor the pride and rebelliousness of the upper nobility:

> Et otrosí de los homes nobles et poderosos non se puede el rey bien servir en los oficios de cada día, car por la nobleza desdeñarían el servicio cotidiano, et por el poderío atreverse hien mucho aína a facer cosas que torneríen como en daño et en despreciamento dél; mas por esto debe tomar de los homes medianos, catando primeramente que sean de buen lugar, et leales, et de buen seso et que hayan algo. (II, ix, 2)

> (Furthermore the king cannot very well employ noble and powerful men in everyday occupations, because their nobility would cause them to scorn the daily chores and their power would very soon make them venture to do things that would be harmful and insulting to him; therefore he must select men of middling degree, having first made sure that their background is solid, that they are loyal and intelligent, and that they own some property.)

Juan Manuel adds that townsmen and *hombres de criazón* are more amenable, because they cannot claim exemption from corporal punishment and do not feel insulted if they are asked to keep a record of the rents which they have collected.

Court officials can be broadly divided into three categories: those who, as counsellors, tutors and favourites, serve the king in confidential matters ('las cosas de poridat'); those who, as domestics, purveyors and minstrels, attend to his personal needs; and those who, either in a judicial or a military capacity, are concerned with the welfare and protection of the king's subjects (*Siete part.*, II, ix, 1). The position of each official in the court hierarchy seems to have been primarily dictated by proximity to the king's person and the honorific value of his services. The household of a medieval monarch possessed, in an embryonic form, the different sectors of a modern bureaucracy: the royal retinue, the Army, the Chancery, the Treasury and the High Court of Appeal. The heads of these departments were respectively the Majordomo, the Constable, the High Chancellor, the Treasurer or Chief Accountant, and the Chief Justice. In the *Siete partidas* priority is given to the court chaplain as the mediator between the king and God. In Juan I's testament he has been supplanted by the Constable, the head of the armed forces, a change which marks the secularisation of government (Blanco-González, 1962, pp. 270–1). This post was not created until the late fourteenth century. The troops had previously been led, in the king's absence, by the King's Standard-Bearer. The position of High Chancellor remained a prominent one, because, with the assistance of a host of clerks and scribes, he supervised all diplomatic correspondence and legal documents. He was thus the mediator between the king and his people (II, ix, 4). The third post mentioned in Juan I's testament was that of Majordomo, the person in charge of royal revenues and court expenses (as there were no separate offices for public and private expenditure). Juan Manuel was himself Majordomo to Alfonso el Sabio from 1278 to 1282. This post had been held by Prince Fernando, the king's eldest son, from 1260 to 1275. Many of his responsibilities were delegated to the Chief Treasurer, later superseded by the Chief Accountant. The highest domestic official was the High Chamberlain or *camarero mayor*, traditionally of noble birth, and beneath him were a large number of officials with specialised skills. An *Audiencia* or Court of Appeal, for civil justice, and a Council, for criminal justice, were created as separate judicial bodies in the late fourteenth century.

An official was sworn into office by a ceremony of vassalage. He took an oath on bended knee, his hands placed in the hands of the king, to uphold the honour of his lord, to offer him good counsel and loyal service, to keep his confidence in word and deed, to defend any property entrusted to him, to obey his lord's commands and to fulfil the duties of his office (*Siete part.*, II, ix, 26). The bond between lord and vassal was here also the bond between king and subject.

Courtiers and poets

In Spain the term *cortesano* did not become current until the fifteenth century. However, by the thirteenth century the *palaciano* or courtier was already a recognisable social type: a polite, deferential and tactful person who knew how to be merry and solemn as the occasion demanded (*Siete part.*, II, ix, 30). Courtiers and court officials had to be well versed in the rules of propriety and conspicuously subservient, because the status of their master would be gauged by their conduct. The protocol governing the seating of guests at table was extremely elaborate, as will become evident from a glance at John Russell's *The Boke of Nurture*, a book of instruction for a young man who intends to become a butler in a noble household.[60] Court officials were, to use Veblen's phrase, a 'vicarious leisure class' (Veblen, 1973, p. 56), because they were trained to stand and wait, to assume the air of the dilettante, and, like their master, to abstain from productive and profitable labour. Some specialised menial, but honorific, tasks, such as those of chief cup-bearer, lady-in-waiting or keeper of the hounds, degenerated into offices which were almost entirely nominal. There were many occupations traditionally reserved for members of the aristocracy, such as cavalry warfare, tourneys, deer-hunting and falconry, from which officials were excluded. They thus had ample time to cultivate literary and musical talents, which were both a sign of good breeding and a means of contending for favours and preferment. Court poetry was simultaneously a form of service and a form of entertainment. The court poet was essentially a non-professional or occasional author. He would not be listed on the court pay-roll as a poet, unless he was a professional *joglar* or minstrel, although skill in poetry was undoubtedly an asset for the diplomat or ambassador, especially in the task of preparing the ground for a royal marriage.

Literary patronage at court

Prior to the invention of movable type, which led to the emergence of a professional class of writers who addressed themselves to a new and predominantly urban book-reading public, almost all forms of secular literature were determined by the tastes and requirements of the aristocracy, because it alone had the wealth, the leisure and the inclination to promote such activities. Since the political and social life of the aristocracy centred on the courts of kings, princes and noble prelates, these courts became the natural meeting-places for writers, poets and patrons, and a circle of friends and acquaintants. It was through a patron that a poet was ensured of a public and immunity from adverse criticism:[61]

> Ce n'est pas chose nouvelle que ceulx qui livres batissent et composent volontiers, présentent leurs ouvrages et labours aux grands seigneurs, adfin de leur monstrer et offrir la très entière affection qu'ilz ont à eulx, et que soubz leur nom leurs livres prennent quelque auctorité et cours.

> (It is a common practice for those who decide to construct and compose books to dedicate their works and labours to men of high rank, in order to display and offer them a sign of their genuine affection, and that, under the protection of the latter's names, their books may acquire some authority and currency.)

The relationship was by no means one-sided, for by surrounding himself with poets the patron added to the splendour of his court and flattered his vanity by having his deeds and virtues immortalised.

The terms 'patron' and 'client' are so alien to modern society that they have become virtually synonymous. For example, the clients of a smart restaurant are also its patrons. The term client is often used as a substitute for customer. Thus Peter Burke, in his sociological study of artistic patronage in Renaissance Italy, distinguishes between the 'patron', who takes writers and artists into his service, and the 'client', who commissions a single work of art (Burke, 1974, p. 103). It would be more sensible to apply the term 'patron' both to the person who formally commissions a literary or artistic work and to the person who accepts a work dedicated to him. The system of literary patronage which prevailed in the Middle Ages was that which J. M. B. Edwards has defined as the 'household system'.[62] In Spain many writers and poets, such as Juan de Mena and Fernán Díaz de Toledo, were court officials; whether or not they received board and lodging, they were guaranteed economic security and a relatively high social status free from any taint of the market place.

Part II

Historical Background to the Troubadour Revival

The period during which Castile and later Aragon were ruled by the Trastámaran dynasty (1369–1516) witnessed the growth of an influential, but increasingly obsolescent, nobility, which was not unnaturally committed to the theoretical structure of society outlined above. As has already been observed, the theory of the three estates had long ceased, by the late Middle Ages, to correspond to the nature of reality, because, with the increasing division of labour, it was unrealistic to make religion, warfare and agriculture the sole criteria for the stratification of society. The competitive meritocratic ethic, which gradually emerged with the development of a monetary economy, eroded traditional status barriers by introducing class divisions based upon income and upon the fluctuations of the labour market, and disseminated bourgeois values[1] – the sanctity of labour, the virtues of thrift and prudence, the concern for respectability – which were incompatible with the *hidalgo* mentality of the leisure class élite. The activities of the urban middle classes began to encroach on those which had previously been reserved for the nobility and the clergy. Wealth, whether earned or inherited, became the conventional basis of esteem:[2]

Sea un omne necio e rudo labrador,
los dineros le fazen fidalgo e sabidores. . . .
Él [el Dinero] faze cavalleros de necios aldeanos
condes e ricosomnes, de algunos villanos;
con el Dinero andan todos omnes loçanos;
quantos son en el mundo le besan en las manos.

(A man may be an ignorant and uncouth peasant, yet money will make him a gentleman and a scholar. . . . Money makes knights out of stupid villagers, counts and high-ranking nobles out of certain

77

commoners; with Money all men go haughtily; everyone on earth today kisses Money's hand in homage.)

It was wealth rather than military status which released nobles and even commoners from the necessity of stooping to commerce and manual labour. The increased circulation of money and the dissolution of the reciprocal obligations of feudalism gave considerable scope for individualism and for the satisfaction of personal aspirations, but it also depersonalised social relations and created the need for new forms of patronage. These changes encouraged nobles to neglect their self-appointed role as the protectors of the oppressed and the upholders of justice, and made inequalities of wealth and privilege more visible and harder to justify on moral and ideological grounds. Insecurity thus became the dominant feature of life at every social level.

This process of social change was greatly accelerated in the late fourteenth century by an increase in the power of the labouring classes and by a rapid inflation of wages and prices, both to some extent consequences of the Black Death (1348–52), a plague epidemic which wiped out at least a third of the population of Europe, thereby causing a serious shortage of manpower. Landlords, who were short of day-labourers or unable to pay the exorbitant wages which were demanded, often sold their estates to peasant farmers or leased them to tenants at low rents. Serfs who were dissatisfied with their lot, or tempted by the illusion of freedom and prosperity, gravitated to the towns (Aragoneses in Viñas y Mey, 1949, pp. 354–5). This urban proletariat, regimented and exploited by industrial entrepreneurs, vented its grievances and its sense of frustration in a series of popular uprisings which occurred throughout Europe in the late Middle Ages, parti-cularly in the years 1378–83, when class friction, racial prejudice and religious fanaticism were intensified by an economic slump: 'The crucial moment everywhere in Europe', writes Vicens Vives, 'was the year 1381, the first certain date we possess for far-reaching changes in the business cycle' (Vicens Vives, 1969, p. 174).

In Spain popular unrest took the form of anti-Semitic pogroms, which erupted with particular virulence in the year 1391, after the premature death of Juan I of Castile, who had himself prepared the way for catastrophe by his approval of racialist legislation and by his decision to impose excessive taxation on his tax-paying subjects for the purpose of repaying war loans and raising more troops. Faced by two alternatives, apostasy or death, Jews in large numbers chose the former. It has been reckoned that the wave of pogroms in 1391 resulted in the conversion to Christianity of about 200,000 Jews in Aragon and Castile.[3] The converts flooded into professions which had once been closed to them, such as the law, the army, the universities, the civil service or royal household, and the church, some of them playing an active part in the Inquisition and in the composition and publication of anti-Semitic propaganda.[4] Jewish communities had traditionally relied on royal patronage. A large number of the *conversos* therefore entered royal service, and soon occupied important offices at court. They were thus able to intermarry with many of the noble families of Spain. As is well known, King Ferdinand was himself of Jewish ancestry on his mother's side.[5] By 1480 there were at least 250,000 New Christians, who 'made up the most powerful, most vital and active segment of the Castilian population in the fifteenth century (Vicens Vives, 1969, p. 292). They greatly enriched the intellectual and religious life of the time, and many of them vied with other court poets in the composition of troubadour lyrics.

In the late fourteenth century and throughout the fifteenth century there was a tendency amongst all social groups to proclaim the king as the messiah who alone could remedy social discord and redress the wrongs to which they had been subjected:

> It was a kind of apotheosis. The nobles for honour and support, the townsmen for wealth and safety, the peasants for protection to live and labour, all looked to the national or territorial ruler by right divine, the embodiment of law, of order, of justice, and of ancient right. (Prévité-Orton, 1936, p. 806)

The decline in the powers and prerogatives of individual status groups was proportionate to the growth of an efficient centralised bureaucracy, administered, for the most part, by men of middle-class origins: 'The more the ruler succeeds in attaching to himself a staff of officials who depend solely on him and whose interests are linked to his, the more the privilege-holding estates are gradually expropriated' (Weber, 1948, p. 298). The transition from a decentralised feudal or patrimonial system to a centralised rational bureaucracy could not be achieved without a struggle. In Spain, for a variety of reasons which will presently be elucidated, the aristocracy triumphed until some years after the accession of Ferdinand and Isabella. Some impression of the waxing and waning fortunes of the aristocracy can be gained from studying a graph of the number of nobiliar titles conferred between 1350 and 1540 (see Appendix 1). In the fifteenth and sixteenth centuries the number of persons in Spain who claimed tax exemption on the grounds of *hidalguía* was probably about half a million.[6] These *hidalgos* were a serious drain on the country's resources, but, as they lost their autonomous powers and were made dependent for a livelihood on royal pensions and payments for services, they ceased to be a threat to monarchical government, although they were an economic liability. The process continued in the seventeenth century. According to Sancho de Moncada, author of a contemporary analysis of the causes of the decrease in Spain's population, there were, by 1619, no fewer than 400,000 persons in the service of the court (Moncada, 1619, p. 19).

The Spanish nobility, whose survival and *raison d'être* were endangered by the socio-economic convulsions which occurred in the late Middle Ages (for which, it must be added, it was partially responsible), attributed the country's ills to the decay of traditional values. The Marquis of Santillana, for example, condemned the introduction of Italian customs and fashions as a source of corruption and recommended a return to the past in his *Lamentación de España* (c. 1450):

> Mas si tu retornasses en ti e cobrasses las antigoas costumbres
> e dexasses las ytálicas que de nuevo cobraste, e la fe e verdat e
> lealdat que son desterrados de los tu[s] términos retornassen en ti e
> fuessen en ti constituydas segúnt la antigua costumbre, entonçe
> creería yo que la altíssima e soberana piedat del magnífico e
> poderoso Dios e soberano piadosamente se toviesse contigo e
> fincasses libre de los tus tan terribles avenimientos. (*Canc. Herberay*,
> p. 22)

> (But if you [Spain] were to look back and recover your ancient
> customs and were to abandon the Italian customs which you have
> recently acquired, and if faith, truth and loyalty, which have been
> exiled from your boundaries, were brought back and re-established
> in accordance with ancient tradition, then I believe that the sublime
> and sovereign mercy of our magnificent, almighty and sovereign
> Lord would be kindly disposed towards you and would free you
> from the very terrible events that have befallen you.)

Ferdinand and Isabella were careful to observe traditions, as is proved by their letter to Diego de Valera, dated 6 July 1480, seeking advice on the correct procedure to adopt in conferring the title of marquis on the *converso* Andrés de Cabrera. Having drawn attention to an error in the *Siete partidas*, which he discussed in *Cirimonial de príncipes* (counts should not be given precedence over marquises), Valera explains how the ceremony should be conducted in accordance with Charlemagne's prescriptions at the general assembly of princes in Mainz in AD 770 (Penna, *Prosistas*, pp. 18–20). Elsewhere he bewails the contamination of chivalry by mercenary interests:

> Ya son mudados por la mayor parte aquellos propósitos, con los quales la cavallería fue comenzada: estonce se buscaba en el cavallero sola virtud, agora es buscada cavallería para no pechar.
> (p. 107)

> (The purposes for which chivalry was first established have now largely changed: then one only sought virtue in a knight, now chivalry is sought to avoid paying tax.)

The troubadour revival must be understood as part of this general nostalgia for the stability and idealism of a past which was of course largely imaginary.

In 1369, after thirteen years of civil war, Enrique de Trastámara, backed by a rebel aristocracy and the White Companies of Bertrand du Guesclin, murdered the king and seized the throne of Castile. By murdering his half-brother, Pedro I (r. 1350–69), known to posterity as 'el Cruel', Enrique avenged the assassination of his mother, Leonor de Guzmán, which had been instigated by the Portuguese favourite Juan Alfonso de Alburquerque. His generous distribution of lands and pensions to those who had assisted him in the war earned him the title of 'el Dadivoso'. The 'mercedes enriqueños' were indeed to become proverbial:

> Nunca yo çesé de guerras
> treynta años contynuados;
> conquerý gentes e tierras
> e gané nobles rregnados;
> fiz ducados e condados
> e muy altos señoríos,
> e di a estraños e a míos
> más que todos los pasados.
> (*Canc. Baena*, no. 304, II, p. 657)

(I never ceased waging war for thirty continuous years; I conquered peoples and lands, and gained noble realms; I made duchies and counties and very noble estates, and I gave more, both to foreigners and to my own subjects, than all my predecessors.)

The beneficiaries included Trastámaran relatives (Guzmán, Manuel, Enríquez), royal favourites and counsellors (Fernández de Velasco, González de Mendoza), and soldiers of fortune (Rodrigo de Villandrando, Count of Ribadeo). These families were by no means exclusively Castilian. Amongst those who infiltrated the new Castilian aristocracy through the munificence of the early Trastámaran kings were the Lunas from Aragon, the Arellanos and Estúñigas from Navarre, the Pachecos, Acuñas and Pimentels from Portugal, and Bernard de Béarn, who, by marrying into the La Cerda family, was the founder of the House of Medinaceli (Moxó, 1970). They were to provide Castile with many poets and patrons. Enrique II, married to Juana Manuel, daughter of the learned Juan Manuel, was more cosmopolitan in his outlook than most of his royal predecessors (with the exception of Alfonso el Sabio). As a political exile, he had served at the court of Pedro IV of Aragon, and had travelled widely in Europe.

The future of Castile seemed to lie with Portugal, although that country had supported the cause of the loyalists. Fernando 'o Formoso' had only one legitimate child, the Infanta Beatriz, and it seemed inevitable that Portugal would be absorbed by her aggressive neighbour. Fernando, having pressed his claim as the grandchild of Sancho IV to succeed to the throne of Castile, decided to support the pretensions of the House of Lancaster. John of Gaunt, Duke of Lancaster, married Constanza, the eldest daughter of Pedro I of Castile and his mistress María de Padilla, in September 1371; and to ensure that the Castilian succession remained with Edward III's sons, Edmund of Cambridge was wedded by the king's command to Constanza's beautiful younger sister Isabel, who was probably the lady addressed by Othon de Grandson in his *Cinq balades ensuivans*, some stanzas of which were translated by Chaucer for John of Gaunt (Braddy, 1947, pp. 75–9, 81–3). Edmund made an expedition to Lisbon in 1381, planning that his son, Edward Langley, should marry the young princess. But Portugal, like Castile, was destined to be ruled by a bastard dynasty. Edmund proved to be utterly incompetent as a military commander, and the betrothal had to be delayed until the king of Portugal had withdrawn his allegiance to the anti-pope Clement VII. The queen, Leonor Teles, was extremely unpopular. Her adulterous relations with the Galician nobleman Juan Fernández Andeiro aroused a scandal, which was further aggravated by news that she was pregnant. Believing that Dom João, the king's illegitimate half-brother, was responsible for the censure of her conduct, she had him and one of his companions arrested. Dom João appealed to Edmund for help, and the latter, after much hesitation and under the pressure of public opinion, intervened to secure the release of the prisoners. In the following year a secret treaty between King Fernando of Portugal and Juan I of Castile provided for the dissolution of the Infanta Beatriz's vows to Edward Langley and for her betrothal to the Castilian king's second son, Fernando (later elected to rule Aragon). When the Portuguese king died on 22 October 1383 at the age of thirty-eight, Juan I took Beatriz as his own bride and set out to annex Portugal. News of the Castilian invasion toppled the queen regent's government in Lisbon and sparked off a popular revolution. Dom João was proclaimed a national hero when he broke into the royal palace and assassinated Andeiro. The common people, opposed to the old feudal regime and united in their desire to defend their country, selected him as their leader. At the Siege of Lisbon in the summer of 1384 both sides suffered heavy casualties from plague, but the city held out bravely, and in 1385 Juan I's imperialistic ambitions were rudely shattered when his troops were put to rout at the Battle of Aljubarrota. Total losses have been estimated at about 7,500. The ancient aristocracy of Portugal, which had fought with the invaders to recover its lands and prerogatives, was virtually annihilated (P. E. Russell, 1955, p. 396 *et passim*).

Juan I's vulnerability encouraged the Duke of Lancaster to make a final, but once again abortive, bid for the Castilian throne. The English Parliament gave the enterprise its official blessing and authorised 1,000 royal archers to enter the duke's service. On 8 March 1386 Richard II formally declared his uncle to be the true heir to Castile, and presented him with a golden crown for use at his coronation. After a magnificent tournament at Smithfield, Lancaster's soldiers embarked for Galicia, accompanied by a large number of craftsmen, household officials and ladies-in-waiting, timing their arrival to coincide with the Feast of Compostela (25 July). A squadron of Castilian ships, surprised at anchor in the port of Betanzos, was easily destroyed. Juan I was so alarmed that he took the unprecedented step of promising the title and privileges of knighthood, including tax exemption, to every man, whether mounted or on foot, who was willing to fight at his own expense for a period of two months (Pescador, 1961, p. 214). The king's fears were in fact exaggerated. Lancaster wasted much precious time in Portugal, arranging a marriage between his daughter Philippa (child of his first wife Blanche) and Dom João d'Aviz, and he tactlessly signed a treaty at Ponte do Mouro, whereby the hated Portuguese were to receive a strip of Castilian territory 80 kilometres wide in order to improve Portugal's defensive position. On 5 January 1387, Pedro IV of Aragon died, and was succeeded by the pro-Trastámaran Joan I. Some days earlier another personal friend of Juan I of Castile, Carlos 'el Noble', had ascended the throne of Navarre on the death of his father Carlos II (who had fought for the legitimist cause with the Black Prince and Lancaster). Dom João and Philippa finally married on St Valentine's Day, 1387. By then about two-thirds of the English troops had perished of plague. Once the campaign was under way more time was wasted in the misplaced gallantry of contests between individual combatants outside the walls of Benavente. Safe-conducts were granted to those who wished to watch jousting between English and French knights, many of them acquaintances from the Hundred Years' War. The fraternisation continued at Salamanca: 'Both Frenchmen and Englishmen dined and jousted happily with each other, behaving like old friends rather than nominal enemies' (P. E. Russell, 1955, p. 483). Yet the Anglo-Portuguese troops had failed to capture a city large enough to serve as a base for any length of time, and the starving Portuguese, excluded from the banqueting, were not unnaturally disenchanted. In June 1387 the English constable, Sir John Holland, nonchalantly took leave of the Portuguese king, taking with him Lady Holland and several of Constanza's ladies-in-waiting. Lancaster's last chance of gaining a crown was now lost, but he characteristically achieved a profitable matrimonial alliance: his daughter Catalina married Juan I's son, the future Enrique III. This marriage, negotiated in 1388, brought Lancaster an annual tribute of 200,000 francs, which was a heavy burden on the Castilian economy.

Juan I regarded his country's defeat at the hands of the Portuguese as an act of divine retribution for his failure to establish justice in the kingdom, and he saw to it that authoritarian and fanatically religious measures were passed by the Cortes of Valladolid in December 1386 and by the Cortes of Briviesca in December 1387. Shopkeepers were obliged to close their premises on Sundays; the laws which demanded that Jews and Moors wear identity marks and that they should be segregated from Christians were to be strictly enforced. Furthermore, ignoring the principle of democratic representation, the king took upon himself the right to nominate members of the Royal Council. 'It is not without irony', writes P. E. Russell, 'that Castile should return to the political policies of Pedro I in the year in which the dynastic struggle caused by Pedro's murder was brought to an end' (p. 496). It can at least be said of Pedro I that he was, in the eyes of his adversaries, excessively tolerant to Jews and Moors.

During the brief reign of Enrique III (1390–1406), known as 'el Doliente' because he was a constant invalid, the court was ruled by lawyers, prelates and bachelors of theology. For the first time in many years there were no occasions for military exploits, and the academic, as opposed to the chivalric, profession momentarily acquired some prestige. The king had been educated by Diego Anaya, the founder of the Colegio Mayor de San Bartolomé at Salamanca, by Álvaro de Isorna, Bishop of Cuenca, later Archbishop of Santiago (one of the reforming clerics who championed the monarchy after Enrique II's death in 1379), and by Juan Hurtado de Mendoza, who joined the king's relatives in a revolt against the Regency Council when Juan I died in 1390. During these years the power of the upper nobility and that of the third estate was gradually checked by the emergence of a new state oligarchy dependent on the royal treasury (Mitré Fernández, 1968). The animosity which existed between the poetic innovators, led by Francisco Imperial, most of whom had been trained in the universities and were of mercantile origin, and the traditionalists, represented by Alfonso Álvarez de Villasandino (who, contrary to the generally accepted opinion, belonged to the rural gentry) seems to have been largely a product of a sudden change in the relative prosperity of different social groups. Villasandino, who became in his old age a target for ridicule and self-parody, had been brought up in the royal household and had been made a member of the Orden de la Banda by Enrique II; he speaks of his houses and wine-presses,[7] and still keeps three pikemen in his service:

Gasté toda mi fazienda
por bien apostar tres lanças
para mis fuertes andanças.
(*Canc. Baena*, no. 72, st. 5)

(I spent all my fortune on suitably equipping three pikemen for my bold knight-errantry.)

That the decline of chivalry was in his opinion clearly correlated with the rise of the schoolmen is illustrated by the following passage:

ya los inorantes andan disputando
las glossas e testos de Santo Agostín;
e los aldeanos fablan buen latýn;
las grandes proezas ya son olvidadas.
(ibid., no. 97, st. 2)

(now the ignorant go about debating the commentaries and texts of St Augustine; and villagers speak good Latin; great deeds of valour are now forgotten.)

Those who, like Villasandino, had received small fiefs from Enrique II could no longer survive on their revenues, while high court officials could not afford to be generous. This change of circumstances is alluded to in a poem addressed to Villasandino by an anonymous bachelor of arts:

Dezidme, señor, hu se foy franqueza
que ia non paresçe nos rrenos de España,
e grant tempo ha que aquesta compaña
que hy fyzo, bive en muy grant pobreza . . .
e poys o señores ia nada non dan
fydalgos cabtivos ora ¿qué farán?
Os pobres e boos son deseredados.
(Ibid., no. 94, sts 2 and 4)

(Tell me, sir, where generosity went, for it no longer appears in the realms of Spain, and the company to which I belong has been living for a long time in very great poverty? . . . And since the lords now give us nothing, what will the wretched *hidalgos* do? The poor and the good have been disinherited.)

Fernán Sánchez Talavera, in a poem in which he speaks of leaving the palace to take the habit of the Order of Calatrava, complains that it is no time for troubadours:

Tyenpo es de renunçiar
ya los ommes el palasçio . . .
no es tiempo de trobadores
e nin de ommes gentiles,
pues son onrrados los viles,
con usos, arrendadores.
   (*ibid.*, no. 535, sts 1 and 3)

(It is time now for men to renounce the palace . . . it is no time for troubadours or gentlemen, since base tenants are honoured with rights of usufruct.)

The distinction in the above passage between *gentiles* and *viles* is the distinction of status between noble and ignoble. A useful definition of *gentileza* is given by Diego de Valencia in *Rregla a los galanes*:[8]

Ciertamente gentileza
es linaje guarnecido
de virtudes e nobleza
según pienso y e leydo.

(In my opinion and according to what I have read, gentility is certainly lineage adorned with virtues and nobility.)

The insecurity of the rural gentry must be seen in relation to the growth of popular authority which reached its zenith in 1391. In that year the Cortes (or parliament) of Madrid was attended by 123 *procuradores* on behalf of the third estate representing forty-nine towns. Never again in Spain's history was a meeting of the Cortes so well attended. But it must not be forgotten that this year of democracy was also the year of Spain's worst pogroms.

Enrique III died in 1406 on Christmas Day, when his son was only two years old. Although the child king, Juan II, did not prove to be the messiah which Spain so desperately needed, prophecies of an aristocratic regeneration were fully realised during his long reign. At the start of his reign there were, according to Diego de Valera's *Crónica abreviada*, only three counts in the kingdom of Castile (Medinaceli, Trastámara and Niebla), but by the 1470s, when Pulgar was composing his *Claros varones*, there were about fifty noble families with the titles of duke, marquis, count and viscount (Pulgar, *Claros varones*, p. xxi). From 1406 until 1419 Castile was ruled by a regency, in which Catalina, the queen mother, acted as regent (until she died in 1418), assisted by Juan II's uncle, Fernando de Antequera, who acted as co-regent until he was called to govern Aragon in 1412. The death of Martí 'el Humá' (the Humane) in 1410, which brought another ancient dynasty, that of Aragon and the House of Barcelona, to an abrupt end, and the election of Fernando, instead of Jaime, Count of Urgel, by a commission which met at Caspe in 1412, enabled a younger branch of the Trastámaras to ascend the throne of Aragon, thus making a flourishing Aragonese culture easily accessible to Castile, and preparing the way for the unification of the two realms under Ferdinand II and Isabella in 1479.

During the fourteenth century, while most of Europe was ravaged by warfare, Aragon and Catalonia had enjoyed comparative peace and prosperity under Pedro IV of Aragon (or Pere III), known as 'el Cerimoniós' (r. 1336–87). He was an astute and remarkably enlightened politician, who prevented his subjects from being drawn into the Hundred Years' War by adopting a policy of neutrality. He was the author of several works, including a book on court ceremonial based on the *Leges palatinae* of Jaume III of Mallorca: *Llibre de les ordinacions de la real Casa d'Aragó*.[9] Such was the fame of the Aragonese court that King Wenzel IV of Bohemia instructed his envoy Robert of Prague to study the customs of the court when the latter visited Joan I in 1388 (see below, pp. 123–6). Pedro IV had been married four times: to María of Navarre (1338); to Leonor of Portugal (1347); to Leonor of Sicily (1349); and to Sibilia de Forcià, widow of Artal de Foces (1377). His successor Joan I (b. 1350; r. 1387–95), son of Leonor of Sicily, inherited a vast maritime empire, comprising Sicily, Mallorca, Corsica and Greece, which was severely hit by the economic depression in the 1380s. It is significant that Joan's wives were all French; in 1370 he married Jeanne de Valois, daughter of Philippe VI of France and Queen Blanche, but she died in Béziers before reaching Aragon; on 6 March 1372 he married Marthe d'Armagnac, who died prematurely in Saragossa in 1378; and in late October 1379 he was betrothed to Yolande de Bar (1365–1431), daughter of Robert, Duke of Bar, and Marie, sister of Charles 'le Sage'. Joan I had an impulsive, sentimental and artistic temperament, as had a large number of contemporary kings and princes, including Richard II of England, Wenzel IV of Bohemia, Duke Philippe of Burgundy, Gaston Fébus, Count of Foix, and King René of Anjou, which was in marked contrast to his father's ironic and realistic turn of mind. It was characteristic of Joan that, on learning that Jeanne de Valois (to whom he had been betrothed but whom he knew only by hearsay) was ill, he crossed the Pyrenees incognito to be by her bedside. His third marriage was a love match which did not meet with his father's approval. Pedro IV had planned that the bride should be his niece María, the heiress of Sicily. He informed his son in 1379 that Guillermo Ramón de Moncada had announced his intention of challenging to a joust any man who asserted that there was a woman in Barcelona more beautiful than María (Rubió y Balaguer, 1943, p. 271). In a letter, dated 13 November 1379, he reluctantly gave his blessing to the marriage with Yolande, but at the same time appended a poem in which he found an outlet for his disappointment, complaining that his son had been ill advised to shun a marriage which would have brought him 'un bon regnat' (Riquer, 1964, II, pp. 534–6). Yolande in fact proved to be a woman of great charm who exerted a profound influence on the Aragonese court in matters of refinement and literary taste (see below, pp. 123–4). It has been said, perhaps as an indication of Joan's veneration for her, that the marriage was not consummated until 1384 (Servais, 1865–7, I, p. 348). This statement is contradicted by the fact that on 11 August 1381 she gave birth to a daughter, Yolande, who in 1400 married Louis II, Duke of Anjou.[10]

In view of the prestige which the Aragonese court possessed in the late fourteenth and early fifteenth centuries, it is significant that some of the leading political and literary figures in Castile during this same period were Aragonese by birth or by education. Iñigo López de Mendoza (1398–1458), the future Marquis of Santillana, was schooled in Aragon: in 1413 he was chief cup-bearer to Prince Alfonso (later to become Alfonso V, 'el Magnánimo') when Fernando de Antequera was still regent; and in 1414 he attended the *jochs florals*, the annual poetry competition over which Enrique de Villena then presided. Villena (1384–1434), son of Pedro de Aragon and Juana, an illegitimate daughter of Enrique II of Castile, was himself an important intermediary between Aragon and Castile. His *Arte de trovar*, of which only a fragment survives, was addressed to Santillana with the express purpose of fostering a troubadour school in Castile (see below, pp. 142–5). Álvaro de Luna (1390–1453), who entered the Castilian court in 1408 on the recommendation of his uncle, Pedro de Luna, the anti-pope Benedict XIII, came from a noble family of Aragon. In addition to his political abilities, he was a lover, a poet, a patron of poets, and the author of a book in defence of women: *Libro de las claras e virtuosas mugeres.*[11] His portrait is given in the *Crónica de Álvaro de Luna*, attributed to Gonzalo Chacón:

Fue muy medido e conpasado en las costumbres desde la su juventud; sienpre amó e honrró mucho al linage de las mugeres. Fue muy enamorado en todo tienpo; guardó gran secreto a sus amores, e muchas bezes declaraba en ellos misterios de otros grandes fechos. Vistióse siempre bien. . . . Fue muy inventivo e mucho dada a fallar invenciones, e sacar entremeses en fiestas o en justas, o en guerra; en las quales invençiones muy agudamente significaba lo que quería. (Mata Carriazo, *Crónica*, p. 207)

(Since his youth his habits had been very moderate and restrained; he always loved and greatly respected the female sex. He was constantly in love; he kept his love affairs very secret, and frequently he used them to expound mysteries concerning other great matters. He always dressed well. . . . He was very inventive, and much given to composing poetic fictions and directing theatrical interludes at feasts or jousts or on the battlefield; in these fictions he expressed whatever he wished with great subtlety.)

The sons of Fernando de Antequera and Leonor of Castile were also responsible for firing the imagination of Spaniards with the fiction of chivalry and courtly love. According to a modern historian, it was chiefly through their influence that 'the splendid fantasy now prevailing in other European courts was introduced into Castile' (Suárez Fernández, 1959, p. 78). Fernando never attempted, like John of Gaunt, to seize the throne of Castile. Yet by employing similar tactics he certainly ensured that his children controlled Spain's destiny.

The eldest of the Infantes de Aragon, whose departure from the stage of history was lamented by Jorge Manrique in his lines on the death of his father, was Alfonso V (r. 1416–58), an outstanding monarch and an enthusiastic patron of the arts who attracted many Castilian poets into his orbit. Much of his later life was spent in Naples, where he established a flourishing court.

Juan II, King of Aragon and Navarre (r. 1458–79), had neither the charm nor the sensibility of his elder brother. In 1418, when the queen regent of Castile died, he fought with his brother Enrique, Master of Santiago, for control of the Regency Council, and in the following year he ruled Navarre in the name of his wife Blanche, refusing, when she died in 1441, to allow his son Carlos to inherit the kingdom. Prince

Enrique, married to Juan II's sister Catalina, was a champion of chivalry, a poet and a literary figure who probably deserves to be better known. An unpublished poem of his is listed by Rafael Floranes as forming part of a miscellaneous collection of prose and verse compiled by Fernán Martínez de Burgos.[12] A fourth brother, Sancho, was Master of Alcántara, and a fifth, Pedro, died in the Siege of Naples in 1438. One of Fernando de Antequera's daughters, María, who was betrothed to Juan II of Castile in 1418 and died in 1445, inspired a number of pro-feminist works, including Juan Rodríguez del Padrón's *Triunfo de la donas* (*Obras*, pp. 88–127) and Diego de Valera's *Tratado en defenssa de virtuossas mugeres* (Penna, *Prosistas*, pp. 55–76). Another daughter, Leonor, married Prince Duarte, heir to the Portuguese throne, in 1430.

Juan II of Castile had the misfortune to be born in an age which demanded no less than extraordinary qualities of leadership in a king. He was an idle, weak and irresponsible man who, instead of assuming the duties of kingship, remained throughout his life under the dominion of others. Fernán Pérez de Guzmán holds him chiefly to blame for the anarchy which prevailed during his reign:

> nunca una ora sola quiso entender nin trabajar en el regimiento
> aunque en su tienpo fueron en Castilla tantas rebueltas e
> movimientos e daños e males e peligros quantos no ovo en
> tienpo de reyes pasados por espacio de dozientos años.
> (*Generaciones*, p. 39)

> (never for a single hour did he wish to understand or turn his mind to
> the task of government, even though during his reign there were in
> Castile more disturbances and uprisings and injuries and crimes and
> dangers than there had been during the reigns of previous kings for
> a period of two hundred years.)

However, he was too intelligent to be ignorant of his defects. In an exchange of verses with Álvaro de Luna the latter extols his charity and *gentileza* and he replies:

> Cierto es que la firmeza
> es raýz de la bondat,
> e muy estranya maldat
> poderío con flaqueza.
> (*Canc. Palacio*, no. 49, p. 157)

(Steadfastness is certainly the root of goodness, and power combined with weakness a very strange evil.)

The prince's guardians, Diego López de Estúñiga, Chief Justice of Castile, and Juan de Velasco, High Chamberlain, died before the boy was old enough to be declared of age (the former in November 1417, the latter in October 1418). The queen mother herself died in 1418, leaving the country in the hands of a Regency Council which was crippled by internal dissension. By this time the king had become infatuated by Álvaro de Luna, who charmed his master through his good looks, social graces, literary talents and, according to some, through the power of magic. He would dance with no one but Álvaro, and would become depressed and irritable when the latter was absent. When the king came of age in 1419, the two contending factions, that of Prince Enrique and that of Prince Juan, approached him through the mediation of his favourite. In 1420 Juan II suffered the indignity of being placed under house arrest for a period of seven months in his palace at Tordesillas by Prince Enrique and the Constable Ruy López Dávalos. By the end of that year a palace revolution had occurred which brought younger men to positions of power, so that of the seven magnates who controlled the council in 1418 only one man, namely Alfonso Enríquez (who had shrewdly cultivated the friendship of Álvaro de Luna), now remained.[13] By exploiting differences and the king's incompetence to govern, Álvaro made himself, by slow degrees, the virtual dictator of Castile. The expulsion of Prince Enrique's partisans from office was, however, politically unwise, because it created a dangerous anti-monarchical element which was extremely jealous of Álvaro de Luna. Initially rivalries found an outlet in tournaments and in song, rather than in actual skirmishes, but the situation soon deteriorated into civil war. Juan II's betrothal to María of Aragon in 1418, the appointment of Álvaro as constable in 1423, and the visit of the king's sister-in-law, Leonor of Aragon, in 1428 on her way to Portugal were all marked by boisterous festivities.

Even on the authority of his most hostile critics, Juan II was a talented musician, a competent Latin scholar, an assiduous reader and a discriminating critic:

Sabía fablar e entender latín, leía muy bien, plazíanle mucho libros y estorias, oía muy de grado los dizires rimados e conocía los viçios dellos, avía grant plazer en oir palabras alegres e bien

apuntadas, e aun él mesmo las sabía bien dizir. Usava mucho la
caça e el monte e entendía bien en toda la arte dello. Sabía dell
arte de la música, cantava e tañía bien e aun en el justar e juegos
de cañas se avía bien. (Pérez de Guzmán, *Generaciones*, p. 39)

(He understood Latin and could speak it, he read very well, he
enjoyed books and stories very much, he was fond of listening to
rhymed *decires* [poems for the spoken voice] and understood their
imperfections, he derived much pleasure from listening to amusing
and well-aimed remarks, and he himself could make some good
ones. He often took part in hunting and the chase, and was well
versed in this whole art. He was familiar with the art of music, he
sang and played well, and even in jousts and in contests with reed
spears he would acquit himself well.)

It must be remembered that his education had been entrusted to
Sh'lomoh Hallevi, better known to orthodox Spaniards as Pablo de
Santa María, once Rabbi and later Bishop of Burgos and Chancellor
of Castile (Serrano, 1942). He took an interest in the study of classical
mythology, as did his chief poet and propagandist Juan de Mena, and
he evidently found much consolation during troubled times in the
stoicism of Seneca's *De vita beata*, a work which was translated into
Castilian by Pablo de Santa María's son, Alfonso de Cartagena.[14]
Leonardo Bruni's lengthy epistle to Juan II, tracing the ancestry of all
Spanish kings to the Roman emperors, is well known (Soria, 1956,
pp. 113–15, 122–5), but Bruni failed to destroy the myth of Gothic
ancestry, and Italian humanism did not begin to take root in Castile
until the closing decades of the fifteenth century. Scholarly and
theological debates were a distinctive feature of the poetry anthology
compiled for Juan II by Juan Alfonso de Baena, but short lyrical
canciones on traditional troubadour themes were predominant in the
later *cancioneros*, and the Castilian court was above all a centre for
courtly and chivalric activities.

The period 1420–50 was throughout Europe, both in life and
literature, one of romance and chivalric enterprise. Several biographical
works about contemporary heroes, such as Pero Niño, Jacques de
Lalaing and Jean Le Meingre (known as Boucicaut), are scarcely
distinguishable from prose romances, such as the anonymous *Curial
e Güelfa*, Antoine de La Sale's *Le Petit Jehan de Saintré* and Rodríguez
del Padrón's *Siervo libre de amor*.[15] In 1429 Philippe 'le Bon', Duke of

Burgundy, married Isabel, daughter of João I of Portugal, and founded the Order of the Golden Fleece, which conceived Jason's quest as an allegory of its purpose to rescue Jerusalem from the Moslems. Equally fantastic was the *paso honroso* of Suero Quiñones. At one o'clock in the morning of New Year's Day, 1434, Quiñones and nine other knights dressed in white armour entertained Juan II, his wife María, his son Enrique and Álvaro de Luna. It was then that he announced his intention of holding a 'pas d'armes' for a month, beginning fifteen days before the Feast of Santiago, in which he vowed to break 300 lances before he considered himself liberated from love's servitude. The jousting match took place, as arranged, in the district of Leon on the pilgrim route to Santiago near the bridge of Orbigo (Puymaigre, 1873, II, pp. 127–38). This extraordinary example of life lived as romance was faithfully recorded by the court notary Pero Rodríguez de Lena in his *Libro del passo honroso* (see Bibliography). The church expressed its disapproval of jousts by refusing to allow those who died in them to be buried in holy ground, but it was impotent to prevent them taking place. In the same year a May Day tournament was organised, which ended with a prize-giving speech read by a poet personifying the king of love, who addressed the king as his standard-bearer (see below, pp. 145–7). In these years many knights, pilgrims and diplomats travelled from Spain to foreign parts. The Council of Basle in 1436 provided a good opportunity for travel. For most of them, however, political and religious considerations were of secondary importance. Pero Tafur, who journeyed to Morocco, Italy and the Holy Land in the years 1436–9, seems to have been primarily motivated by the love of adventure and the curiosity of a tourist (Tafur, *Andanças*). A chronicler, explaining why Pedro of Portugal, the second son of King Duarte, had been to Germany in 1428, writes quite simply 'que abía ydo allá a ver mundo' (Carrillo de Huete, *Crónica*, p. 30) (that he had been over there to see the world). Knight-errantry had become once again a fashionable pursuit. The writer Diego de Valera, son of the Jewish doctor Alonso Chirino, witnessed the coronation of the Holy Roman Emperor, Albert V, in Prague in 1437, and won many awards for his skill in jousting.[16] Many other Spanish knights, who, like Diego de Valera, were critical of the way Castile was governed, went abroad to win renown.

Some Castilian knights and poets entered the service of Alfonso 'el Magnánimo'. Alfonso set sail on his first expedition to Italy in 1420, leaving his wife Doña María, sister of Juan II of Castile, to rule Aragon in his absence. Whilst in Sardinia, he received an embassy from Joanna II, Queen of Naples, begging him to assist her against Louis III of Anjou and promising him, as a recompense, the title of Duke of Calabria and the succession to the kingdom of Naples. Alfonso took up the offer and repulsed Louis of Anjou's fleet, which was threatening the port of Naples. Under the influence of her lover Caracciolo, the old queen then changed her mind and transferred her allegiance to the House of Anjou, which provoked a fresh war in 1423. The queen barricaded herself in the castle of Capuana and Alfonso took Naples by force. The city was no sooner taken than he had to hasten back to Spain, on learning that his brother, Prince Enrique, Master of Santiago, had been imprisoned on the orders of Juan II of Castile. In 1422 Ruy López Dávalos (d. 1428), the Constable of Castile, was deprived of his estates and titles, and these were bestowed on Álvaro de Luna in the following year. Dávalos is reported to have said to one of Álvaro de Luna's servants, who had come to visit him in Valencia where he lived in exile:[17]

> Dezilde al señor don Álvaro, que qual es fuimos, y qual somos será. Porque tan de vidrio es su fortuna, y la de todos los privados: como lo fue la mía.

> (Tell your master Don Álvaro that we once were what he is now, and that what we are now he will become. Because his fortune and that of all court favourites is so brittle; just as mine was.)

In 1432 Alfonso 'el Magnánimo' embarked on his second expedition to Italy, this time accompanied by his brothers, King Juan of Navarre, Enrique and Pedro, and by many Castilian nobles who had been exiled or disinherited through their opposition to Álvaro de Luna.

Amongst the refugees from Castile were many knights who wrote poetry, including several sons and step-sons of Ruy López Dávalos: Alfonso Dávalos and Iñigo Dávalos (later Marquis of Pescara); Iñigo and Fernando de Guevara (children of Ruy López's second wife Elvira de Guevara); Rodrigo Dávalos, a *criado* of Prince Enrique, Master of Santiago (Alfonso V's brother); Diego Gómez de Sandoval, Count of Castro, portrayed by Fernán Pérez de Guzmán as a robust and ambitious gentleman with a passion for horses and war (*Generaciones*, p. 28); Gonzalo de Quadros, who had aroused Juan II's displeasure by wounding Álvaro de Luna in a tournament in honour of the king's

betrothal in 1418; Lope and Juan de Estúñiga, sons of Juana, an illegitimate daughter of Carlos III of Navarre, and Iñigo López de Estúñiga,
Juan II's chief bodyguard; and Juan de Dueñas, who had been banished
from the Castilian court for having written a poem in which he pro-
tested that poor and honourable knights were scorned while the
undeserving rich were shown excessive favour (Vendrell de Millás,
1933, pp. 73–8). Several of these Castilians shared imprisonment with
Alfonso V after the naval Battle of Ponza, a defeat which inspired a
long poem on the mutability of Fortune by the Marquis of Santillana,
entitled *Comedieta de Ponza* (1436). The Genoese handed Alfonso over
to the Duke of Milan, Filippo Maria Visconti, who set him free
without a ransom, even recognising his claim to the kingdom of
Naples. Juan de Tapia, one of the most talented of the Castilian poets in
the service of Alfonso, addressed a panegyric to the Duke of Milan's
illegitimate daughter Bianca, who pleaded for his release (Vendrell
de Millás, 1933, pp. 105–13). The troops of Louis III's brother, René
d'Anjou, were vanquished, and on 26 February 1443 the Aragonese
king made a magnificent triumphal entry into Naples through an
artificial breach in the walls, seated in a gilded chariot drawn by white
horses. In pageantry, refinement, scholarship and the practice of the
fine arts the court of Naples soon surpassed that of Castile.

At the Neapolitan court Latin humanism and traditional Spanish
court poetry seem to have coexisted without any appreciable inter-
change between them:[18]

> The first thing to notice is that during the reign of Alfonso V two
> literatures flourished simultaneously, although entirely independent
> of one another: one was that of the Italian humanists and their
> Spanish disciples, written in the Latin tongue; the other was that of
> the court poets, generally written in Castilian and sometimes in
> Catalan.

These two very different aspects of Neapolitan court culture reflect
the complexity of Alfonso V's own character. For Jacob Burckhardt he
naturally typified the Renaissance prince:

> Among the secular princes of the fifteenth century, none displayed
> such enthusiasm for antiquity as Alfonso the Great of Aragon, King
> of Naples. . . . He had in his service, either successively or at the same
> time, George of Trebizond, the younger Chrysoloras, Lorenzo

Valla, and Bartolommeo Fazio and Antonio Panormita, who were his historians; Panormita daily instructed his court in Livy, even during military expeditions. These men cost him 20,000 gold florins annually. (Burckhardt, 1960, p. 175)

He would often arrange after-dinner readings from Virgil, which all who were serious were welcome to attend, especially those of low condition, and such was his intellectual curiosity that he used to put books under his pillow when he went to bed so that he could read them as soon as he woke up (Beccadelli, 1552, fols 104^r and 108^r). Yet in his thirst for knowledge, his love of ceremonial, his tender, sometimes credulous, piety, his craving for fame, and his passionate courtship of Lucrezia d'Alagno there was a strange blend of Renaissance and medieval qualities. As an example of his piety, it is sufficient to recall his custom of secretly washing and kissing the feet of sixty of the poor every Thursday, giving them food, clothes and alms (fols 96^v–97^r). When, late in life (probably in 1448), he met Lucrezia and became infatuated by her beauty, he conformed to the true picture of the courtly lover before his idol. Pope Pius II describes her as follows:

She was a beautiful woman or girl, the daughter of poor but noble Neapolitan parents (if there is any nobility in poverty) with whom the King was so desperately in love that in her presence he was beside himself and could neither hear nor see anything but Lucrezia. He could not take his eyes off her, praised everything she said, marvelled at her wisdom, admired every gesture, thought her beauty divine. He had made her many presents, had given orders that she was to receive the honours of a queen, and at last was so completely dominated by her that no one could get a hearing without her consent. Marvellous is the power of love! (Piccolomini, *Memoirs*, p. 74)

She is reported to have claimed that she would die rather than permit the king to ravish her maidenhood, but Pius II expresses some scepticism with regard to the sincerity of such noble words, observing that after Alfonso's death she became the mistress of Giacomo Piccinino's secretary and had a child by him. Alfonso was only six years old when he married his cousin, María of Castile, and he failed to obtain Calixtus III's authorisation for a divorce when his wife had caused one of his mistresses, Marguerite de Híjar, to be murdered (Puymaigre, 1873,

II, p. 183 n.). On 7 November 1457 Lucrezia travelled to Rome to seek an annulment of the marriage on the grounds of sterility (Riccio, 1543, fol. 63ᵛ). However, her mission was unsuccessful, and Alfonso died several months later, leaving Naples to his illegitimate son, Ferrante (whose real father, some say, was a Valencian Jew).

Few Spaniards wished to remain in Naples under the rule of Ferrante, who was, by most accounts, of a despotic and sadistic disposition. (One exception was Juan de Tapia. He entered the service of the new king and wrote a panegyric for him, describing him as a 'mountain of diamonds'.) Instead they returned to Spain to swell the tide of baronial anarchy which existed both in the kingdom of Castile and in the Crown of Aragon. In Castile victory for the pro-monarchical faction at the Battle of Olmedo in 1445 failed to rehabilitate the royal authority. In 1447 Álvaro de Luna contributed to his own downfall by arranging Juan II's second marriage to Isabel of Portugal (1425–96), for it was under her influence that, in 1453, the king agreed to have Álvaro beheaded. Juan II outlived his favourite by only one year, and was succeeded by his much maligned son, Enrique IV (1425–74), who was even less successful at appeasing the nobility than his father. Meanwhile in Navarre and Catalonia, where there was growing discontent, the hopes of the populace crystallised successively around two young princes whose lives were brief and tragic: Carlos, Prince of Viana (1421–61), and Dom Pedro, Constable of Portugal (1429–66). Both were poets, men of letters and bibliophiles, and both wrote in Castilian.

Carlos – he actually signed himself Charles – was the son of Alfonso V's brother, Juan II of Aragon, by the latter's first wife, Blanche of Navarre, widow of King Martin of Sicily. One of the conditions of his parents' marriage in 1420 was that the throne of Navarre should pass to their issue. In 1425 the prince's grandfather, Carlos 'el Noble', died, and on 15 May 1428 the Cortes declared that Carlos was the rightful heir. When Blanche died in 1441 she stipulated that Navarre should be governed by Carlos, but added that he should not employ the title of king without his father's consent. This consent was never granted, and when in 1451 Carlos was forced to make a pact with Juan II of Castile without consulting his father, the latter sent his second wife, Juana Enríquez, daughter of the Admiral, to govern Navarre as co-regent. This action provoked a civil war which rekindled the ancient feud between *agramonteses* and *beaumonteses*. Carlos was defeated. A treaty, arranged through the mediation of Alfonso V's wife, Doña María, was broken in December 1453. Two years later Juan of Aragon signed a treaty with his son-in-law, Gaston de Foix, disinheriting Carlos and Blanche, the children of his first marriage. In that same year, 1455, Blanche's marriage to Enrique IV of Castile was annulled on the pretext that it had never been consummated. Carlos fled to France, where he encountered little sympathy for his cause. He then travelled to Naples to seek the advice and support of his uncle. However, he was too late, for Alfonso had just died, and, fearing lest his sudden arrival should be misinterpreted as a bid for the Neapolitan throne, Carlos proceeded to Sicily. Here, where his mother had once been queen, he was well received. After spending several quiet months at the Benedictine monastery of Messina, he returned to Spain, reaching Catalonia in August 1459. A new pact with his father was short-lived. Juan II of Aragon was disliked intensely by the Catalans; he was therefore galled by the enthusiasm which greeted his son's entry into Barcelona. It was moreover rumoured that the Navarrese prince aspired to marry Princess Isabella of Castile, whom Juan wished to reserve for Carlos' half-brother Ferdinand (1452–1516). Carlos was imprisoned in 1460, accused of secretly plotting with the Castilians. The Catalan uprising in 1461 led to his release and to his appointment as Governor or *lugarteniente* of Catalonia. He made a formal request for Isabella's hand in marriage. The answer never reached him because the ambassadors were intercepted in Saragossa on their return journey. On 23 September he died. Popular opinion attributed his death to poisoning by his scheming step-mother, Juana Enríquez, but it is more probable that he died of pleurisy or pulmonary consumption (Desdevises, 1889, p. 393). Miracles were reported to have occurred at his tomb, although it seems that these could have been rigged by the municipality.[19]

Although he was somewhat effete, Carlos obviously had much of Alfonso V's magnetism. A flattering portrait of him is given by one of his uncle's chaplains:

fonch criat e nodrit ab molta perfecció de virtut, fonch molt bel, molt savi, molt soptil, molt agut et molt clar enteniment, gran trobador, gran e bel sonador, dansador, cavalcador, complit de tota amor e gracia, hac encara molta sciència: tot lo temps de la sua vida ama estudi; fonch molt verdader e devot cristià; hac gracia e amor de totes gents del món. O goig e alegria de pare, tenint hun tal fill! (Sanchis i Sivera, *Dietari*, pp. 251–2)

(he was educated and nurtured to be most accomplished in virtue; he was very handsome, very learned, very subtle, with a very clear and penetrating mind; he was a great troubadour, a great and fine musician, dancer and rider, fully endowed with love and grace; he also possessed much knowledge; throughout his life he loved to study; he was a very sincere and devout Christian; he was loved and favoured by everyone in the world. Oh what joy and happiness for a father to have such a son!)

He wrote an uninspiring chronicle concerning the kings of Navarre; he translated Aristotle's *Ethics*; and he addressed an open letter to the courts of Castile, Aragon and Portugal, inviting scholars to realise a project, which he outlined, for reconciling Aristotelian ethics with Christianity.[20] There is evidence that he participated in poetry debates with Juan Ruiz de Corella, Juan Poeta, Antón de Montoro and others, but his poetry is not extant. One of the dilemmas proposed for debate was as follows: if a man were shipwrecked with two ladies, one of whom he is able to save, should he select the lady whom he loves, but who does not reciprocate his love, or the lady who loves him, but whose love he does not share? It was suggested that the former course of action would indicate the blindness of passion, whereas the latter would indicate the blindness of reason.[21]

Much care was taken over the prince's education. His tutor, Don Juan de Beaumont, invited the Jewish convert Alfonso de la Torre to compose a treatise on the liberal arts for the boy's instruction. This work, the *Visión delectable*, which Ernst Curtius considered to be symptomatic of Spain's cultural belatedness, was composed in 1430 or soon after.[22] Alfonso the Magnanimous took an interest in his nephew's education: Pere Torroella (Torrellas in Castilian) and Giovano Pontano were sent from Naples in 1438 to give him lessons (Ametller y Viñas, 1903–23, III, p. 409). These new tutors do not seem to have inspired a taste for Italian culture. Torrellas, best known for his misogynistic *Coplas de maldecir de mujeres* (for which he was put to death in a sadistic fashion in *Grisel y Mirabella*, a prose romance by Juan de Flores), wrote a long Catalan *poème à citations* (*Canc. cat.*, ed. Baselga y Ramírez, pp. 183–206), containing excerpts from the poetry of Arnaut Daniel, Bernart de Ventadorn, Peire Vidal, Othon de Grandson, Guillaume de Machaut and Alain Chartier. As this list suggests, the predominant foreign influence on Spanish court poetry was French and Provençal. By marrying Agnès de Clèves, sister of

Marie de Clèves (1426–87), Carlos became in 1439 the brother-in-law of Charles d'Orléans (1391–1463). Whether or not the Prince of Viana ever met Charles d'Orléans is uncertain. Carlos was a close friend of the brilliant Catalan love poet, Ausias March. He was also a friend of the poet and knight Fernando de Guevara, who visited the Navarrese court several times. We know, for example, that in 1439, on the latter's return from jousting in Germany, a splendid banquet was given in the palace of Olite (Vendrell, 1933, p. 71).

Dom Pedro, Constable of Portugal, was son of Pedro, Duke of Coimbra, and Isabel, daughter of Jaime, Count of Urgel. In 1443 at the age of fourteen he succeeded his uncle King João as Constable and Master of the Order of Aviz. After being knighted by Henry the Navigator at the monastery of Coimbra, he entered Castile with an army of 2,000 horsemen and 4,000 footsoldiers to assist Álvaro de Luna against the Infantes de Aragón. He arrived too late to witness the triumph of Álvaro at Olmedo in 1445, but the king greeted him with festivities at Mayorga. It was on this occasion that he met the Marquis of Santillana, with whom he formed a lasting friendship. During this period he wrote his *Sátyra de felice e infelice vida* (Paz y Melia, *Opúsculos*), an allegorical prose romance interspersed with poetry modelled on Rodríguez del Padrón's *Siervo libre de amor*, which he dedicated to his sister Isabel, Afonso V's wife. When Afonso V, 'el Africano' (1432–81), son of King Duarte and Leonor of Aragon, assumed power in 1448, his counsellors persuaded him that his uncle, Dom Pedro, Duke of Coimbra, was plotting to overthrow him. The duke was killed at Alfarrobeiro in 1449, and his son, Dom Pedro, who was disinherited, sought refuge in Castile, where from 1449 until 1457 he lived in exile. When Isabel died in 1455 he wrote his *Tragedia de la insigne reina doña Isabel*.²³ He corresponded with Juan de Mena and composed a long moralistic poem in Castilian entitled *Contempto del mundo*.²⁴ The oldest manuscript version of this poem, dated 1457, was dedicated to Afonso V, perhaps as a gesture of reconciliation. In that year Afonso invited Dom Pedro to return to Portugal and to repossess his estates. In 1463, whilst in Ceuta, where the Portuguese were engaged in a disastrous campaign against the Moors, Pedro received an embassy from Catalonia calling him to be their king. On 21 January 1464 he was proclaimed Count of Barcelona and Pedro V of Aragon. However, he did not rule for long, because in February 1465 his army was defeated by the Count of Prades and the young Prince Ferdinand (who was later to rule Spain jointly with his wife Isabella of Castile). Having escaped the battlefield, Dom Pedro took up headquarters at Vich. Here he conceived the plan of marrying Margaret of York, sister of Henry IV of England, hoping no doubt that the English would offer him military assistance, as they had done in Portugal in the late fourteenth century. As in the case of the Prince of Viana, his plan to marry was interrupted by his untimely death, which occurred at Granollers on 29 June 1466. (Margaret married Charles 'le Téméraire', Duke of Burgundy, in 1468, and was a generous patroness to William Caxton, for many years a resident of Bruges.)

Afonso V (1432–81), a cousin both of Carlos, Prince of Viana, and of Dom Pedro, Constable of Portugal, has a minor, but none the less significant, place in the history of the Castilian love lyric. He was only six years old when his father, King Duarte, died in 1438. In order to avoid civil war, his mother, Leonor of Aragon, in 1440 abdicated her authority as regent in favour of her deceased husband's brother, Prince Pedro (the constable's father). In February or early March 1453, while Álvaro de Luna was being hounded to his execution, Prince Enrique, the future king, having failed to consummate his marriage to Blanche of Navarre, rode to Extremadura to speak to his young cousin Afonso about the possibility of a match between himself and that monarch's sister, Juana. Afonso encouraged his sister to agree to the marriage, although he knew that it would probably prove to be barren:

> Afonso, ruler of a country bordering on Castile and cousin both of the repudiated and the repudiator, was however easily convinced that this farce of a marriage might offer him an opportunity for territorial expansion, when he should have realised that it would, on the contrary, only add to his ignominy . . . it is said that he urged his sister, with great impatience, to decide whether she would accept a barren match, content with the mere name of queen, and that she had replied, amongst other things, that she would prefer to be the queen of a very powerful state than to have the good fortune to conceive offspring by another husband. (Palencia, *Crónica*, I, p. 168)

Ten years later, in December 1463, the two monarchs were to meet again to discuss another marriage. Enrique had come south on the eve of civil war to visit his beloved and only faithful companion, Miguel Lucas de Iranzo, Constable of Castile, and to attempt to pacify the feud which existed between the Guzmán and Ponce de León families.

He learnt that Afonso was in Ceuta. A meeting, mediated by Beltrán de la Cueva, was arranged in Gibraltar (Mata Carriazo, *Hechos del condestable*, p. 192). It was decided that Afonso, now a widower, should marry Enrique IV's half-sister, the Infanta Isabella. The Portuguese king seems to have approved of the donation of Gibraltar to Beltrán, although he must certainly have known of the illicit relationship between Beltrán and his sister. In 1464 interviews took place between Afonso and Isabella at Guadalupe, the site of a Hieronymite monastery and hospital, which was to become the queen's favourite country retreat.[25] There is a series of poems in the *British Museum Cancionero* and the *Cancionero general* by Guevara, Pinar and Florencia Pinar which seem to have been prompted by these betrothal negotiations. One poem in the *British Museum Cancionero* (ed. Rennert, no. 159, p. 81) was probably composed by Afonso himself, because it bears the rubric 'El Grande Africano', which was the title which he had earned through his conquests in North Africa and his predilection for Moorish dress. The song is short and sorrowful:

> Nunca cesarán mis ojos
> por do fueren de llorar,
> ni la vida de penar.
>
> El grave dolor que siento
> nunca dexará de ser,
> pues no se puede perder.

(Never will my eyes cease to weep wherever they are, nor will life cease to weigh with sorrow. Since it cannot be lost, the heavy grief which I feel will never stop existing.)

Afonso may also have been the author or, at any rate, the singer of a 'Canción' glossed by Pinar: an invitation to the funeral of the lover's heart, which explores the traditional paradox of observing the precept of secrecy while at the same time satisfying the need for self-expression:

> Venid, venid amadores
> quantos en el mundo son,
> venid todos a la muerte
> de mi triste coraçon;
> que muero públicamente,

de una secreta afiçión;
y más quiso que muriese
que dexase su pasión,
porque nunca vió esperança
que esperase gualardón.
(*Canc. Brit. Mus.*, no. 164, p. 84)

(Come, lovers, come, as many of you as there are in the world, come all of you to the death of my sad heart; for I am openly dying of a secret affection; and it [my heart] preferred to die than to abandon its passion, because it never saw hope that hoped for recompense.)

The Portuguese majordomo João Manuel, in 'Que yo cyen bocas tuviese' (*Canc. geral*, fol. 54ʳ) (Would that I had a hundred mouths), and Guevara, in 'a complaint that he made in Guadalupe, remembering how he fell in love there' (*Canc. gen.*, fol. 107ʳ), both revisit in memory the beautiful scene of a lost love set in Guadalupe. These and other poems would seem to indicate that Afonso had been genuinely captivated by the headstrong girl of thirteen. She was sent to Portugal with Queen Juana in 1465, to be out of harm's way and to seek military assistance because the aristocratic League, established at Tudela in 1460, was closing in. Although Enrique IV continued to press her, she had set her mind against the match. Afonso belatedly intervened in the Castilian civil war on behalf of Juana 'la Beltraneja' (b. 1462), reputedly the daughter of Beltrán de la Cueva. In May 1475 Afonso entered Castile, and on the twelfth of the month in Placencia he was betrothed to Princess Juana, then scarcely thirteen years of age. His troops were defeated at Toro in 1476, and he made a fruitless journey to France to seek the support of Louis XI. Disillusioned and fearing the ridicule which would meet him on his return to Portugal, he entered a monastery at Honfleur in 1477 and wrote to his son to inform him that he intended to make a pilgrimage to the Holy Land. Afonso then changed his mind. Louis XI provided him with a fleet of ships to take him home, and he arrived on 15 November 1478, five days after his son's coronation. His son resigned his crown to his father. Sixtus IV was persuaded by the court of Castile to overrule the dispensation previously granted for Afonso's marriage to Princess Juana. The unfortunate princess entered the monastery of Santa Clara at Coimbra. Afonso resolved to follow her example. It was as if he were the jilted lover in the popular song recorded by Pinar: 'Pues por mi desventura/ya no me queredes ver,/frayle me quiero meter' (*Canc. Brit. Mus.*, ed. Rennert, no. 169^b, p. 91) (Since owing to my ill fortune you no longer wish to see me, I want to become a friar). He had no sooner made preparations to retire to the monastery of Varatojo when, on 28 August 1481, he died (Prescott, 1841, I, p. 221).

Enrique IV (1425–74) was in some ways the least courtly of Spanish monarchs, but, like his father, he played the lute and was passionately fond of music; and, again like his father, he was not very interested in the task of being a king:

> Era grand músico y tenía buena gracia en cantar y tañer y en fablar en cosas generales. Pero en la execución de las particulares y necesarias algunas vezes era flaco, porque ocupava su pensamiento en aquellos deleites de que estava acostumbrado. (Pulgar, *Claros varones*, p. 7)

> (He was a good musician and was very gifted at singing and playing [the lute] and discussing general matters. But in the performance of the necessary particulars he was sometimes irresolute, because those pleasures to which he was accustomed would occupy his mind.)

He preferred the company of commoners to that of the sons of the rich, which was one cause of his undoing. He disliked royal ceremonial and formal social gatherings, and was happiest when alone hunting, 'He always wore clothes that were lugubrious in appearance' (Palencia, *Crónica*, I, p. 12). Usually he wore a black cloak and a Moorish turban (see plate 8). In his contempt for chivalry and his passion for the chase, he resembled Louis XI of France, although he lacked the latter's political cunning (Kendall, 1974, p. 142). He was a pacifist, drank no wine, and had little respect for the church. At the start of his reign, in March 1455, he sought to please the papacy and the aristocracy by marching into the kingdom of Granada with a vast army of 10,000 horsemen and two or three times as many footsoldiers, but they did not engage in any serious combat. Enrique reluctantly agreed that the destruction of crops was a necessary preliminary to the conquest of Granada. However, he ordered that the fruit trees should be spared; 'He insisted that, at least for the time being, they should respect the fruit trees which are so slow to take root and grow, and so quick to die after the slightest injury' (Palencia, *Crónica*, I, p. 180). Some soldiers who disobeyed this order had their ears chopped off. 'Odd man', comments Townsend Miller, 'to prize Moslem olives more than Catholic ears' (Miller, 1972, p. 78). Enrique allowed his knights to measure their skill in single combat with the Moors, but, according to Alonso de Palencia, he failed to contain his sadness when the Spaniard was victorious, and would chide the victor: 'It is very stupid of a soldier to brag that he has put to death another more worthy than he, not through his natural or acquired expertise, but because his fate so willed it!' (Palencia, *Crónica*, I, p. 181). When he reached the plain of Granada, he halted for four days within sight of the city as if he were more intent upon contemplating it than upon conquering it (p. 182). He then forbade his troops to fight, saying that life was too precious to be squandered:

> decía que pues la vida de los hombres no tenía prescio, ni avía equivalencia, que era muy grand yerro consentir aventuralla, e que por eso no le plascía que los suyos saliesen a las escaramuzas. (Enríquez del Castillo, *Crónica*, p. 107)

> (he said that since man's life is priceless and irreplaceable, it was a very great mistake to agree to it being placed at risk, and that therefore he did not wish his men to take part in skirmishes.)

These attitudes were not such as were likely to endear him to the ambitious and belligerent magnates. It was said, with some justification, that the king's habits and beliefs were tainted by Islam, and that he was well disposed to Jews and Moors. His homosexual proclivities were common knowledge, and the general sexual permissiveness of Queen Juana and her retinue was cause for scandal:

> the continual peals of laughter that punctuated the conversation, the constant coming and going of go-betweens, carrying indecent messages, and the restless craving that devoured them night and day were all more habitual among these ladies than in the very brothels. (Palencia, *Crónica*, I, p. 194)

The verdict had been given by a physician that the king was sexually impotent, and the alleged illegitimacy of Juana 'la Beltraneja' was a useful pretext for his symbolic deposition at Ávila in 1462. Yet the real source of grievance was the king's refusal to appoint aristocrats to positions of trust at court, and his total disregard for the titles and privileges of the nobility, which he handed out with abandon, even to his muleteers, in a vain effort to win support (Carmen Carlé, 1961, p. 70). The young men who surrounded him were, with the exception of Beltrán de la Cueva, social upstarts, some of them selected more for their looks than for their administrative abilities: Miguel Lucas de Iranzo, Constable of Castile (1458); Gómez de Cáceres, Master of Alcántara (1455); his brother, Gutierre de Cáceres, Count of Coria (1469); Andrés de Cabrera, Marquis of Moya (1480); Juan de Valenzuela, Prior of San Juan (1455); and Diego Arias, the Chief Accountant. The chief villains who conspired against him, Juan Pacheco, Marquis of Villena and Master of Santiago, and his brother, Pedro Girón, Master of Calatrava, were also men of humble origins.

A petition drawn up by the League in 1464, signed by Alfonso Carrillo, Archbishop of Toledo, by Juan Pacheco, and by Álvaro de Estúñiga, Count of Plasencia, will provide the reader with much information about the character of the king, the changing climate of opinion with regard to religious and sexual matters, and the causes of the civil war during the period 1464–84. It was considered scandalous that the king should be accompanied by a Moorish bodyguard, and that he should be on such intimate terms with these Moors:[26]

suplicámosle que por cuanto de la grand familiaridad que vuestra Alteza tiene con los moros que en su guarda trae, vuestros súbditos e naturales están escandalizados e a todas las gentes de vuestros regnos e de fuera dellos parece muy mal enjemplo, e contra la fe católica que la vuestra Alteza los haya de tener cerca de sí, dándoles grandes favores.

(we beseech you, with regard to the intimacy between Your Highness and the Moors employed in the royal bodyguard, your vassals and subjects are shocked, and it seems to all people within your realms and abroad a very bad example, and contrary to the Catholic faith, that Your Highness should keep them by his side and accord them great favours.)

The Moors at court are charged with having sexual relations with Christian virgins and married women and of committing other abominable, but unspecified, crimes. It is proposed that they be sold into slavery and that the money raised in this fashion be used either to ransom

Christians from Moorish captivity or to compensate the victims for the crimes perpetrated. It is distressing to learn that the king weakly relinquished his Moorish bodyguard to the ecclesiastical authorities. Criticism is also levelled against him for elevating Jews to high office and for permitting them to extort money from Christians through the practice of usury:

> e los judíos que habían de ser esclavos e siervos de los cristianos en
> vuestros regnos son señores dellos por los grandes oficios públicos,
> e mando e señorío que tienen sobre los cristianos en las cibdades,
> e villas e lugares dellos; e con las grandes usuras que cometen,
> destruyen a muy muchos cristianos, e beben la sangre e sustancia
> dellos en tal manera que los empobrecen, e los judíos quedan
> ricos. (p. 373)

> (and in your realms the Jews, who should be the slaves and servants of
> Christians, are masters, because they hold important public offices
> and have authority and dominion over the Christians in the cities,
> towns and villages; and, as a result of the high interests charged on
> loans, they ruin a great many Christians, and they drink their blood
> and substance so that the latter become improvised, and the Jews
> remain rich.)

The king is made to revoke the laws which he had passed in Toledo favouring the Jewish money-lenders and to enforce the law which stated that Jews and Moors must wear identity marks. He is warned that if he does not make confession at least once a year and take Holy Communion at Easter he is liable to excommunication and will be denied the rites of Christian burial. The heretics and unbelievers whom he is accused of harbouring are to be delivered into the hands of the Papal Inquisition to be imprisoned and punished. Ecclesiastical and administrative posts must in future be given to those who are deemed worthy of them, namely to nobles, sons of knights and university graduates.

That many of these allegations were not without some foundation is attested by an independent account of the anarchical state of Castile in 1466 by a group of Bohemian travellers:[27]

> The old King has many [heathens] at his court and has driven out
> many Christians and given their land to the heathen. Also he eats and
> drinks and is clothed and worships in the heathen manner and is an
> enemy of Christians. He has committed a great crime and follows

un-Christian ways. . . . The Queen marvelled at our hair. She is a brown and handsome woman, but the King is at enmity with her and does not lie with her.

The Bohemians were astonished to find that in several towns and noble households Christians and Moslems lived together in amity, and Enrique IV was not the only person whose religious orthodoxy was suspect. Concerning Pedro Fernández de Velasco, Count of Haro (1399–1470), Tetzel wrote: 'In his town, also at his court, are Christians, heathens, and Jews. He leaves each one to his own belief. The Count is said to be a Christian, but no one knows what his belief is' (*ibid.*, p. 78). There were likewise contacts between the Moors and members of the rebel aristocracy. For example, in February 1448 Rodrigo Manrique joined forces with 2,000 Moors from Granada and attacked several towns in Andalusia (Carrillo de Huete, *Crónica*, pp. 494–5). One must also remember that Juan II had his *caballeros moriscos*. In 1447 they were acutely short of pay and were deemed to be at some risk of reconversion (Colmeiro, *Cortes*, III, pp. 559–61). However, among the younger generation there seems to have been far less tolerance towards both Jews and Arabs. Indeed the Count of Haro's eldest son, Pedro, was one of the ringleaders of the League, and at a secret conclave in 1464 he urged the nobles to rebel and denounced the king with inquisitorial vehemence:

> Nor could he understand, he added, what kind of madness drove everyone to extol so enthusiastically and so unanimously, and to treat with such humble deference, a man immersed since his tenderest childhood in infamous vices, and who, with unequalled audacity, had not only dared to relax and destroy the military order and discipline recommended by ancient authorities but, even in his dress and deportment, in his meals and habit of reclining to eat and in other secret and more depraved excesses, had preferred the customs of the Moors to those of the Christian religion, of which not the slightest trace could be found in him, but instead a whole series of depravities contrary to honour, harmful to religion, dishonourable to his reputation and liable to corrupt the entire human race. (Palencia, *Crónica*, I, p. 190)

The atmosphere of sexual permissiveness and religious heterodoxy which prevailed at the Castilian court during the reign of Enrique IV was soon dissipated by the austere Isabella, whom the king had been obliged to recognise as his successor at Toros de Guisando in 1468. Through emissaries she obtained reports on the character and appearance of her various suitors. In selecting Ferdinand of Aragon, she was motivated not only by her own preferences and those of the grandees, but, as Menéndez Pidal points out, by 'the voice of her ancestors', because her grandfather, Enrique III, had expressed the wish that 'there should always continue to be new matrimonial connections' between the royal families of Castile and Aragon.[28] The marriage, solemnised by the Archbishop of Toledo, Alfonso Carrillo, was hastily celebrated during the king's absence in 1469. The country's social and economic problems became more acute. In 1470 there was a serious shortage of bread, wine and other foods, and many people died of starvation. The value of money was more than halved by the circulation of false currency and the minting of new coins. According to Diego de Valera, the king permitted the number of minting houses to rise from five to 150 within the space of three years.[29] In 1473 the Jewish ghettos were sacked in Jaén, Andújar and Córdoba. In 1474 Enrique IV died, and the Portuguese invaded Castile on behalf of Juana 'la Beltraneja'. Isabella's troops won a decisive victory at the Battle of Toro in 1476, which was interpreted by Bachiller Alonso de la Palma as a reprisal against the Portuguese for the defeat suffered by the Castilians at the Battle of Aljubarrota in 1385, and as the completion of a cycle of divine retribution against the sins of the Trastámaran kings (see Appendix 2). Three years later Juan II of Aragon died at the age of eighty-one, leaving Ferdinand and Isabella the joint rulers of Spain.

Isabella instructed her chronicler, Fernando de Pulgar, to employ on every occasion the magic formula 'el rey y la reina', and she insisted that, even when her husband was absent, orders should be issued in the name of both husband and wife, 'for though necessity separated their persons, love held their wills together'.[30] However, although Ferdinand enjoyed the status of a Castilian monarch, his wife took precedence over him in the government of the kingdom, reserving for herself the right to draw funds from the royal treasury and to make royal appointments. It is very much to Ferdinand's credit that he saw the political advantages of such an arrangement. Nicolaus von Poppelau, who witnessed the Christmas Eve celebrations at Seville in 1484, was rather shocked to discover that no letter could be sealed by the king without his wife's approval. It seemed that he could do nothing without her permission:

It is necessary to record here a strange paradox concerning this kingdom: the queen is king and the king is her servant... the nobility fears the queen more than the king, who at all times thinks only of fulfilling her orders, mandates and wishes.... The king can do nothing without the queen's permission; on the other hand, what she desires he must set out to accomplish. (García Mercadal, *Viajes*, p. 319)

Despite his infidelities, Ferdinand was courteous in his manners and couched his letters from Aragon in the language appropriate to a courtly lover: 'Un día volveréis a vuestro antiguo afecto. Si no, yo moriría y vos seríais culpable'[31] (One day you will return to your former affection. If not, I would die and you would be the guilty one).

Queen Isabella had been brought up to believe that, in restoring law and order, suppressing heresy and conquering Granada, she was fulfilling a divine mission. Some writers and poets even likened her to the Virgin Mary:[32]

Bien se puede con verdad desir, que así como nuestro Señor
quiso en este mundo nasciese la gloriosa Señora nuestra, porque
della procediese el universal Redentor del linaje humano, así
determinó, vos, Señora, nasciésedes para reformar e restaurar estos
reinos e sacarlos de la tiránica governación en que tan luengamente
han estado.

(It can in truth be said that, just as our Lord desired that our glorious Lady might be born in this world, because from her would proceed the universal Redeemer of the human race, so he decided that you, my lady, would be born to reform and restore these realms and liberate them from the tyrannical government which they have so long endured.)

It seemed, as Hieronymus Münzer says, that this exceptional woman had been sent by God to save Spain from imminent ruin.[33] This mission devolved on her when her younger brother, Alfonso, died on 5 July 1468. On 14 November 1467 Alfonso had received a poem from Gómez Manrique, in honour of his fourteenth birthday, in which nine ladies of the court including Isabella play the part of the nine Muses prophesying a glorious future.[34] In another poem the young prince is portrayed as a new Caesar who will establish an overseas empire and conquer 'las bárbaras nasciones' (*ibid.*, no. 417, pp. 149–50). Perhaps the key to Isabella's success was that by combining the role of a popular messiah with that of a courtly *dame sans merci*, she was able to canalise the energies of the aristocracy, which had previously been vented on internal rebellion, into the completion of the Reconquest. This task had long been deferred, and might well have been achieved by her father in 1431, if he had set his mind to it, or by her half-brother Enrique IV. The political expediency of a 'holy war' had been put to Enrique IV by the *converso* Juan de Lucena in 1463:[35]

> Alhora la casa está sin ruydo quando los puercos son al monte . . .
> ¡Qué gloria de rey! ¡Qué fama de vasallos, qué corona d'España,
> sy el clero, religioso y sin regla, fuesen contra Granada, y los
> cavalleros con el Rey erumpiesen en Africa! Sería, por cierto,
> ganar otro nombre que de rico. Mayor riqueza sería crescer reynos,
> que thesoros amontonar.

> (The house is silent when the pigs are out on the hill. . . . How glorious [would be] the king, how famous his vassals, how great the crown of Spain if the secular and regular clergy were to march on Granada, and if the knights with the king were to burst through into Africa! It would certainly earn a very different reputation from that of being rich. Greater wealth would there be in accumulating kingdoms than in piling up treasure.)

In the short term the strategy was excellent. In the long term it was disastrous, because Spain became intoxicated by delusions of grandeur, and made territorial expansion almost an end in itself, unrelated to the country's economic needs. Lucena refused to see this because, like most Spaniards, he had been infected by what can best be described as the *hidalgo* mentality. By declaring war on Granada Isabella simultaneously confronted the problem of baronial anarchy and the genuine threat of the Moorish presence, thereby acquiring prestige and public acclaim as a political saviour and a defender of the faith.

Von Poppelau was amazed by the fear and respect which Isabella inspired amongst the nobles and by the alacrity with which they obeyed her orders. She commanded great authority through her virtue, feminine charm and masculine strength of mind. The last of these qualities was praised by several of her contemporaries. 'Oh male heart in female apparel,' exclaimed Juan de Lucena, 'an example to all

1 Knights fighting; dancing; lover worshipping a lady; devil carrying off a lover's soul. From Matfré Ermengaud's 'Breviari d'amor'. Catalan; early fifteenth century (British Library, MS Royal 19 C I, fol. 204ᵛ). This sequence is unusual in that it represents an unequivocal condemnation of the courtly and chivalric way of life.

2 Tree of battles sprouting from the jaws of a monster, symbolising hell, topped by the blind-folded figure of Fortune standing within her wheel; angels and devils struggle for possession of the souls of dying soldiers. From Honoré Bonet's 'Livre des batailles'. French, in Latin; fifteenth century (Musée Condé, Chantilly, MS 346/1561, fol. 10ᵛ). This miniature conveys the mood of the late Middle Ages: the uncertainty of life, particularly for the knight, and the uncertainty of man's fate after death. Bonet's work was widely read; it was translated into Castilian by Antón de Zurita, in the service of the Marquis of Santillana.

3 Death riding a bull; Office of the Dead. From the 'Prayer book of
Alfonso V of Aragon'. Spanish; c. 1442 (British Library, MS Add.
28962, fol. 378ᵛ).

4 A figure at the foot of the tomb of Doña Teresa de Chacón. Spanish; late fifteenth century (Victoria and Albert Museum).

5 (i) Queen and attendants listening to musicians; (ii) Two kings playing chess, interrupted by the arrival of a messenger. From 'Le Roman du Roi Meliadus de Leonnoys', attributed to Hélie de Borron. Written 1352–62, dedicated to Louis II, King of Naples (British Library, MS Add. 12228, fols 222^v and 23^v).

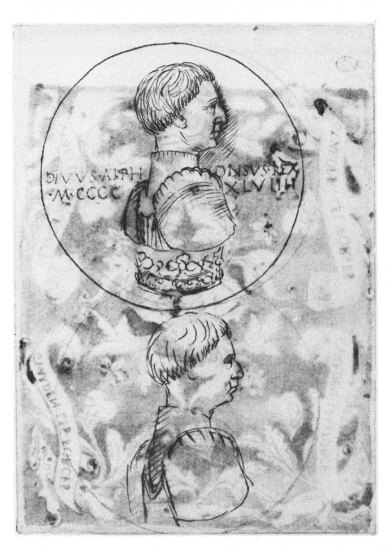

6 Design for a bronze medal, portraying Alfonso V, the Magnanimous, of Aragon (b. 1394, ruled 1416–58), by Pisanello, in pen and brown ink, executed 1448–9 (Louvre, Cabinet des Dessins, 2306).

7 John II of Navarre and Aragon (b. 1397; ascended the throne of Navarre with his wife Blanche, 1425; of Aragon, 1458; d. 1479). Legend: Hans, by God's grace, King of Navarre and of Arragon, Duke of Venion and of Munblanck, Count of Ribbagorsa, Lord of the town of Ballager. John is clad in a long brown cloak with a red collar. The shoes are black. The sword-case is black with a gilt tip. He wears a heavy gold chain round his neck. Coloured drawing from Jörg von Ehingen's 'Diary', executed *c.* 1460, based on a contemporary sketch. German; written 1453-9 (Landesbibliothek, Stuttgart, MS Historia 4to, 141).

8 Henry IV, the Impotent, of Castile (b. 1425; r. 1454-74). Legend: Hainrich, by God's grace, King of Castilia and of Leon, Toledo, Galicia, Sevillia, Cordua, Mortza, Jaen, Algarbe, Algezira, Lord of Wisgeia, Mollina. Henry's dress reflects his contempt for ceremony and his partiality for the Arabs: he wears a black cloak, slashed to show his linen, a red cap or fez, and yellow shoes (*ibid.*).

9 Afonso V, the African, of Portugal (b. 1432; ascended the throne, 1438; d. 1481). Legend: Afonso, by God's grace, King of Portugal and Algarbe, Lord of Sept and Algogiro. The hat, coat and hose are black, the shoes black with brown linings. He wears a black sword-case with a gilt tip and a gold necklace (*ibid.*).

10 (i) Juana 'la Beltraneja' (1462-1530). Detail from one of eleven leaves of an unfinished 'Genealogy of the Royal Houses of Spain and Portugal', probably executed by Simon Benichius or Bening, after designs by Antonio d'Olanda, for Dom Fernando, third son of Manuel I of Portugal. Flemish; early sixteenth century (British Library, MS Add. 12531, Table 10); (ii) Queen Isabella of Spain (b. 1451; r. 1474-1504). Painting; Spanish School, early sixteenth century (Windsor Castle. Reproduced by gracious permission of Her Majesty the Queen).

11 Queen Isabella with her daughters and a young man, presumably Philip
the Fair, presenting her with a book. From Pedro Marcuello,
'Devocionario de la Reina Doña Juana la Loca'. Written, and illustrated
by a Burgundian artist, 1482-1500, for the wedding of Princess Juana and
Philip the Fair, son of the Emperor Maximilian, in 1498 (Musée Condé,
Chantilly, MS 604/1339, fol. 54ᵛ).

queens, a model for all women and for all men a subject worthy of literature!'[36] Fray Iñigo de Mendoza wrote:[37]

¡ O alta fama viril
de dueña maravillosa
que el estado feminil
hizo fuerça varonil
con cabtela virtuosa!

(Oh what masculine renown of an astonishing lady, whom the female estate has endowed with manly strength and virtuous cunning!)

The Venetian ambassador, Andrea Navagiero, spoke of Isabella's 'animo virile' and remarked that, even in men, such valour was very rare (Navagiero, 1563, fol. 27^r). Virility was, as Charles Aubrun says, 'a fashionable virtue which the most faint-hearted woman tries to assume, and which is ascribed to her without hesitation by lovers and poets' (*Canc. Herberay*, p. lxii). The anthology edited by Aubrun, known as the *Cancionero d'Herberay*, was presented to Leonor, Countess of Foix, whom Diego de Sevilla calls 'la viril infanta'. This tough and ambitious woman ruled Navarre in place of her half-brother the Prince of Viana from 1457 to 1461. Juan de Mena maintains in his *Laberinto de Fortuna* (ll. 605–8) that if Queen María of Castile had been transformed into a man, she would have established justice in the kingdom. Thus when Isabella appeared, like Joan of Arc, mounted on a war-horse and dressed in knight's armour at the Siege of Alhama in 1481, she clearly answered the mood of the country (Prescott, 1841, II, p. 343).

It was later recognised, with some regret, that chivalric idealism would never be the same without a Moorish Granada to serve as a stimulus to noble exploits. For example, the humanist Juan Ginés de Sepúlveda wrote as follows:

I sometimes wonder whether it would not have been better for us if the Moorish kingdom had been preserved in Granada instead of disappearing completely. For if it is indeed certain that we have extended the kingdom, we have also thrown the enemy back beyond the sea, deprived the Spaniards of the opportunity to practise their valour, and destroyed the magnificent motive for their triumphs.

Wherefore I fear a little lest, with so much idleness and security, the valour of men may grow weak. (Castro, 1971, pp. 83–4)

Fray Alonso de Cabrera, preacher to Felipe II, gave a sermon in which he evoked the age of youth and innocence which, he imagined, had existed prior to the conquest of Granada:

> Our grandfathers, my lords, lamented the winning of Granada from the Moors, because on that day the horses fell lame and the cuirasses began to rust, and the shields to rot. And the most distinguished cavalry of Andalusia was finished, and it was the end of youth and all its well-known and estimable gallantries. (Castro, 1971, p. 84)

The fall of Granada symbolised the passing of an era, because it was the last war of its kind based on courtly and chivalric principles, and the last European war in which firearms were scarcely used:

> Fu gentil guerra, non vi erano anchor tante artigliarie come sono venute dopoi, & molto più si potevano cognoscere i valent'huomini, che non si ponno hora. . . . Tutta la nobiltà di Spagna vi si trovava, & tra tutti era concorrentia di portarsi meglio, & acquistarsi più fama. . . . Oltra la concorrentia che ecitava ogn'uno a far più di quel che poteva; la Regina con la corte sua dava grande animo a ogn'uno. Non vi era Signor che non fusse innamorato in qual ch'una delle Dame della Regina, le quali essendo presenti, & certi testimoni di quanto si faceva da ciascaduno: & dando spesso le arme di sue mani a quelli che andavano a combattere, & spesso alcun suo favore, & forsi alle volte dicendoli parole che gli facessero cuore, & preganoli che ne i portamenti loro, facessero cognoscere quanto le amavano, qual è quel huomo si vile, si di poco animo, si di poca forza, che non havesse vinto ogni potente & animo adversario: & che non havesse osato perder mille volte la vita, più presto che ritornar alla sua Signora con vergogna; per il che si può dir che questa guerra fusse principalmente vinta per Amore. (Navagiero, 1563, fol. 27)

(This was a polite war; there were not as many firearms as have since become customary, and it was much easier to recognise men of prowess than it is nowadays. . . . All the nobility of Spain was there, and each sought to emulate the other and earn more renown. . . . In addition to the competitive spirit which spurred each man to do more than he was able, the queen with her court breathed courage into every heart. There was scarce a cavalier who was not in love with one of the queen's ladies. Being present, these ladies were reliable witnesses of each man's achievements, frequently handing them their weapons as they went out to do battle, and frequently offering several a token of favour, and perhaps at times uttering words of encouragement, and beseeching them to make known by their conduct the degree of their passion. There is surely no man so base, so weak-hearted or so lacking in strength who would not have vanquished the stoutest adversary, or who would not sooner have lost his life a thousand times, than return dishonoured to the lady of his love. One can therefore truthfully say that this war was chiefly won through Love.)

As soon as the Catholic monarchs had gained control of Castile, they introduced measures which were designed to curb the power and diminish the wealth of the aristocracy without forfeiting their co-operation. In 1476 they authorised the formation of a rural police force subordinate to the Crown, the Santa Hermandad, the ancestor of the modern Guardia Civil, which in Aragon was exploited as an instrument of repression by the Inquisition. In 1480 the Cortes decreed that the grants and pensions of the nobility should be reduced in the interests of the national economy, and that all income usurped since 1464 should be returned to the Crown (Vicens Vives, 1969, p. 295). In the same year the aristocracy was permitted a limited voice in the Royal Council, which was to consist in future of eight or nine lawyers, three nobles and one cleric. The judicial system continued to be entrusted to men of middle-class extraction who had been trained in the universities. In 1481 serfdom was officially abolished, although it has been said that this freedom was in reality little more than 'the freedom to die of hunger' (*ibid.*, p. 299). In the years 1494, 1495 and 1496 strict sumptuary laws were passed condemning excessive expenditure on weddings and funerals (Sempere y Guariños, 1788, II, p. 20). These and other measures indicate that a new climate of opinion, favouring austerity, rationality and restraint, had begun to prevail. Thus for a variety of social and economic reasons, as well as for the lack of chivalric enter-prise, the royal court ceased after 1492 to be a place of frivolity, gaiety and extravagance. King Ferdinand had in any case the reputation of being something of a miser. According to the Florentine ambassador who visited him in 1512, his meals were frugal and, save on special occasions, he would dine alone in the presence of his servants. The upper nobility nevertheless continued to live in comparative luxury:

> the grandees ... keep a well-stocked table, and are waited on with such ceremony and marks of respect that one would have taken each of them for a king; men speak to them on bended knee and, in short, they expect to be worshipped, which illustrates the haughty character of this nation. (García Mercadal, *Viajes*, p. 621)

In 1501 there were still, to judge by Antoine de Lalaing's account, eleven duchies, seven marquisates and thirty-eight counties with a combined revenue of 627,300 florins (*ibid.*, pp. 489–90).

The most vulnerable sector of the community in the late fifteenth century was not the aristocracy but the *converso* bourgeoisie which looked in vain to the monarch for protection against the envy of the masses. An article by R. O. Jones on 'Isabel la Católica y el amor cortés' seems to confirm the impression that the majority of those who addressed panegyrics to Isabella at the beginning of her reign were Jewish by birth or origin: Pedro de Cartagena, Juan Álvarez Gato, Antón de Montoro, Juan de Lucena, Fray Iñigo de Mendoza and Diego de Valera (Jones, 1962). Isabella is portrayed by these authors as the object or potential object of an idolatrous cult. The controversy aroused by Antón de Montoro's poem, which claimed that, had Isabella been alive, God would have selected her as Christ's mother is well known (*Canc. gen.*, fol. 75ᵛ). Some verses by Pedro de Cartagena can be taken as an apt commentary on Montoro's blasphemy:

> Que loaros, a mi ver,
> en vuestra y agena patria,
> silencio devéys poner,
> que daros a conoscer
> haze la gente ydolatria.
> >   (*ibid.*, fol. 87ᵛ)

(In my opinion you ought to silence the eulogies addressed to you in your own and in other countries, because in making you known the people commit idolatry.)

R. O. Jones was sceptical about Lida de Malkiel's theory that the tendency to sacred hyperbole in fifteenth-century Castilian poetry might be connected with the influx of *conversos* into Christian society (Lida, 1946). Yet I think that much of the messianic zeal and self-mockery that one finds in these love poems cannot really be understood except within the context of the *converso* problem. Despite her reliance on the administrative and financial skills of the New Christians, Isabella betrayed their trust in her: she gave her consent to the establishment of the Inquisition, which began its iniquitous operations in 1481, and she signed an edict on 30 March 1492, banishing all unconverted Jews from Castile and Aragon. It cannot be denied that she was guilty of racial, as well as religious, prejudice.[38] Historians, dazzled by her truly remarkable qualities, have generally been anxious, like her contemporaries, to condone this aspect of her character.

Isabella died, after a period of illness, on 26 November 1504. On 18 March 1506 Ferdinand married Germaine, daughter of Jean de Foix, Viscount of Narbonne, and one of the sisters of Louis XII. The marriage was celebrated in Dueñas, where thirty years previously Ferdinand had been united to Isabella. On 23 January 1516 Ferdinand died, and Germaine, having failed to produce a male heir, pursued a gay social life in Valencia. The court of Germaine and her third husband, the exiled Prince of Calabria, is depicted in Luis Milán's *El cortesano* and the poetry of Juan Fernández de Heredia. It is significant that Valencia was one of the last places to abandon the conventions of troubadour poetry: 'The focus and centre of this belated troubadour school, which continued its practices even into the middle of the sixteenth century, was the court of the Dukes of Calabria' (Menéndez y Pelayo, *Antología*, III, p. 408). It was a city that remained very much under the influence of the old aristocracy. Münzer, who was struck by the affable and courtly character of the Valencian people, observed in 1494 that there resided in the city two dukes, the Duke of Valencia and the Duke of Gandía (who was Juan Borjia, son of Pope Alexander VI), several counts, including Juan de Próxita, Count of Aversa, and Serafín Centelles, Count of Oliva (to whom the *Cancionero general* was dedicated), about 500 knights, and over 2,000 merchants, artisans and clerics. This traveller also remarked on the seductive appearance of Valencian women:

The men wear long garments, and the women dress with unusual but excessive coquetry, for their neck-lines are so low that their nipples are visible; furthermore, they all paint their faces and use perfumes and cosmetics, a thing which is truly reprehensible. (García Mercadal, *Viajes*, p. 344)

Except for snatches of popular song, the poetry written at the Valencian court is mediocre and contrived. The themes had become hackneyed; the concepts had lost their vigour. Juan del Encina had already sensed this turn of events in 1496, and seriously doubted whether any further progress was possible in the craft of poetry.[39]

Part III

Documents on the Troubadour Revival

I

17 February 1388. Joan I of Aragon (r. 1387–95) issued a decree making it illegal for court officials to frequent brothels or to have relations with prostitutes.

Ordenació feta per lo dit senyor Rey en Johan en qual manera los officials de sa casa deuen viure e honestament conversar en aquella.

Que nengú de casa del senyor rey gós tenir fembre en lo bordell.

Per esquivar peccats e vicis mals, los quals se pertanyen mills guardar a la reyal magestat que a altres persones, e per clar bon eximpli a nostres servidors e sotsmeses: volem e ordinam que tot hom, de qualque condició sia o stament, qui de nostra casa, de la reyna, e de tots nostres infants seran, no gosen tenir fembra o fembres en bordell: e siu fan que de present sien dampnats de carta de ració e sien foragitats de nostra casa e merçè. . . .

Que les fembres públiques no gosen tenir per amichs hòmens qui sien de casa del dit senyor.

Encara volem e ordonam quel dit algutzir de continent diga a alguns de son offici què facen manament a totes las fembres públiques que d'ací avant no tenguen per amichs hòmens qui sien de casa nostra ne de la dita reyna ne de nostres infants: e si·u fan e no·u denuncien, que hajen a correr la vila açotan, e aprés que sien exellades de tots nostres regnes e terres. E semblantment ho haje a fer denunciar lo dit algutzir als hostalers dels bordells que hajen a denunciar si algun de càsa nostra e de la dita reina e infans tindran alguna de les dites fembres: e si·ls dits hostalers no·u denuncien, que sien encorreguts en la dita pena o que paguen mil sous a la cort sens tota mercè.

Que los damunt dits continuament no mengen ne jaguen en los bordells.

Item que no gosen participar continuament axí en menjar com en jaura en los bordells ne en los hostals de aquells sots encorriment de les dites penes.

Fo publicada la present ordinació en Barcelona a XVII dies del mes de febrer del any MCCCLXXXVIII presents los honrats mossèn Thomas jutge algutzir del dit senyor, en Guillem Oliver scrivà de ratió de la dita reyna, en Bernad Çafort de offici de ratió del dit senyor, en Francesch de Vallsecca de offici de comprador del dit senyor, e molt d'altres senyors e molt d'altres presens. (Bofarull y Mascaró, *Colección*, V, cxxii, pp. 392–4)

(Decree issued by the said King John concerning the manner in which officials of his court should live and decently converse with one another.

That no one who was a member of the royal court should venture to keep a mistress in the brothel.

In order to avoid sins and evil practices, which ought to be more thoroughly shielded from his royal majesty than from other persons, and in order to set a good and clear example to our servants and subjects, we wish and command that no man, whatever his condition or rank, who belongs to our household, to the queen's household or to the households of the royal princes, may venture to keep a mistress, or mistresses, in the brothel; and should he do so, he will immediately be dismissed from the pay-roll and expelled from our household and favour. . . .

That prostitutes shall not take as friends men who belong to the household of the said king.

Further we wish and command that the said constable shall forthwith instruct some members of his profession to issue a mandate to all prostitutes that henceforward they are forbidden to take as friends men who belong to our household, or to the queen's and princes' households; and if they do so and do not report it to us, they will be whipped through the town and afterwards banished from our realms and territories. And similarly the said constable should advise the keepers of the brothels that they must make it known whether any member of our household, or of the queen's and princes' households, has relations with any of the said women; and if the said innkeepers do not report it to us, they shall be punished with the said penalty or they will pay one thousand *sous* to the court without any appeal for mercy.

That the above-mentioned shall not continually eat and lie in the brothels.

Further that they shall not continually venture to eat and to lie in the brothels or the hostels belonging to the brothels on pain of incurring the said penalties.

This decree was published in Barcelona on the 17th day of the month of February of the year 1388 in the presence of the honourable Sir Thomas, chief constable of the said king, Guillem Oliver, clerk of payments of the said queen, Bernad Çafort appointed distributor of rations for the said king, Francesch de Vallsecca appointed purchaser for the said king, and many other gentlemen and many others present.)

2

July 1388. Queen Yolande was served by many noble ladies; she encouraged the study of courtesy, and she organised dances, poetry recitals and other courtly entertainments. Joan I sent an embassy to Charles VI of France, seeking permission to establish a poetic academy in Spain to teach the Gay Science of the troubadours.[1] Robert of Prague visited Joan I to observe the customs of the Aragonese court and to propose marriage between Princess Juana and King Wenzel IV of Bohemia.

(i)

la Reyna doña Violante . . . tenía en su casa muchas damas hijas de los príncipes señores destos Reynos, y avía tanto estudio y cuydado en favorecer toda gentileza y cortesanía, que ordinariamente era seguida la corte del Rey como la mayor Príncipe que avía en la Christiandad. Mas introdúxose tanto excesso en esto, que toda la vida se passava en danças, y salas de damas: y en lugar de las armas y exercicios de guerra, que eran los ordinarios passatiempos de los Príncipes passados, sucedieron las trobas y poesía vulgar, y el arte della, que llamavan la gaya sciencia, de la qual se començaron a instituyr escuelas públicas, y

lo que en tiempos passados avía sido un muy honesto exercicio, y
que era alivio de los trabajos de la guerra, en que de antiguo se
señalaron en la lengua Limosina muchos ingenios muy excelentes
de cavalleros de Rossellón y del Ampurdán, que imitaron las
trobas delos Proençales, vino a envilecerse en tanto grado que
todos parecían juglares. Para mayor declaración desta bastara
referir lo que affirma aquel famoso cavallero destos mismos
tiempos don Enrique de Villena, que para fundar en su Reyno una
gran escuela de aquella gaya sciencia, a semejança de las proençales,
y para traer los más excelentes maestros que avía della, se embió
por el Rey una muy solenne embaxada a Francia: lo que es mucho
de maravillar, prevaleciendo tanto las armas dentro de sus estados.
Concurrió en el mismo tiempo Venceslao Rey de Romanos y de
Bohemio, que como en competencia se deleytava en los mismos
passatiempos: y fue muy afficionado al Rey de Aragón: y por el
mes de Iulio deste año embió un su camarero, que se llamava
Roberto de Praga, para que se informasse de la orden de la casa y
corte de Rey, y con el le embió a dezir, que se holgava, que se
conformassen tanto en sus passatiempos y exercicios de la caça, y
música: y le embió a pedir, que le diesse por muger a la Infanta
doña Iuana su hija, y le avisava, que su hermano Sigismundo Rey de
Ungría: y Marqués de Brandanburch gozava de pacífica possessión
de su Regno, que pertenecía a la Reyna María su muger hija de
Luys Rey de Ungría. (Zurita, *Anales*, 1610–21, II, fols 393^r–394^r)

(Queen Yolande ... had many ladies in her household who were
daughters of the chief lords of these realms, and such was the care
and consideration with which she encouraged all forms of courtesy
and good breeding that in general the court of the king was attended
as though he were the greatest prince in Christendom. But this was
taken to such exaggerated lengths that all life was spent in dances and
in ladies' assemblies; and arms and exercises of war, which were the
normal pastimes of past rulers, were now replaced by troubadour
songs and vernacular poetry and the poetic art known as the Gay
Science, for the teaching of which public schools were established;
and what in bygone days had been a very respectable exercise, a
relief from the travails of war in which many excellent knights of
Roussillon and Ampurdan (who were skilled in the Limousin tongue
and imitated the troubadour songs of the Provençals) distinguished
themselves, became debased to such a degree that all men appeared

to be minstrels. For fuller confirmation of this it is sufficient to refer to what has been said by the famous knight Enrique de Villena, who witnessed these events. He states that the king sent a solemn embassy to France, in order that a large school of the Gay Science, similar to the Provençal schools, might be set up in his kingdom, and in order that the most excellent teachers of the art might be recruited, which is astonishing at a time when arms were rife within his domains. During this same period Wenzel, King of the Romans and of Bohemia, arrived, who, as if in emulation, delighted in the same pastimes. He was very fond of the King of Aragon; and in the month of July of this year [1388] he sent his chamberlain, who was called Robert of Prague, to gather information about the organisation of the household and court of the king, and with him he sent a message, saying that he was pleased that they should conform so closely in their pastimes and in their practice of hunting and music; and he begged [the King of Aragon] to give him his daughter, Princess Juana, as a wife, and informed him that his brother Sigismund, King of Hungary and Marquis of Brandenburg, was in peaceful possession of his kingdom, which belonged to Queen Mary, his [Sigismund's] wife, daughter of Louis King of Hungary.)

(ii)

Iulio mense Robertus Praga Venceslai Romanorum Regis legatus Regem salutat. Begnina is oratione retulit: Venceslaum conciliari Regi ad benevolentiam, quam maxime cupere: et ut Iohannam filiam illi in matrimonium collocet. Similitudo magna morum illicere, atque attrahere hos maxime Principes visa est. Ambo aucupio atque venationi supra modum dediti, belli studia deposuerant. Symphonia, et cantu vocum, nervorum, et tibiarum totae regiae personabant: intempestiva semper convivia, multarumque deliciarum comes extrema, ut ille inquit, saltatio: et molli, et effeminata copia omnia ad voluptatem referebantur. Adeoq[ue] more et instituto id usurpatum, ut Henricus Viliena, non minus multiplici et recondita literatura, quam antiquissima Regum Aragoniae, et Comitum Barcinonensium stirpe, et Henrico Castellae Rege avo materno clarus, referat, haud secus ac de suis rebus maximis Regem legatos ad Francorum Regem, sollemni, publicaque legatione misisse, ut vernaculae linguae celebres poetae in Hispaniam ex Narbonensis provinciae scholis traducerentur: et studia poetices, quam Gaiam scientiam vocabant, instituerentur. His vero, quorum ingenium in eo artificio elucere videbatur, magna praemia, industriae, et honoris insignia, monumentaque laudis esse constituta. Postremo Rex desidiae atque inertae deditus, non modo patris, flagrantis animi Principis, et regio plane spiritu praediti, sed ceterorum Regum omnium longe dissimilis comissationibus, et voluptatibus affluens, uxorio arbitrio se, et gubernacula regni, et rempublicam tradiderat. (Zurita, *Indices*, 1578, fol. 363)

(In the month of July Robert of Prague, emissary of Wenzel King of the Romans, greets the king [viz. Joan I of Aragon]. He declares in a courteous speech that Wenzel greatly desired to be united in friendship with the king and wished that the latter might give him his daughter Juana in marriage. It is evident that these princes were drawn and attracted to each other by a close similarity of customs. Both of them, inordinately devoted to falconry and hunting, had abandoned the study of war. Their palaces were filled throughout with song and with the music of stringed and wind instruments. There were banquets at all hours and seasons, and dancing which, he said, was the boon companion of many delights; everything amidst a decadent and unmanly surfeit was geared to the pursuit of pleasure. These practices had so far appropriated the customs and institutions of the state that Enrique de Villena (a man no less famous for his manifold and recondite writings than for his descent from the ancient line of the Kings of Aragon and the Counts of Barcelona and from his maternal grandfather, King Henry of Castile) reports that the king had sent ambassadors to the King of France in a solemn and public embassy—just as he would have done concerning the highest affairs of state – in order to have celebrated vernacular poets brought to Spain from the schools of the province of Narbonne to institute the poetic studies which are called the Gay Science. Indeed great prizes, emblems of industry and honour and marks of praise were bestowed upon those whose skill in this craft was apparent. Finally the king, quite different not only from his father, a prince of ardent soul and fully endowed with kingly spirit, but from all other kings, being naturally disposed towards sloth and idleness and indulging in revelries and pleasures, had through the influence of his wife betrayed himself, the government of the kingdom and the common weal.)

3

Valencia, 20 February 1393. Joan I established the festival of the Gay
Science, to be held annually in March on the Feast of the Annunciation
of the Virgin Mary or on the following Sunday. He appointed Jaume
March, a knight, and Lluís d'Aversó, a citizen of Barcelona, as
'mantenedors', granting them authority to judge the poems and
literary works submitted in the competition and to award prizes.

Pro Jacobo Marchi et Ludovico d'Aversone. Nos Johannes etc.
Quot et quantis amor origo fuerit subscript[a]e scienci[a]e, sui
vocabuli nomen pr[a]estans, per quem unigenitum Dei Filium ad
summovendum primi parentis noxam carnem ex virginali utero
suscepisse, et multa alia mirifica facta fuisse perlegimus, mentis
nostr[a]e cellula revolventes, et ipsius scienci[a]e qu[a]e uno amoris
vocabulo gaya vel gaudiosa, et alio nomine inveniendi sciencia
noncupatur, effectum et escienciam arbitrantes, qu[a]e purissimo,
honesto et curiali nitens eloquio, rudes erudit, inertes excitat,
ebetes mollit, doctos allicit, [h]irsuta crinit, occulta elicit, obscura
lucidat, cor l[a]etificat, excitat mentem, sensum clarificat atque
purgat, parvulos et iuvenes haustu sui lactis melliflui nutrit et
attrahit, faciens eos in puerilibus annis anticipare modestiam
senectutis et ante capescere mentem gravissimam, quam possint
annorum [a]etate canescere numerosa, edocens eos ut in ipso
[a]etatis iuvenilis fervore, morum regimine temperentur, senes
delectabili recreacione confovens morum gravitate venustos quasi
in pristina sustinet iuventute, utrosque dulci modulamine gaudii
pernimii recreans et delectans. H[a]ec nempe qu[a]e morum est
aula virtutum socia, honestatis conservatrix et custos, ac viciis
penitus inimica, cuius utilitas lucet, magnificencia virtutis apparet,
operacio arridet fructuosa, vitalia iubens, noxia prohibens, errata
dirigens, terrena removens, celestia persuadens, non solum in
sermone set eciam in virtute, maiores, mediocres et minores
corrigens, reformans et informans [fol. 149ᵛ], exules fovet,
afflictos relevat, consolatur et tristes, et illos ad propria ubera
nutriendos colligit quos sui docmatis esse filios recognoscit
nutritosque, et a maternis erectos uberibus imbutosque nectare
suavissimi fontis sui per eorum delectabilia carmina auditum
mulcibilia in noticiam et graciam mittit Regum, prelatorum,
principum et magnatum mediocrium et eciam infimorum; amoris

vocabuli nominacione attrahimur et aliis pr[a]edictis inducimur et movemur excellencia dict[a]e scienci[a]e attenta pr[a]ecipue qu[a]e pr[a]edictis et aliis iugiter meretur attolli concessionem et auctoritatem dare et facere infrascriptis. Quamobrem supplicantibus nobis humiliter pro subscriptis vobis, dilecto et fidelibus nostris Jacobo Marchi, milite, et Ludovico de Averçone, cive Barchinon[a]e, quos ad huiusmodi scienciam promovendam credimus firmiter debitum habere propositum, vestra condicione attenta et quod obsequiosi eidem nedum surculos sed ramos eciam in eius [h]ortulo collegistis flores et fructus uberrime afferentes, vobis ei[s]dem Jacobo et Ludovico ad augmentacionem dict[a]e scienci[a]e, et ut nostri dilecti et fideles regnicol[a]e, nobiles, milites, cives generosi et alii quos dilectabit circa presentem laborare scienciam, possint peramplius in eadem proficere, et ad id locum ac facultatem habeant oportunos; ipsam quoque scienciam magis subtiliter practicari, doceri ac adisci valeat in civitate Barchonon[a]e pr[a]edictam secundum veram et approbatam artem, omni depulso errore, ad laudem et gloriam omnipotentis Dei et gloriosissim[a]e Virginis Matris su[a]e, ad quorum laudem et gloriam per opifices scienci[a]e huius multa fieri et concini speramus. Tenore presentis vos, dictos Jacobum et Ludovicum, peritos admodum in hac sciencia, super infrascriptis preferimus, ac vos magistros et defensores eiusdem scienci[a]e facimus et creamus, vobisque concedimus et auctoritatem et plenissimum damus posse quod singulis annis, die seu festo Beat[a]e Mari[a]e mensis marcii, possitis et liceat vobis libere et impune festum comemoracionem ac solemnitatem pro huiusmodi scienciam celebrare et facere ac fieri et celebrari eciam facere, necnon tenere sigillum in quo imagines Beat[a]e Mari[a]e Virginis, angeli Gabrielis et obumbracio Sancti Spiritus sub nostri regalis signi pallio figurentur; et taliter et non aliter volumus sit huius sigilli impressio et sic in eo Beat[a]e Virginis Concepcio denotetur. Possitis insuper, vobisque liceat, omnia carmina, opera sive dictamina vobis per illos qui se volent peritos in hac sciencia titulari, die qua fiet dicta solemnitas presentanda iudicare, corrigere et emendare, ac illa, si vobis videbitur auctorizare, reprobareve, reicere seu eciam refuctare, et illis carminibus sive operibus, qu[a]e dicti sigilli impression[a]e digna videbitis, ipsam impressionem apponere, ut sic apparere lucide valeat de eorum excellencia et composicione vel operacione condigna. Et iocalia pro pr[a]edictis assignanda dicto festo Beat[a]e

Mari[a]e Virginis seu [fol. 150] sequenti die dominica, pericioribus
in hac sciencia ac quibus volueritis et vobis videbitur dare, tradere
et assignare, dum tamen celebracioni solemnitatis et festi
huiusmodi sint presentes; Ordinaciones necminus quascumque pro
pr[a]edictis et infrascriptis libere facere quas ad ea noveritis
oportunas. Possitis, inquam, omnia alia facere qu[a]e alii magistri
aut pr[a]efecti huic scienci[a]e in civitatibus Parisius et Tholos[a]e
ac aliis civitatibus et locis consueverunt et possunt facere seu
eciam exercere. Nos enim illas et illa, cum fuerint per vos fact[a]e
et facta, nunc pro tunc et e contra laudamus, approbamus,
auctorizamus et eciam confirmamus, dum tamen per eas et ea
iura et Regali[a]e nostr[a]e aliquatenus non l[a]edantur. Mandantes
per hanc eandem de certa sciencia et expresse Gubernatori
Generali, necnon Gubernatori Cathaloni[a]e principatus, vicario,
subvicario, baiulo, consiliariis et probis hominibus Barchinon[a]e
et aliis universis et singulis officialibus nostris et subditis ad quos
spectet presentibus et futuris quatenus creacionem concessionemque
nostras huiusmodi et alia omnia supradicta iuxta sui seriem
pleniorem observent tenaciter, observarique faciant inconcusse
vobisque si et quociens fuerint requisiti assistant officiales
pr[a]emissi in et super pr[a]emissis effectui deducendis, servandis
eciam et tenendis consilio, auxilio et favore efficaciter et solerter
nil in contrarium ullatenus pr[a]esumpturi. In cuius rei testimonium
hanc iussimus fieri nostro pendenti sigillo munitam, Datum
Valencie vicesima die ffebruarii anno a nativitate Domini
MCCCLXXXXIII. Regnique nostri septimo. Rex Joh. Dominus
Rex mandavit michi Bartolomeo Sirvent. (ACA, Reg. 1924, fols
149ʳ-50ʳ; Torres Amat, 1836, pp. 59–61; Aversó, *Torcimany*, ed.
Casas Homs, Appendix I, pp. 441–3; there is a MS. of this
document in the Biblioteca Colombina, cited in Amador de los
Ríos, 1861–5, VI, p. 12 n.)

(On behalf of Jaume March and Lluís d'Aversó. We John, etc.
In so far as love was the origin of the science described below, the
thing itself excelling the name whereby it is known; whereby, so we
read, the only begotten son of God was conceived in a virgin's
womb to absolve the guilt of our first parent and through which
many other wondrous things were brought to pass; turning the
matter over in our minds, and considering the effect and essence of
the said science, which is known by one of love's terms as the

Joyous or Gay Science and by another as the Science of Invention; that science which, shining with the most pure, honourable and courtly eloquence, civilises the uncouth, vitalises the slothful, softens the coarse, entices the learned, trims the hirsute, discloses hidden things, sheds light on things obscure; rejoices the heart, stimulates the mind, clarifies and purges the senses; nourishes and allures children and young men with the draught of her mellifluous milk, making them while yet in youth, before the years have whitened their heads, take on the seriousness of mind and sobriety of old age, teaching them while still in the full fervour of their youth to restrain themselves by a strict code of morals; nurturing old men, charming in the dignity of their ways, with delightful entertainment, it sustains them as though in the freshness of their youth; it refreshes and delights both young and old with a sweet melody of surpassing joy; that science which is indeed the hall of manners, companion of virtues, preserver and guardian of honour and sworn enemy of vice, whose utility shines forth, whose magnificent qualities are apparent, whose fruitful labour is pleasing; she commands what is wholesome, forbids what is harmful and guides what is in error; all earthly things are moved by her; she influences the heavenly bodies in their courses; corrects, reforms and informs those of high, middling and lowly degree not only in word but also in deed; she cherishes exiles, relieves the afflicted, consoles the sorrowful, and gathers to her udders to be fed all those whom she recognises to be the sons and fosterlings of her doctrine. These, invigorated by her maternal milk, imbued by the nectar of her sweet font, she sends forth to gain the notice and favour of kings, prelates, and grandees of lesser and even lowly rank by virtue of their pleasant soothing songs. Attracted by the mention of the name of love and especially bearing in mind the excellence of the said science which, for the foregoing and other reasons, justly deserves to be extolled, we are induced and persuaded to give and to grant concession and authority to those named below. Wherefor we do most humbly beseech almighty God on behalf of the beneath-mentioned Jaume March and Lluís d'Aversó, believing you both to be firmly committed to the furtherance of the said science, mindful and duly respectful of your status – for you have gathered in the garden [of love or rhetoric] no mere shoots but branches already heavy with rich flowers and fruit. We pray on behalf of the said Jaume and Lluís that the said science may prosper; and in order that our beloved and faithful officials, nobles, soldiers, generous citizens and others who used to love to labour in the science whereof we treat may the more fully profit therein, and that they may have at their disposal a place and faculty for it, we pray that the said science be more subtly practised, taught and studied in the city of Barcelona according to the afore-mentioned true and approved art, all error having been banished, to the praise and glory of almighty God and his most blessed Virgin Mother, to whose praise and glory we hope that great things be done and sung by the craftsmen of this science. By these presents we do promote you, the said Jaume and Lluís, being sufficiently adept in this science, to positions superior to those named below, and we hereby make and create you magistrates and guardians of the said science, and we concede and grant you authority and supreme power to celebrate and perform freely and with impunity, and cause to be celebrated and performed, the feast, commemoration and solemnity of the said science every year on the feast of the Blessed Virgin Mary in the month of March, and to carry the seal on which images of the Blessed Virgin Mary, the Angel Gabriel and the overshadowing presence of the Holy Spirit shall be represented under our royal crest; and thus and not otherwise do we wish the stamp of this seal to be, that the Conception of the Blessed Virgin may be denoted by it. Moreover you can and are entitled to affix the stamp of the said seal to those poems and compositions which you deem to be worthy thereof, that it may clearly appear as a testimony of their excellence in construction and craftsmanship. And furthermore, on the said feast of the Virgin Mary or on the following Sunday, you are entitled to grant, make over and assign the trophies set aside for the aforementioned works to those skilled in this science and to whomsoever you wish and see fit, so long as they are present. You may also freely make any decrees which you deem appropriate favouring the things specified above and below. Indeed you may perform all other things that other magistrates and prefects of the said science in the cities of Paris and Toulouse and other cities and places are accustomed and able to execute and perform. Moreover we praise, approve, authorise and endorse the appointments and awards which will have been made by you, now and henceforward, provided that our laws and royal prerogatives are in no wise impaired thereby. We expressly and with sure knowledge command that the Governor General, and also the Governor of Catalonia, the vicar, subvicar, bailiff, councillors and upright men of Barcelona, and all our officials and subordinates, universally and individually, to whom it may concern may now and henceforward strictly observe and cause to be observed our nomination and concession, and all the foregoing, according to the full and proper protocol thereof; and that the officials appointed over and above those appointed to safeguard and conduct the execution of the above shall efficaciously and skilfully wait on you with advice, help and goodwill if and as often as they shall be required to do so; nor shall they presume to act in any way at variance with the above. In witness of which we order that this statement be stamped with our pendant seal. Given at Valencia on the twentieth day of February in the year of grace 1393, the seventh of our reign.)

4

Perpignan, 19 February 1396. Joan I sent a letter, composed by Bernat Metge, to the councillors and worthy citizens of Barcelona asking them to continue to hold an annual festivity in honour of the Gay Science and to offer the same prizes as in the previous year.

The king gives his assurance that among the good decrees issued in every important town there should be one providing an occasion whereby men of all ages, especially those living off their revenues and inherited property, might avoid idleness, and the most effective way of motivating them to abandon idleness is through the achievement of profitable and agreeable things. Since these two things cannot be easily accomplished, except through some branch of learning, there must be a place where many men may have a chance to study, especially if it be to study a science such as the Gay Science which can be achieved without much work or trouble. Enlightened men may appropriately learn it and take pleasure in it, and often derive profit from it, because it is based on rhetoric, which (when combined with wisdom, without which it is practically worthless) has been a course of honour and profit for many communities and individuals throughout the world, as the history books attest and as everyday experience shows. Therefore, moved by this consideration and bearing in mind the beautiful festival that was held last year in honour of the said Gay Science, which inclined men to shun idleness and to learn how to speak with knowledge and elegance, we beseech you that, continuing what you have begun and bringing the work to completion, a similar festival shall be celebrated this year in the city [of Barcelona], and as a result shall be celebrated regularly in future years, at which jewels [rewards] similar to those given last year shall be given to the troubadours who, through their learning and inventiveness, best deserve them. And this will be a thing most agreeable to us, and one which will redound to the great honour of the city. Given at Perpignan under our secret seal on the nineteenth day of February of the year 1396, King John.

The king commands me, Bernat Metge, to address the counsellors and honest men of Barcelona.

(ACA, Reg. 1967, fols 87ᵛ–88ʳ; Rubió y Lluch, *Documents*, I, pp. 384–5; Sanpere y Miquel, 1878, p. 209; Riquer, *Història*, I, p. 567)

5

Saragossa, 1 May 1398. Martí I (r. 1396–1410), extolling the benefits of all branches of learning, granted the rectors and judges or 'mantenedors' of the Gay Science in Barcelona an annual sum of 40 florins of gold to pay for the gold and silver prizes. The king reserved the right to nominate the judges, and stipulated that in that year, and in subsequent years, payment should be made for the expense of the prizes at Pentecost.[2] On 12 August 1399 he confirmed the nomination of Jaume March and Lluís d'Aversó as 'mantenedors' (Rubió y Lluch, *Documents*, II, pp. 352–3).

In favorem Gay[a]e scienci[a]e. Nos Martinus Dei gratia Rex Aragonum etc. Quoniam sola sciencia dicitur summa nobilitas in hac vita, Cum per eandem Teologus Regnum adquirat c[a]eleste; per eam legista iam statuat, iubeat, vindicet, puniat ac interpretetur clarissime; per eandem ac eciam canonista, ecclesi[a]e robur firmissimum et fidei orthodox[a]e columpna inmobilis, solvat quascumque ambiguas qu[a]estiones, et facta causarum predubia dirimat; per eam ulterius moderator human[a]e natur[a]e naturalisque scienci[a]e inquisitor sagacissimus phisicus, valida corpora in sanitate plenaria auxiliis phisic[a]e preconservet, et [a]egra ad pristinam temperantiam peroptatam reducat; per eam astrologus perspicaci corruscans ingenio, disposiciones c[a]elestium corporum intuatur, cursus inspiciat planetarum c[a]elique iam signa duodecim contempletur, stellas connumeret, zodiacum atque spheram firmamento in ipso proprio intellectu comprendat, unde

133

se dicit plenarie de futuris iudicare iam posse; per eam interea
Arismeticus numeros colligat, et in isto non modicum glorietur;
per eam mensuras Geometra amplectens, triangulos atque
quadrangulos recte designet; per eam iam Musicus modulamina
vocum eructet predulcia; per eam orator alliciens eius colloquia
vocis munimine gloriose corroboret, necnon et habeat copiam
dicendorum, et dulci sermone suabilique exordio et affabili
ratione animos alienos utiliter atrahat ad se ipsum; per eam
necminus dialecticus veritatem et falsitatem inquirat; per eam
gramaticus recte loquatur, recte et aret cum penna; per eam res
publica gubernetur, cultus iustici[a]e immoletur, timida pr[o]elia
comittantur; per eam terribiles machin[a]e erigantur, et hostium
expulsiva propugnacula construantur; per eam novalia renoventur,
et public[a]e libertatis quies, ambita atque confinium populorum
benevolenci[a]e reformentur; per eam postremo alia universa,
qu[a]e toto sub orbe intra laudabilis racionis s[a]eptageruntur
exitu concludantur felici. Quid ergo tam dulcius, quid tam
iocundius, quid tan utilius esse debet quam sciencia[m]
peramplecti? Porro universos et maxime nostros fideles subiectos,
scienci[a]e et doctrinis ac aliis moribus virtuosis continue militantes,
favore et graciis atque donis prosequimur, s[a]epius ut ad
pr[a]edictam vel aliqua ex eisdem habenda ferventius animentur,
Cum ex scientificis viris et regna et terr[a]e reluceant. Quia et
eciam Barchinon[a]e in urbe, qu[a]e fertilitatis ut ager assiduitate
cultur[a]e fecundior fructus uberrimus proferens viros virtutum
proflua ubertate fecundos producit, quorum fecunditas graciosa
in alios affluenter affunditor, parvos magnificans, rudes erudiens et
debiles virtuosos efficiens, sint viri quamplures qui inter alia
scienci[a]e docmata circa pr[a]ecepta et practicam oratori[a]e
facultatis, qua principum atque regum iam gratia capitur, ling[u]a
prerudis acuitur et possessor eiusdem de infimis [fol. 72] ad
honoris fastigia sublevatur sub rithimis atque metris et prosis
mesuracione sub certa protensis exercitare, pr[a]ecipue per eosdem
et qu[a]e inde vulgariter sciencia gaya vocatur, sic modo insudant
laudabili quod carmina eorundem modo Parisius modo Tholosam
huiusmodi et aliarum quarumlibet artium obtima quippe
gi[m]nasia ut inibi corrigi valeant destinata abinde remittuntur
s[a]epiissime laudis corona penitus illustrata, tanquam ab incude
malleo atque lima dict[a]e amen[a]e seu gay[a]e scienci[a]e,
quibuslibet viciis exinde relegatis, protracta fideliter atque pure;

unde et civitas Barchinon[a]e, cui non parum afficimur, cum ipsa
iam semper extiterit ac existat peravida, pervigil et actenta in
illis qu[a]e celebrem ad honorem et regi[a]e domus nostr[a]e
augmentum tunc dicerentur et possint spectare non modicum
commendatur, quod nobis ad placitum cedit permagnum. Tenore
presentis ut illi Civitatis pr[a]etens[a]e et alii universi, qui inibi
dicte amene seu gaye sciencie nunc vel de cetero vaccare
curaverint melius ad eandem habendam et practicam ipsius
exercendam induci tunc valeant, communitati eorum et ipsis
necnon Rectoribus et Defensoribus ac Manutentoribus eiusdem
amen[a]e seu gay[a]e scienci[a]e, Quadraginta florenos auri de
Aragonia annuales sub condicione inferius posita, ut ex ipsis iocalia
infrascripta emantur generosius ducimus concedendos, quos in
atque super emolumentis et iuribus universis officii baiuli[a]e
Civitatis Barchinon[a]e iam dicte eciam assignamus. Mandantes
serie cum presenti baiulo civitatis eiusdem, presenti atque futuro
et cuilibet alii, ad quem hoc spectet quovismodo, quatenus in hoc
festo Pentecostes venienti de proximo, et eciam singulis annis, de
cetero termino in eodem, Rectoribus et defensoribus ac
manutentoribus antedictis dictos Quadraginta florenos
convertendos per ipsos in iocalia infrascripta, nostri Thesaurarii
executoria seu mandato ad istud nullatenus expectato, exsolvat
plenarie. Recuperaturus ab ipsis apocas de soluto, in quarum
priori contextus huiusmodi penitus inseratur, in reliquis quidem
specialis solummodo mencio habeatur. Nos enim tenore presentis
nostro Racionali magistro vel alii cuicumque super iam dictis a
baiulo antedicto compotum audituro iubemus, quod tempore
raciocinii ipsius dictos Quadraginta florenos in suo recipiat
compoto supradicto nullam eidem pro isto qu[a]estionem facturus.
Volumus autem et tradimus in mandatis dictis Rectoribus et
defensoribus ac manutentoribus pr[a]efat[a]e amen[a]e seu gay[a]e
scienci[a]e, quod ex dictis Quadraginta florenis, illud vel illa
iocalia argenti vel auri, qu[a]e proinde videbuntur eisdem emenda,
emant, totaliter illi vel illis eorum, qui iuxta pr[a]ecepta et leges
dict[a]e amen[a]e seu gay[a]e scienci[a]e, alique carmina vel eciam
opera, secundum ipsorum iudicium melius aliis ediderint,
texuerint, fecerint seu ordinaverint in honorem et gloriam
aliqual[a]e et bravium hinc adquisita, penitus conferenda et danda
per eos. Quia [fol. 72^v] eisdem super iam dictis plenarie vices
nostras cum ista comittimus, nobis ipsis expressius retinentes, et

concessionem huiusmodi condicione sub ista eciam facientes,
quod dicti Rectores et deffensores ac manutentores pr[a]efat[a]e
amen[a]e seu gay[a]e scienci[a]e nominari et eligi ac·creari et poni
a nobis omnino nunc et de cetero habeant. Sin autem presentem
pro viribus et effectu carere nos volumus, quam in memoriam et
testimonium pr[a]emissorum fieri fecimus, nostro sigillo pendenti
munita. Datum C[a]esarauguste prima die madii anno a nativitate
Domini millesimo Trecentesimo .xc. octavo Regnique nostri
tercio. Matias vicecancellarius. Dominus Rex mandavit mihi
Jacobo Tavaschani. Vidit eam dominus Rex. Berengarius Sarta.
(ACA, Reg. 2254, fols 71ᵛ–72ᵛ; Aversó, *Torcimany*, Appendix II,
pp. 444–6; Bofarull y Mascaró, *Colección*, VI, pp. 469–75; Torres
Amat, 1836, p. 171)

(Knowledge alone is said to be the noblest thing in life, since the
theologian seeks out the kingdom of heaven thereby; and thereby
the man of law legislates, commands, vindicates, punishes and
interprets with clarity; thereby the canon lawyer, the church's
tower of strength and a staunch pillar of orthodoxy, resolves
ambiguities and confused and dubious issues; thereby the physician,
a great moderator of human nature and a most wise investigator of
natural science, preserves healthy bodies from disease with the help
of medicine and leads the sick back to their original and most
desirable balance of humours; thereby the astrologer, with brilliant
insight and understanding, observes the dispositions of the heavenly
bodies, considers the planets in their courses and contemplates the
twelve signs of the zodiac; by it he numbers the stars and compre-
hends within his intellect the zodiac and sphere in the firmament,
whence he claims to be able to foretell the future; thereby, meanwhile, the arithmetician brings numbers together and in no small
measure enhances his reputation; and the student of geometry,
taking measurements thereby, correctly draws triangles and quad-
rangles; by means of science also the musician pours forth modula-
tions of voice with surpassing sweetness; thereby the persuasive
orator reinforces his discourse with the wonderful weapon of his
voice and finds matter in plenty to dilate upon; and by the sweetness
of his speech, his convincing exordium and affable reasoning, he
profitably draws the minds of others to his point of view. Furthermore, through science the dialectician investigates truth and false-
hood; through it the grammarian correctly speaks and wields the

pen. By science the state is governed, justice paid her due homage and battles waged; thereby terrible weapons are constructed and defences for repelling the enemy are built; by means of science lands which are fallow are renewed; the peace of domestic freedom and the good will of neighbouring peoples are restored; and, finally, all things throughout the world performed within the bounds of reason are brought by science to a happy conclusion. What therefore can be as sweet, as pleasant and as profitable as to take up the pursuit of learning? Forthwith we shower with goodwill, esteem and gifts all our faithful subjects who perpetually struggle on behalf of the doctrines and practices of science that they may be more keenly motivated to embrace it, or to take up any of its doctrines or practices, since kingdoms and countries reflect the glory of their scholars and scientists. In the city of Barcelona (which – like a fertile field that by careful tillage bears more and richer fruit – produces men of abundant virtue who can, through their prolific fertility, easily and richly influence others, exalting the lowly, instructing the ignorant and making the weaklings brave); in the said city of Barcelona, there are many men who, besides being learned in other doctrines, labour in the precepts and the practice of the art of oratory, whereby the favour of princes and kings is won, the uncouth tongue refined and its owner raised from the lowliest condition to one of honour; who through rhythms, metres and measured prose labour especially in that art popularly known as the Gay Science. Their efforts deserve to be praised, because the poems which they compose, after being dispatched to Paris and Toulouse and the best schools of this and other arts to be corrected, are sent back crowned with laurels, purged of all flaws, perfected by the anvil, hammer and file of the said Pleasant or Gay Science, purified and faithful to its precepts. On this account the city of Barcelona (peerless in that she has always seemed, and is, most keen, vigilant and attentive to whatever might have, or may, concern the far-famed honour and prosperity of our royal house) is not a little commended, which greatly pleases us. Therefore, in order that these men of the said city of Barcelona, and all others who care to devote themselves to the said Pleasant or Gay Science, shall now and henceforward cherish and practise it more fervently, we do hereby most generously concede to their community, and also to the rectors, guardians and presidents of the said science, the annual sum of forty gold florins of Aragon on the conditions stated below, namely that the trophies described below shall be purchased; and we assign this sum over and above the emoluments, laws and perquisites of the office of bailiff of the said city of Barcelona. We hereby earnestly enjoin the present or future bailiff of the said city, or any other person in any way concerned, that he shall, on the coming feast of Pentecost, and annually henceforward on the same date, pay the said sum of forty florins in full to the rectors, guardians and presidents aforementioned, to be exchanged by them for the trophies described below, without waiting for an order or mandate from our treasury to this effect, and he shall recover from them receipts, in the first of which he shall place a copy of this present letter, whilst in the remaining receipts there shall be only a private memorandum. Therefore we hereby command our chief accountant, or any other person who shall audit the account received from the said bailiff, that when he audits the said account, he note the payment of the said forty florins therein, and that he may in no wise question the bailiff concerning it. We wish and charge the said rectors, guardians and presidents of the said Pleasant or Gay Science to purchase from the said forty florins the silver or gold trophy or trophies which they deem it necessary to purchase, to be by them conferred on and awarded to the person or persons who, in accordance with the precepts and laws of the said Pleasant or Gay Science, produce, compose, make or set down any poems or compositions commissioned from here, in honour of whomsoever, which they judge to be better than the rest. We do hereby fully entrust our fortune to the above-named with this express reservation, and making the said grant on the following condition: that the said rectors, guardians and presidents of the aforementioned Pleasant or Gay Science shall be named, elected, created and appointed entirely by us now and henceforward. If, on the other hand, we wish this document to lack force and effect . . . which we cause to be stamped with our pendant seal in memory and witness of those appointed. Given at Saragossa on the first day of May in the year of grace 1390, the eighth of our reign.)

6

Nantes, 6 January 1401. Charles VI of France, at the request of Philippe, Duke of Burgundy, and Louis, Duke of Bourbon, established a court of love, the purpose of which was to praise and serve ladies, and thereby to promote fine manners and deeds of prowess. It was planned that the society should hold a poetry competition or 'puy d'amours' on the first Sunday of every month at a pre-arranged place, and that the poems should be based on a set refrain. Two rods of gold, inscribed with the refrain in letters of enamel, would be offered as prizes. The twenty-four ministers of the court were to take turns in organising the monthly 'puys'.³ The charter of the society was to be made public on St Valentine's Day (14 February). On this day ladies would be selected to judge the best 'balades', which could be based on any refrain, and to award the golden rods. This feast was to be repeated every year. A dinner would also be given annually on one of the five feasts of the Virgin Mary. A competition would be held in the composition of 'serventois' in honour of the Virgin Mary, based on love poems previously submitted by the contestants either in May or in the monthly 'puys'. A silver crown and chaplet would be the prizes on this occasion. After a choral mass, the prize poems would be presented as an offering before the altar. If any members of the society propose a jousting match in May, the king undertakes to participate in person. Anyone found guilty of slandering women, or making a defamatory statement about any prince, lord, prelate, knight or squire, is liable to have his arms defaced and his shield painted the colour of ashes. The charter was read by a person who had been appointed the Prince of Love in the presence of a large number of princes and dignitaries.

One reason given for instituting the 'Court d'amours' was, as in the case of Boccaccio's *Decameron*, to provide some distraction from the terrors of a plague epidemic. Another possible motive was to entertain Charles VI, who temporarily recovered his wits in the first week of January 1401, after a bout of insanity which had lasted four months. Quite apart from the folk ritual associated with St Valentine's Day, I suspect that it was the king's affection for Valentine de Milan, the mother of Charles d'Orléans, which determined the choice of this day as one of special celebration. In 1399, when the king suffered from several fits of delirium, Valentine was the only woman who could calm him and tend to his needs. He recognised neither his wife, Isabeau, nor his children (Thibault, 1903, p. 224). The physicians recommended sports and amusements as a form of therapy. It is therefore quite possible that Isabeau herself had a hand in the establishment of the 'Court d'amours'. It is known that Valentine observed the traditional customs of St Valentine's Day:⁴

She used to hold a court of love at which it was expected that every knight should select a lady, whom he would serve and celebrate in song for one year, with the freedom to be faithful to her for longer.

Above all the society enabled an affluent and decadent aristocracy to evade the social and economic problems that had to be resolved.

From the Prince of the bailiwick of Love. To all noblemen and other renowned persons who shall now and hereafter see or hear this amorous epistle. Greetings. . . .

We do hereby humbly command and lovingly order all our amorous subjects, now and hereafter, to uphold, sustain, uplift and maintain this present decree, each according to his authority, degree and capacity, so strenuously and so perfectly that in their humble allegiance they will be shining exemplars worthy of honour and praise throughout all lands, that the sovereignty and majesty of love may thereby be an aid and gracious comfort to them in all their affairs and acts of service, contributing to the honour and eulogy of the good and lasting renown of all ladies and damsels throughout the universe, for it pleases us that it shall thus with much love be done, despite the murmur of slanderers, the scorn of the haughty, the distress of the envious, the disparagement of braggarts and all other hostilities opposed to love.

Humbly granted in the royal hall at Nantes, on the sixth day of January in the year of our Lord 1400, and in the first year of our joyful reign.

By the Prince at his amorous council, attended by Charles King of France, Philip Duke of Burgundy, Louis Duke of Bourbon, Louis son of the Duke of Bavaria, Peter son of the King of Navarre, William Duke of Bavaria . . . signed Jalle Noussel. (Potvin, 1886, pp. 191–220)

7

Barcelona, 17 March 1413. Fernando de Antequera (r. 1412–16) confirmed the concessions granted to the Gay Science by his royal predecessors, repeating verbatim Martí's praise of learning. In addition, he permitted the consistory or college to elect four rectors or presidents, and to hold celebrations throughout the year.

Pro gaya sciencia habentur ista. Nos Fferdinandus Dei gracia Rex Aragonum. . . . Et carmina eorundem, ea videlicet qu[a]e fidelia

extiterint et correcta per dictos rectores, deffensores et
manutentores secundum legem scienci[a]e ipsius, tam in die festi
pr[a]edicti quam infra annum et tociens quociens fieri contingat,
et prout ipsis rectoribus, deffensoribus ac manutentoribus
pr[a]efat[a]e amen[a]e seu gay[a]e scienci[a]e extiterit bene visum,
valeant auctoritate nostra laudis corona, ut moris est, penitus
illustrare, ipsaque sigilli assueti munimine insignire. Quia eisdem
super iam dictis plenarie vices nostras cum ista comittimus, nobis
ipsis expressius retinentes, et concessionem huiusmodi condicione
sub ista eciam facientes, quod dicti rectores et deffensores ac
manutentores pr[a]efat[a]e amen[a]e seu gay[a]e scienc[a]e nominari
et eligi ac creari et poni habeant a consistorio, collegio seu c[o]etu
inventorum dict[a]e amen[a]e seu gay[a]e scienci[a]e
quocienscumque necesse eis extiterit, qui dum electi, creati et
positi fuerint, illos pro rectoribus, deffensoribus et
ma[nu]tentoribus habeant, dum ipsis manutentoribus fuerit vita
comes, et quos mutare nequeant neque eciam variare, nisi
superveniente morte alius seu aliorum eorumdem, aut per
absenciam aliorum aut alicuius ipsorum. In cuius seu quorum loco
alium seu alios deffensores seu manutentores scienci[a]e ipsius
eligere et ponere valeant ac creare illam et eandem potestatem
habentes. Volumus inquam quod dicti rectores, deffensores et
manutentores sint quatuor numero, qui potestatem habeant in
eorum examine, et iudices alios consocios in dicta sciencia peritos
adiungere sibi, et ipsos tociens quociens voluerint variare, possint
eciam consistorium celebrare infra annum et tociens quociens
voluerint in anno, tam pro iocalibus specialibus quam generalibus,
et in ipso ritus et assuetas cerimonias observare. Et quascumque
ordinaciones facere, ad honorem, commodum et utilitatem totius
communitatis seu collegii amen[a]e scienci[a]e supradict[a]e, et
alias, prout antiquis temporibus erat fieri consuetum. In cuius rei
testimonium presentem fieri fecimus nostri sigilli munimine
insignitam. Datam Barchinone XVII die Marcii, Anno a
Nativitate Domini MCCCCXIII, regnique nostri secundo. Rex
Ferdinandus. Dominus Rex mandavit michi Paulo Nicholai.
(ACA, Reg. 2393, fols 43ᵛ–45ʳ; Bibl. Nat. de Paris, MS. esp. 225;
Aversó, *Torcimany*, Appendix III, pp. 447–9)

(These things are held in favour of the Gay Science. We Ferdinand
by the grace of God King of Aragon. . . . The said rectors, guardians

and presidents shall have full power by our authority (both on the aforementioned feast day and annually, and as often as the occasion arises, and according to the wishes of the said rectors, guardians and presidents of the said Pleasant or Gay Science) to crown the poems of the aforementioned which they deem to conform to the precepts of the said science with the traditional laurels and to dignify them with the seal prescribed by custom. We do hereby fully entrust our fortune to the above named with this express reservation, making the said grant on the following condition, namely that the said rectors, guardians and presidents of the aforementioned Pleasant or Gay Science shall be named, elected, created and appointed by a consistory, college or assembly of troubadours of the said Pleasant or Gay Science, to be held as often as they deem it good. And once they have been elected, created and appointed, they shall be maintained as rectors, guardians and presidents for life, nor shall there be any changes or alterations made in them except in the event of the death or absence of one or more of their number. Whereupon, in their place or places, other guardians and presidents of the said science, having the same authority, may be elected, created and appointed. It is our wish that the said rectors, guardians and presidents be four in number, empowered as a body to attach to themselves other associate judges, and to vary these as they wish. Moreover the consistory may be held annually, and as often as is desired during the course of the year, for the award both of special and of general trophies; and the usual rituals and ceremonies may be observed on these occasions, as well as making any appointments to office, to the honour, use and benefit of the whole community or to that of the college of the said Pleasant Science, and any other appointments to office in conformity with the precedent of former times. In witness of which we cause this document to be stamped with our seal. Given at Barcelona on the seventeenth day of March in the year of grace 1413, the second of our reign.)

8

An account of the events which led to the establishment of the consistory of the Gay Science in Barcelona and a description of the manner in which the poetry festival was conducted are to be found in Enrique de Villena's *Arte de trovar*, addressed to the Marquis of

Santillana, of which only a fragment survives. Villena (1384–1434) had been charged with the task of reforming the consistory during the reign of Fernando de Antequera. The following is an excerpt from this work. It will be observed that in the list of topics for poetry love is linked with manners, which implies that it was considered a social art.

So great is the benefit which civil life derives from this doctrine, which removes idleness and causes noble and inventive minds to be engaged in a most honourable inquiry, that other nations desired and obtained for themselves a school of this doctrine; and thus it was disseminated to various parts of the world.

With this object King John I of Aragon, son of King Peter II [his father was actually Peter IV of Aragon, III Count of Barcelona], sent a solemn embassy to the King of France, asking him to command the college of troubadours to come and establish the study of the Gay Science in his kingdom; his request was granted, and a school was established in the city of Barcelona by two 'maintainers' [i.e. guardians of the art] who came from Toulouse for that purpose; it was decreed that in the school and consistory of this science in Barcelona there should be four 'maintainers': one a knight, another a Master of Theology, another a Master of Law, another an honest citizen; and that when one of them passed away another of his condition was to be elected by the college of troubadours, and his appointment endorsed by the king.

In the reign of King Martin his brother the revenues and concessions assigned to the consistory were increased, for running expenses, such as the cost of repair-work on the books of the poetic art, the seals of the consistory and the silver rods of the vergers who walk ahead of the 'maintainers', as well as the prizes that are given every month,[5] and for the expense of celebrating the regular festivities. And during this period some very remarkable works were composed, which were considered worthy of recompense.

After the death of King Martin dissension in the Kingdom of Aragon over the royal succession made it necessary for some of the 'maintainers' and principal members of the consistory to leave for Tortosa [Toulouse?], and the college in Barcelona closed down.

[King Fernando was afterwards elected, Enrique de Villena, who was in his service, brought about the reform of the consistory, and they appointed him to be their president.]

[The topics proposed at Barcelona whilst Enrique was there were as follows]: sometimes praise of the Virgin Mary, sometimes praise of arms, sometimes praise of gallantry and good manners.

And on the appointed day the 'maintainers' and troubadours would assemble in the palace, where I used to stay, and we would leave there in an orderly fashion with the vergers preceding the 'maintainers' and heading the procession, carrying the books of the poetic art and the register. And when we arrived at the said chapter-house, preparations had already been made: the walls round the room were bedecked with tapestries, and in front seats had been erected in tiers; Enrique would sit in the middle, flanked by the 'maintainers', and the scribes of the consistory would sit at our feet, the vergers lower down; and the floor was covered with carpets; and there were two circular rows of seats where the troubadours sat, and in the middle there was a square construction as high as an altar, covered in gold cloth, on top of which were placed the books of the poetic art and the prize. And on the right was the throne of the king, who was usually present; and many other people would sit there.

And when everyone was silent, the Master of Theology, who was one of the 'maintainers', would rise to his feet and make a discourse on a chosen topic and on possible objections to it, praising the Gay Science and the subjects to be treated at that consistory, and he would sit down again; and then one of the vergers would tell the troubadours who had assembled there to divulge and make public the works which they had composed on the topics assigned to them; and then each in turn would stand up and read the work which he had composed in a clear voice, and these had been written on damask paper of diverse colours in letters of gold and silver with beautiful illuminations, the very best that they could produce; and after they had all been made public, each would present his work to the scribe of the consistory.

Afterwards two sessions were held, one in private, the other in public. At the private session everyone swore to judge fairly according to the rules of the art, without being at all biased, which was the best work examined by them; and as the works were meticulously read aloud by the scribe, each judge noted down the defects contained in them; and these were marked down in the outer margins. And when all had been corrected, the consistory would elect to present the jewel to the work found to contain no defects, or to the one with the least.

At the public session the 'maintainers' and troubadours would assemble in the palace; and, as before, I would accompany them from there to the chapter-house of the friar preachers; and when they had taken their seats and were silent, I would address a discourse to the troubadours, praising their compositions, and explaining in particular which one deserved the prize; and this composition had already been written down on finely illuminated parchment by the scribe of the consistory, with the crown of gold placed on top of it; and I would sign it at the foot of the page, and then the 'maintainers' would do likewise, and the scribe would seal it with the pendant seal of the consistory, and he would carry the prize to me, and when the author had been summoned, I would hand it to him, with the crowned work, to commemorate the occasion. The prize was recorded in the register of the consistory, giving licence and authority for the poem to be sung and spoken in public.

And after this, we would return in procession to the palace, and between two of the 'maintainers' would walk the prize-winner, and a boy would carry the prize in front with minstrels and trumpeters, and on our arrival at the palace, they would be given wine and sweetmeats; and then the 'maintainers' and troubadours would leave with the minstrels and the prize, to escort the prize-winner to his lodgings. (British Library, MS. Add. 9939, fols 119^r-120^v; Sánchez Cantón, 1919; Bullock, *Villena*, pp. 3-6)

9

Valladolid, 2 May 1434. Juan II of Castile and Álvaro de Luna organised a magnificent jousting match, in which they both participated, followed by dancing, jesting and feasting. The prize-giving ceremony was conducted as a court of love over which the god of love himself presided. The king, Love's standard-bearer, was awarded a horse as first prize. Álvaro de Luna received a helmet, adorned with Love's plumes, as second prize. Juan Niño received a sallet, forged by Vulcan, and Pedro de Acuña a rod belonging to Mars. The ladies were encouraged to be gracious to those who had fought so valiantly for their sakes.

When King John was in Valladolid, on 26 April in the year of our Lord 1434, he ordered that a joust should be organised on 1 May in the following manner. . . . This feast was not celebrated on 1 May because it was a Saturday, and the Constable had to hold a reception on that day; and it was postponed until the following Sunday. . . . And this joust ended at sunset, and the king, accompanied by the queen and the prince, and all the jousters and knights and squires, and the ladies and damsels who had been spectators, went to San Pablo where His Majesty was lodged and where his reception had been arranged by the Constable. And there was much dancing by many men in handsome costumes and by the queen with many ladies in splendid attire. And many fine theatrical entertainments were performed, both by them and on their behalf; and it was there in the reception-room that they dined.

At the king's table dined Queen Mary his wife, and Prince Henry his son, and Lady Beatrice, daughter of King Dinis [Duarte] of Portugal, granddaughter of King Henry [III of Castile] and the present king's aunt. Among those who dined at the reception given by the said Constable were the Archbishop of Santiago, and the Archbishop of Seville, the Constable's brother, and the Governor Pero Manrique, and Count García Fernández Manrique, and Count Pero Niño and many other knights, each as befitted his station.

And after they had dined, the following judgment was given and pronounced by the judges:

'We the god of love, seated at court on our throne of justice, ministering the latter to all plaintiffs according to ancient custom, with Mars seated on our left, after considering the hardships endured by these thirty enamoured knights, our vassals and most loyal servants, who this very day, trained by Mars, our dearly beloved cousin, and wounded by our darts,[6] which have never met with any resistance, have exercised themselves in arms, ruthless to their own sufferings and even to death should it befall them, and considering the advice of our judges, elected and chosen by the great Constable of Castile, who is very dear and devoted to us, to discover and judge the virtues of each of the litigants, we find King John, our dearly beloved standard-bearer, both by reason of his excellence and the magnificent valour of his royal person, worthy to receive the gifts of our divine bounty, for he has acquitted himself with extreme courage on this occasion, breaking lances and making noteworthy encounters. And I therefore command that our horse shall be presented to him as a recompense for his labours.

'Further, inasmuch as the great Constable, being endowed with our grace, has jousted beautifully and has made some great and noteworthy encounters and has won a piece of harness, we command that from our precious gifts a helmet with a plume of amorous feathers from our wings shall be given to him.

'Further, inasmuch as Juan Niño has endured longer and has done more bold deeds than those with whom he has jousted, we command that, as a recompense for so much labour, he be given from our chamber of arms a sallet, forged by Vulcan, Jupiter's armourer.

'Further, inasmuch as Pedro de Acuña has conducted himself very well on this occasion, and has laboured hard, and has performed some very noble tilts, we command that he be given a rod of the god Mars our cousin.

'Further, inasmuch as Juan de Merlo and Carlos de Arellano and Alfonso Niño, sheriff of Valladolid, after those to whom these prizes are given, have shown themselves to be the best at observing the rules and making encounters, and have performed more and better tilts than any of the rest, we graciously pray and beseech their ladies and girl-friends to embrace them and give them good cheer as a recompense and reward for their labours. This supplication we likewise make on behalf of Diego Manrique to his lady. Further, with regard to all the other knights and gentlemen who happen to have participated in this noble feast and vigorous joust, we remind them with all our strength that, for the sake of their good deeds, they should entreat and win favour from their ladies and girl-friends, since we elect and judge that, in our opinion, he who has accomplished the least has accomplished a great deal. We cordially beseech that this shall be done as ordained.' (Carrillo de Huete, *Crónica*, pp. 154–60)

10

A poetry anthology associated with the Navarrese court (*c.* 1463), known, after the owner of the manuscript, as the *Chansonnier d'Herberay*, contains an anonymous piece of prose, addressed to 'mossén ugo' (probably Mosén Hugo de Urríes whom Aubrun believes was the compiler of the collection), which expounds and reinterprets the troubadour theory of love. The author discusses love's contradictory effects, and debates what part the disposition of the stars might play in love. He makes some interesting observations on the differences between male and female honour, which, he believes, would explain why love is so rarely reciprocal. A woman must rebuff her lover's advances or dissimulate in order to test his sincerity. The author stresses the need in love for a concord of wills, and ends by evoking the delights resulting from such a union.

Love reduces two wills to one; he intimidates the valiant, makes the judicious vain and rejuvenates the old. Wisdom into ignorance, baseness into nobility, avarice into generosity, cowardice into audacity, he turns everything upside-down; the quality itself is transformed into its contrary. He causes men to pursue death, to hate pleasure, to enjoy suffering and to cast away riches. In short, he commands reason, governs will and rules understanding; and it is he who imposes strange laws on human customs and natural affections, whereby, being the vanquisher of all things, he can be vanquished by none but himself. His power is in fact so clearly evident from experience that one must be content to say in response to his activities: 'It so pleases Love.' But although to others this answer is sufficient, from my intimate acquaintance with him I would say, in reply to your question, that it is not possible for Love to suddenly rob the powers of the will without any previous knowledge of the other person by means of sight alone. And this is the reason. As you know all men naturally find women more pleasing than any other thing; and if one of them, whose beauty and grace can be easily and swiftly perceived, is seen by a youth, who, with a carefree will, ardent blood and noble spirit, wanders in search of love, the flint being prepared and the tinder of good quality, it is small wonder that, through the impact of the eyes alone, the fire of love soon kindles. At other times this force proceeds from the heavens; this occurs as a result of the congruence of the houses of the planets and the degrees of the signs in relation to human beings, so that when those born and conceived under a similar constellation see each other, they are drawn to love one another by that natural impression, and they are attracted to a greater or a lesser extent depending on the degree to which it exists.

But, you object, if this force derives from that equal resemblance, why do the two parties not love each other equally? Here is the reason. The celestial congruence only elicits an inclination to love, which, having overcome prudence, and finding the things that love requires, such as beauty, elegance and noble bearing, very quickly makes a person fall in love. But if a lover lacks these things, do you think that in such a situation the congruence of the heavens can prevail over love's deformity? No, because this master of mine only likes things that allure him, and abhors and destroys all others as if they were hostile to him, so much so that if the unbecoming lover strives to love he will elicit hatred from his beloved, whereas in any other connection such conduct would have seemed agreeable. Besides, as you know, ladies are entitled to fear and reject what we desire and request, for to love many women and moreover to be loved by them is to us an honour, and to be loved by merely one man is to them a risk. What makes us healthy makes them grow sick. To love few members of the opposite sex, or none, does not befit us, whereas in them it is considered a good thing. This is the reason why men surrender themselves entirely in order to possess women, while women come to Love's obedience at a slow and timid pace, believing that a person who complains about love is preparing to regret it. Thus a similar constellation can operate on our desires to a very limited extent, and has only the slightest influence over the desires of women.

It may likewise happen that the lady conceives for her suitor that first degree of affection that prepares her for love, but dissimulating it, knowing that it is better to pass judgment before loving than to do so after having loved, she begins to examine his habits, whence love is strengthened or diminished, and perchance she may find him base, conceited, dirty, importunate, ill mannered, and deficient in the three things which women lack and therefore seek in men, namely ardour, secrecy and sincerity. Believe me that, should this occur, these or similar crimes, ignoble qualities or disablements will cause the pleasure of the first inclination, to which the will had consented, to turn to displeasure after this second knowledge. And do not imagine that everyone may love, even should they wish to do so. Noble, sincere, sweet and gracious qualities are Love's friends. But these can never, or only belatedly, take root in the very covetous, enter into the base, become secure in the fickle or harmonise with the very wicked.[7] As regards the ill-bred person, we would say that he may love well [i.e. in the courtly manner]. But since no one loves beyond that which he knows, and since he is deficient in knowledge, he will inevitably be deficient in the art of loving well. Nor should one believe that there is any means whereby Love may lodge amidst the baffled senses of the madman. Since such persons cannot give love, we should not demand it of them, even if some apparent qualities make them lovable. There are other men whom I have seen, and whom you have met, who are so naturally dull-witted and inept that, detested by all men, they are unable to appear agreeable to anyone. And there are others so gifted and attractive that they are loved by all who know them. It is more than likely that the latter will inspire love very quickly and the former never at all. And assuming that the above obstacles were eliminated, it could happen that the loved one had set his or her heart on another love and was consequently unable to comply with the lover's will; because two persons cannot be loved simultaneously.

These, Master Hugo, are the laws related to your question which Love is in the habit of observing. It is true that occasionally through slovenliness, excessive appetites, mad obsessions, or because Love wishes to display his might, they are sometimes interrupted, yet it is still firmly maintained that love cannot derive very much strength from one party alone. Since nothing increases love so much as love, to earn the perfect name of *enamorado* [or lover] a concord of wills is necessary. Nor should it be imagined that numerous disparities in wisdom, temperament and habits can be united and fastened in the bonds of love, or if they are, that they can be quickly broken. On the other hand, should the celestial and acknowledged congruence befall two persons disposed with a free will to receive love, it is inevitable that sooner or later they will plough their soil, jointly subdued by the yoke of love, and that after sowing, they will pluck that delicious fruit and sweet taste which cannot be compared with any other pleasure. (British Library, MS. Add. 33382; *Canc. Herberay*, ed. Aubrun, pp. 24–6)

Conclusion

The main aim of this study has been to seek an explanation for the unexpected revival of troubadour poetry and chivalric idealism in late medieval Spain. Part I analysed the theoretical structure of medieval society with special reference to the Iberian Peninsula. Part II outlined the history of the period. Part III illustrated certain aspects of the troubadour revival by means of contemporary documents in Latin, Catalan, Castilian and French. It was my general conclusion that this cultural phenomenon was a form of archaism, that is to say a response by the dominant minority to the disintegration of medieval values and institutions.

In the late Middle Ages many European countries were dominated, both politically and culturally, by an aristocracy which was in danger of becoming professionally redundant as a result of its inability to adapt to sudden changes in the nature of society, chief of which were the absence of chivalry in the methods and motives of mechanised warfare, the growth of centralised bureaucracy and the development of a non-seigniorial economy. This was especially true of Spain where, contrary to the experience of most other countries, the nobility expanded rapidly during the course of the fifteenth century (for reasons discussed in Part II). The principle of primogeniture and the duty of non-derogation, whereby a person of noble birth was debarred from participating in trade and commerce, produced a large leisured class in which there was a preponderance of unattached males, most of whom had no material or political responsibilities. This social group looked back with nostalgia to a largely imaginary chivalric age, and rejected as subversive and heretical any social concepts or intellectual theories which denied the immutable providential character of the status quo. The Provençal ideal of *fin'amors* answered the needs of this dominant minority because, being based on the feudal principles of fealty and subservience, it inculcated a respect for status and the existing hierarchy and was a means of evading unpleasant social and political realities.

Part I studied the theory of the three estates, traditional forms of patronage and the nature and functions of the court. The theory of the three estates flourished in literature when it had long ceased to be realistic or practicable. According to this theory, society was divided into three occupational categories: *defensores, oratores* and *laboratores.* Each of these estates of man had its specific duties and prerogatives, which made social mobility and intermarriage almost impossible, and caused the significance of the growing bourgeoisie to be greatly underestimated. Mankind was perceived as a body, knit together by a web of individual contracts, branching out from the king to the lowliest of his subjects. Almost all human relations – kingship, feudalism, court tuition and service, patronage in knighthood, the tutelage of saints, and the bond between the courtly lover and his lady – were influenced by the concept of patronage. This concept was defined as a reciprocally beneficial and reciprocally binding relationship between individuals, or groups of individuals, of unequal status, based upon an exchange of protection for services rendered. It moreover implied the idea of moral education by example, because a patron was expected to serve as a model for his client (the two words 'patron' and 'pattern' being etymologically related), and the client was under an obligation to fulfil his pledge. The *Siete partidas*, a law book prepared by Alfonso el Sabio's legislators which retained its authority until the end of the fifteenth century, thus prescribed how a king should conduct himself in his daily life, in his speech, table manners, dress and other seemingly private matters. I observed that, as in the Islamic *Sharī'a* or religious law, no sharp differentiation was drawn between private morality and public life. It is possible that the rights which a Spanish lord exercised over the person and property of his *criado* owed more to Roman than to Visigothic law. Patronage, in the original sense of the word, was a legal contract between a master and his ex-slave. The status of the medieval court official was in some ways not unlike that of the Roman *cliens*. In the Middle Ages the concept of patronage even extended into the religious sphere, since it was customary for men to dedicate themselves, either individually or as members of a profession or nation, to a patron saint. The centre of patronage and justice was the royal court. It was a place of leisure and play and a school of courtesy, the cardinal social virtue. The archetypal court was of course the court of love. Here the composition of love poetry was a sign of good breeding, a means of contending for favours and one of the most popular forms of entertainment. It was essentially a non-professional activity in which all those who attended the court were encouraged to participate.

Part II studied the historical background to the court culture of fifteenth-century Spain, and briefly described the character of several Castilian and Aragonese monarchs who appear to have exerted some influence on contemporary poetry and cultural attitudes. The revival of courtly and chivalric ideals during the reign of the Trastámaran dynasty (1369–1516) seems to have been closely associated with the fortunes of the nobility and with the assimilation of Aragonese culture by the Castilians. It was with the aid of a rebellious dispossessed aristocracy, which fought to re-establish its ancient power and prerogatives, that in 1369 Enrique de Trastámara defeated the loyalist forces and murdered his half-brother, Pedro 'el Cruel'. Hopes of an aristocratic regeneration were diminished by the rout of the Castilian troops by the Portuguese in 1385 and by the economic slump which afflicted Europe during the final decades of the fourteenth century. The messianic mood of the period is conveyed by many poems in the *Cancionero de Baena*. Although Juan II (1406–54) did not prove to be the long-awaited saviour, he and his son, Enrique IV, permitted the emergence of a new aristocracy which they vainly attempted to propitiate by the lavish distribution of lands and titles. At the start of Juan II's reign there were only three counts in the kingdom of Castile, but by the 1470s, when the country was torn apart by civil war, there were at least fifty noble families with the titles of duke, marquis, count or viscount. A large proportion of the poets whose poems were published in the *Cancionero general* were members of this aristocracy, and the majority were composing amidst the baronial anarchy which prevailed before and immediately after the accession of Ferdinand and Isabella.

Many of the leading political and literary figures in Castile during the fifteenth century were Aragonese by birth or by education, which is significant in view of the fact that Joan I and Martí 'el Humá', the last descendants of the ancient Counts of Barcelona, had promoted the theory and practice of Provençal poetics. The former established a poetic academy at Barcelona in 1393 based on the Toulouse Consistori dels Sept Trobadors. The latter founded a faculty of Limousin at the University of Huesca in 1396. Fernando de Antequera's election to the Aragonese throne in 1412 and Álvaro de Luna's political supremacy in Castile dismantled the cultural barriers which had previously existed between Aragon and Castile. Juan II and his Aragonese favourite were both poets and patrons of poetry, as were several leaders of the rebel faction. A considerable number of Castilian poets, many of whom were hostile to Álvaro de Luna's leadership, were attracted into the service of Fernando's eldest son, Alfonso the Magnanimous, who made a triumphal entry into Naples in 1443.

The key to Isabella's political achievements lay in her ability to combine the role of a popular messiah with that of a courtly *dame sans merci*, thereby earning the support of the common people and the admiring respect of the nobility. She was thus able to focus the energies of the belligerent aristocracy into the completion of the Reconquest, an event which was seen by later historians as marking the end of an era. The chief stimulus to noble exploits disappeared with the fall of Granada. Many poets of Jewish origin addressed panegyrics to Isabella because they were deceived into thinking that she would protect their interests. The traditional love lyric was still fashionable in the aristocratic environment of Valencia under the government of Ferdinand's second wife, Germaine de Foix. However, after 1492 the old ideals and sentiments had lost their vigour.

Part III quoted various passages from royal decrees, charters, chronicles and other sources which illustrate different aspects of the Spanish troubadour revival. These were arranged chronologically from 1388 to *c.* 1463. They revealed that in the late fourteenth century Aragon was renowned for its court ceremonial and that the standards of sexual morality at court were so lax that Joan I considered it necessary to introduce certain moral reforms. The study of *fin'amors* may well have been regarded as part of this programme. His embassy to Charles VI in 1388, seeking permission to establish a poetic academy in Barcelona, also obviously served as a useful diplomatic gesture, since this was the year of the French king's coronation. Documents from the royal archives show that Joan I and Martí 'el Humá' attributed almost miraculous properties to the art of troubadour poetry known as the Gay Science. The capacity of this art to transform qualities into their opposites – polishing the uncouth, sharpening the dull-witted, rejuvenating the old, etc. – was precisely that which, according to a tradition originating in the Arab world, had long been associated with love. (This subject was discussed in *The Origin and Meaning of Courtly Love*, Appendix II, and is mentioned in an anonymous prose fragment quoted from the *Chansonnier d'Herberay*.) The French 'Court d'amours', an aristocratic poetry society founded in 1401 to amuse the half-witted

Charles VI, was in many respects analogous to the Barcelona consistory. Both institutions owed something to the fraternities of minstrels or 'puys' which had existed in France since the twelfth century. These 'puys' held poetry competitions at regular intervals which were often judged by a Prince of Love. The most important festivity was generally that which was celebrated in the spring. In 1413 Fernando de Antequera confirmed the concessions granted to the poetic academy by his royal predecessors. In this year or soon after this date Enrique de Villena, who had been appointed by the king to reform the institution, witnessed the pompous and academic ritual surrounding the election of a poet laureate, of which he was later to give such a vivid account. In 1434 Juan II and Álvaro de Luna organised a joust at which the prizes were distributed by a poet impersonating the god of love. This passage illustrates the pervasive influence of the fiction of courtly love. The final passage, quoted from the Navarrese poetry anthology known as the *Chansonnier d'Herberay*, demonstrates the persistence of traditional psychological opinions about the nature of love during the latter half of the fifteenth century.

Part IV

Appendices

Appendix 1
Number of Titles Granted to the Spanish Titular Nobility by Name of Title: 1350–1540

TABLE 1

Decade	Total	Dukes	Marquises	Counts and Viscounts
1350–60	3	–	–	3
1360–70	6	–	–	6
1370–80	2	1	–	1
1380–90	5	3	–	2
1390–1400	5	1	–	4
1400–10	–	–	–	–
1410–20	1	1	–	–
1420–30	8	3	–	5
1430–40	8	1	–	7
1440–50	17	2	3	12
1450–60	14	1	–	13
1460–70	24	4	1	17
1470–80	26	8	2	16
1480–90	12	6	4	2
1490–1500	9	2	4	3
1500–10	4	1	2	1
1510–20	6	1	4	1
1520–30	5	1	2	2
1530–40	8	1	7	–

Sources: (1) Atienza, 1954 (2) Cadenas, 1956 (3) Blanco-González, 1962, p. 275 (4) Salazar de Mendoza, 1608

Note: given the above sources, the data cannot claim a very high degree of accuracy. The coverage of Castile is more complete than that of Aragon and the Aragonese kingdom of Naples. However, despite its shortcomings, and assuming that the margin of error is more or less the same over time, the figures show an extraordinary inflation of the Spanish titular nobility between 1440 and 1490. The worst period for the nobility, both titular and non-titular, was between 1400 and 1420, during Juan II's minority, as is corroborated by the complaints of impoverished knights in the *Cancionero de Baena*.

FIGURE 1

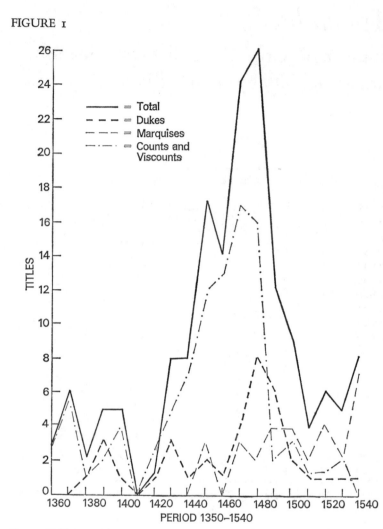

Source: Table 1

Note: Cf. Gerbet, 1972. This article uses a series of graphs to illustrate a correlation between the number of knighthoods, concessions of *hidalguía*, etc., conferred and outbreaks of war.

Appendix 2
Prophecies of Catastrophe and of the Emergence of a New World Order

Archaism and messianism are, as I have argued earlier, two sides of the same coin: attempts to resuscitate a courtly and chivalrous past coincided with messianic expectations and predictions. Francesc Eiximenis, for example, predicted that by the year 1400 all Christian kingdoms would have been destroyed save that of France. This prophecy, which was mentioned by Joan I of Aragon in a letter to Pere d'Artés, dated 17 November 1391, occurs in chapter 466 of his *Regiment de Prínceps*:

> La reformació del món, la qual diuen que s'ha a fer dins lo centenar present, en que comptan 1385, après d'aquest centenar ço dien, se mudarà la seu papel en Jerusalem, e dien que aquí haurà novell papa e novell emperador, e seran abdós de linatge dels jueus convertits a la fe.... Dien encara que, açò fet, tota potestat reial cessarà en lo món, sinó solament en la casa de França, qui durarà longament.... E dien que lavors regnarà per tot lo món la justícia popular, que sols regirà sots un papa e sots un emperador, fins a la fi del món, aixi que non hi haurà altre príncep ne rei pus, sinó aixi como dit és, e cascuna comunitat regirà si mateixa e serà feta pau per tot lo món fins a la fi del món.

> (It is said that the reform of the world will take place within this present century, which they would reckon from 1385; after this century, so they say, the reform will begin in Jerusalem, and they say that there will be a new pope and a new emperor, and that both will be descended from Jews converted to the Christian faith.... They also say that, when this happens, all royal authority will cease in the world, save only for the royal house of France which will long endure.... And they say that then the justice of the people will rule throughout the world, that it alone will rule beneath one pope and beneath one emperor until the end of the world, as there will be no other prince or king, apart from what has been stated, and each community will rule itself and there will be peace throughout the world until the end of the world.)

Appendix 2

The same 100-year period had an apocalyptic significance for Bachiller de la Palma, whose *Divina retribución sobre la caída de España en el tiempo del noble rey Don Juan el Primero* was completed in 1479. On the last day of June 1478, the year in which the Catholic monarchs defeated the Portuguese at the Battle of Toro, Queen Isabella gave birth to a son christened Juan. According to Palma, this child was destined to redeem Spain from the evil which had befallen the country since 1385, when the troops of the child's namesake, Juan I, were defeated by the Portuguese at Aljubarrota:

> Y el desseado príncipe don Juan es el verdadero esposo prometido destos rreynos de Castilla e de León, de la estirpe natural e rreal de Castilla, de amas partes, del Rey e Reyna nuestros sennores, desçendientes del noble rrey don Johan, del noble linaje de los godos. (p. 73)

> (And John, the long awaited prince, is the true promised spouse of these realms of Castile and Leon, descended on both sides of the family from the native royal stock of Castile, from the king and queen, descendants of the noble King John, of noble Gothic ancestry.)

The genealogy of the Trastámaran kings from Juan I to Prince Juan is explained figuratively by means of the statue in Nebuchadnezzar's dream (Daniel, ii): the head of gold is Juan I; the arms of silver are Enrique III and Fernando de Antequera; the belly and thighs of brass are represented by Juan II, the father of Isabella (who was 'fija de su vientre'); the legs of iron and clay symbolise the union of Enrique IV and Queen Juana (because they are substances that do not mix). The stone which destroyed the feet of the statue is Pedro González de Mendoza, Cardinal of Spain, who fought so valiantly at the Battle of Toro. The statue was shattered, but the head of gold remained in the form of Prince Juan (Palma, *Divina retribución*, pp. 75-7). Isabella is compared to Salome, demanding from her mother Herodiade (Castile) the head of St John:

> su madre, Castilla, le aconsejó que non le demandase otra cosa, salvo la cabeça de san Juan, que avía más menester, e estava en deseo de aver tal cabeça de oro preçiosa e de tal seso, que fue del ya dicho rrey don Juan el primero. (pp. 78-9)

> (her [Isabella's] mother Castile advised her to ask for nothing less than the head of St John, which was what she needed most, and she desired to have such a precious head of gold and of such wisdom as that which was possessed by the above-mentioned King John the First.)

An apocryphal work of Arnau de Vilanova, written in about 1420 by a supporter of the anti-pope Pedro de Luna, and based on Joachim da Fiore's *Summa concordiae*, predicts that Fernando de Antequera will be the golden head prophesied by Daniel. A similar prophecy, announcing the imminent union of Castile and Aragon through a princess and a king described as Daniel's head, was reported by Joan de Bur in 1412, who had learnt of it from an Egyptian hermit (Bohigas y Balaguer, 1920–2, pp. 41–3). The meaning of Nebuchadnezzar's dream, which is an important messianic text, is discussed by John Gower in his *Vox clamantis* (bk VII, i–v; *Complete Works*, ed. Macaulay, III, pp. 272–85), and in the *Confessio amantis* (Prologue, ll. 584–890; I, pp. 21–9). He does not forecast the advent of a messiah but merely uses the dream to support a theory of universal degeneration and division that calls for urgent action. Gold, silver, brass and iron represent the Babylonian, Persian, Greek and Roman empires respectively, all of which have passed away:

> But in this wise a man mai lere
> Hou that the world is gon aboute
> The which welnyh is wered out.
> (ll. 869–71; pp. 28–9)

Elsewhere he argues that if human nature were of a single substance, instead of being a compound of body and soul, hot and cold, wet and dry, and so forth, then man would be incorruptible. But since human nature and the whole cosmos are founded on contraries, ageing and decay are inevitable. It is difficult to understand how Gower was able to reconcile this pessimistic and deterministic view of the historical process with his belief that love was a remedy for social ills and a Phoenix in the wilderness (*Vox*, bk VII, iv, ll. 345–6), unless perhaps we consider the paradox that love both creates and resolves all contraries:

> Non amor unicolor est set contrarius in se,
> Qui sine temperie temperat esse vices. . . .
> Est amor iniustus iudex, adversa maritans
> Rerum naturas degenerare facit . . .
> Mors vivens, vita moriens, discordia concors.
> (*Vox*, bk IV, ii, ll. 39–40, 43–4, 69; pp. 202–3)

(Love is not all of one colour but is self-contradictory, mingling the changes of fate without measure. . . . Love is an unjust judge, which, marrying opposites, causes the nature of things to degenerate . . . a living death, a dying life, a united discord.)

The idea of cosmic degeneration is expressed by several poets in the *Cancionero de Baena*, but it is usually accompanied by a vision of regeneration. Ruy Páez de Ribera, who was writing during the regency of Fernando de Antequera, lists the names of the old nobility and predicts that, with the help of the child king Juan II, these families will recover their former estates:

Perdieron la fuerça de los sus cabellos
por el rrodamiento del mundo aborrido,
e agora por este señor que es nasçido
los vienes perdidos tornáronse a ellos.
(*Canc. Baena*, no. 289, st. 13; II, p. 602)

(They lost their strength through the rotation of the weary world, and now by this prince who is born their lost fortunes have returned to them.)

The poet enters a meadow where he sees three thrones on a dais: a golden throne on which the child king is seated; a throne draped in black where the queen mother sits in mourning; and a throne covered in white and blue silk where Fernando is seated. Behind them a respectful crowd is gathered together; in front of them a multitude clamours for justice. The poet is informed by his guide that the child will be Castile's 'redemption' and that the queen mother will be the author of peace and protector of the nobility ('through her the *hidalgos* will shortly recover their former estate'). Similar expectations were aroused by the birth of Charles VI of France, which occurred on the first Sunday of Advent 1368. It was observed that at the time of his birth the priests in Notre-Dame were singing: 'Voici que vient le Roi! Accourons au-devant de notre Sauveur!' (Here comes the King! Let us hasten to our Saviour!) At the feast of his baptism a large crowd made a procession through the streets, bearing torches and singing 'Noël! Noël! que bien peut-il estre venu?' (Thibault, 1903, p. 97) (Nowel! Nowel! Can it be that he has really come?).

Unlike Eiximenis, Páez de Ribera and the Bachiller de la Palma both placed their hopes in a Spanish monarch. The chief difference between them is that the former was a partisan of the old nobility and the rural gentry, whereas the latter spoke on behalf of the common people, voicing populist sentiments that would have been unacceptable to Isabella's royal forebears.

Appendix 3
Pedro Manuel Ximénez de Urrea
(1486–c. 1530): a Late Medieval Troubadour

A biographical inquiry

Pedro Manuel Ximénez de Urrea is generally cited by literary historians as one of the more interesting of the minor poets who flourished in the early years of the sixteenth century. Born too late to be included in the *Cancionero general* (1511), and writing too early to participate in the poetic revolution initiated by Boscán and Garcilaso, Urrea has – despite his literary merit and the interest of his life – received scant attention from scholars and critics.[1] This appendix is primarily concerned with his life and his attitudes to poetry and poetic theory. It also offers for the first time a full listing of his known works. Archival research in Spain would no doubt resolve some of the remaining problems, but I hope that the present study, which makes extensive use of sixteenth-century chronicles not drawn on by previous students of the poet's work, may provide a helpful basis for further investigation.

Pedro Manuel Ximénez de Urrea y Fernández de Híjar was born into one of the most powerful and distinguished families of Aragon: his mother's father, the Duke of Híjar (a title conferred in 1487), was a descendant of Pedro Fernández, a bastard son of James I of Aragon; his own father, Don Lope Ximénez de Urrea, was the first Count of Aranda (a title conferred in 1488), Viscount of Rueda, lord of Almonacir, Epila, Trasmoz, Mata, Castalviejo, Salinas and Casanueva.[2] Through marriage, he was related to almost all the principal families of Aragon: Luna, Cardona, Fernández de Heredia and Sesé. These connections were, however, no guarantee against adversity, because, from an early age, he inherited a private vendetta against Alonso de Aragón, Count of Ribagorza (a title conferred in 1469), a bastard son of John II of Aragon, and against his successor, Juan de Aragón (who briefly held the post of Viceroy of Sicily in 1507).[3] The Counts of Ribagorza were dangerous opponents, since they could rely on military support from another illegitimate prince, Alonso de Aragón (1470–1530), who was not only the Archbishop of Saragossa and the son of King Ferdinand but also the commander of the troops of the Santa Hermandad, a rural police force and a judicial tribunal controlled by the Crown. Furthermore the premature death of the poet's father was, during his childhood, a constant source of anxiety.

In a poem dedicated to his wife Doña María de Sesé, Urrea addresses the ghost of his dead father:[4]

y así andando viviendo
hasta diez y nueve años
de mi edad.
Después, fortuna el dolor
volvió plaziente alegría
dando me tal compañýa
qual tu tuviste señor.

(and thus life continued until I was nineteen years of age. Afterwards Fortune transformed my suffering into pleasant joy by giving me the same companionship as you had my lord.)

Urrea states in this poem that he was married at the age of nineteen, and that he was only four years old when his father died:

Un dolor me veo tener,
entrando tu en blancos paños;
por no pasar de quatro años,
no te pude conocer.
(fol. xiv; p. 114)

(I recollect my grief when you were wrapped in white shrouds; being no more than four years old at the time, I never came to know you.)

From the poet's marriage documents in the Tarazona municipal archives, which are dated 28 and 30 April 1505, and from his age at marriage, Martín Villar was able to calculate, in his introduction to the 1513 *Cancionero* (p. viii), that Pedro Manuel Ximénez de Urrea was born in 1486, which means that his father must have died in 1490, or thereabouts. (A rubric above the list of contents in the 1513 *Cancionero*, which states 'acabado todo lo que enel se contiene hasta veynte y cinco años', tallies with Villar's deduction, since it implies that Urrea could not have been born after 1488.)

Don Lope was almost certainly a victim of the ancient feud between the Urrea family and the Counts of Ribagorza, a feud which was rekindled in 1487 and which, in 1513, nearly deteriorated into a civil war.[5] The Urreas were jealous of their hereditary rights, and therefore they resented interference from either the Inquisition or the Hermandad. When King Ferdinand and the Chief Inquisitor called a meeting of the Cortes at Tarazona in 1484 in order to clamp down on Jewish *conversos* who were suspected of having reverted to their old beliefs, a group of Old Christians sought the assistance of Don Lope Ximénez de Urrea to oust the Inquisition. Don Lope was obliged to remain tactfully neutral, since he had been appointed Deputy of the Realm for the year 1485. The plotters were on the point of pushing Martín de la Ruya, 'assessor del Santo officio', into the river Ebro when Don Lope and Felipe Castro stepped forward and foiled their plans. The Chief Inquisitor, Pedro de Arbués, was nevertheless assassinated in the cathedral of Saragossa on 14 September 1485 (Zurita, 1579–80, bk XX, ch. lxv). It would appear that Don Lope was accused of giving his tacit support to the conspirators, because he, together with other members of the nobility, was subsequently arrested and imprisoned.[6] He is last mentioned by Zurita as one of the rebellious nobles who met in October 1487 to oppose the Santa Hermandad, which suggests that he may have died fighting (Zurita, 1579–80, bk XX, ch. lxxvii). This hypothesis concerning Don Lope's death would, at any rate, account for the vehemence with which the feud flared up again between 1510 and 1513, when the deployment of 2,000 soldiers under the command of the Archbishop of Saragossa, who was entrusted with the task of forcing the towns to join the Hermandad, gave the Counts of Ribagorza the opportunity of attacking their traditional rivals, the Counts of Aranda, with royal and ecclesiastical approval.

Amongst the nobles who met in 1487 to resist the Hermandad were two persons who were closely associated with the poet's upbringing: Don Luis de Híjar and Don Pedro de Luna. Luis Fernández de Híjar, who became, in 1496, the Count of Belchite, seems to have acted as the boy's guardian; it was to him that Pedro Manuel dedicated his poem on the lawsuit between his mother and his elder brother over his father's inheritance (fol. vii^v; pp. 56–7). Pedro de Luna's eldest son, Don Juan, was engaged to marry the poet's elder sister, Doña Catalina, but he was killed at the Siege of Baza in 1483 at the age of twenty;[7] another of his sons, Don Jaime, married her instead. It was to Don Jaime that Urrea dedicated his *Fiestas de amor* (fols xviii–xix^v; pp. 144–61), a poem deeply influenced by the allegorical style of Petrarch's *Trionfo d'Amore* (at least in the opening stanzas) and by the erotic hells of the Marquis of Santillana, Garci Sánchez de Badajoz and others. Don Jaime, the Count of Belchite, and the two brothers, Don Miguel and Don Pedro Manuel de Urrea, fought together in the wars of Navarre in 1512.[8] It is also possible that the poet accompanied Don Jaime to the Italian wars. The poet's brother, Miguel, was certainly amongst those who sailed to Naples with King Ferdinand in 1506 (Dormer, 1697, p. 92). Moreover, Don Jaime was evidently familiar with the Italian language, because Urrea quotes the first six lines of the *Trionfo d'Amore*. Don Jaime was, it would seem, his patron in knighthood: the language which he uses in his letter to this gentleman demonstrates feudal humility and alludes to an obligation which is greater than that of kinship. On 7 September 1510 Don Jaime was promoted from his position as Lord of the King's Bedchamber to that of Lieutenant-General of Catalonia (Zurita, 1579–80, bk VI, ch. xxvi); and in July 1528 he and Don Luis de Híjar, the Count of Belchite, were amongst the chamberlains upon whom honours were conferred. In 1533 the Emperor Charles V bestowed some favours upon his widow, 'Doña Catalina de Urrea, viuda de Don Jayme de Luna, Señor de Yllueca' (Dormer, 1697, p. 398). Don Jaime must therefore have died between 1528 and 1533.

Another person linked with the poet's youth was Juan Fernández de Heredia, a distant cousin of the poet of the same name. He was Lieutenant-General of Aragon in 1481[9] and became Count of Fuentes in 1508. His brother, Lorenzo, was fighting beside Don Luis de Híjar near Venice in 1509 (Zurita, 1579–80, bk VI, ch. xxvi). He himself fought in Navarre in 1512 (Zurita, 1579–80, bk IX, ch. lx). He married the poet's sister, Doña Beatriz, and later distinguished himself in the service of the Emperor (Dormer, 1697, p. 459).

The characters of the poet's two sisters, Doña Catalina and Doña Beatriz, are revealed by the nature of the poetry addressed to them. Doña Catalina received a 'credo glosado' (fol. iv; pp. 22–3) because, according to the accompanying letter, it was a poem which she particularly liked and one which she had persuaded her brother to publish, a decision which he seems to have had cause to regret, because in the prologue to the *Cancionero* he refers to the work as 'un voluntario desastre' (fol. ii^v; p. 9). Doña Beatriz has very different tastes; she is the recipient, not of devotional works, but of *villancicos*, poems written to be sung to music (fol. xxxiv^v; pp. 328–9). Her name occurs several times in a poem entitled *Disparates donde ay puestas muchas damas y señoras de Aragón* in the *Cancionero de Juan de Ixar*, an anthology of poetry compiled for the Dukes of Híjar (II, pp. 785–94).

The poet had a younger brother, Juan de Urrea, who became Abbot of Montearagón; he was one of the chaplains who received payment for his services in 1533 (Dormer, 1697, p. 562). His elder brother, Don Miguel, inherited most of his father's property and the title of Count of Aranda (on 19 June 1508). In 1503 he fought in the wars of Calabria, and in 1506 he attended the celebrations which marked the arrival of Germaine de Foix at Fuentearrabía. After a second journey to Italy he returned to Spain in order to fight in the wars of Navarre. He served as a page in the household of Prince Juan (Fernández de Oviedo, *Libro de la cámara*, p. 21), the heir to the Spanish throne who died in 1497. In 1518 the emperor was a guest at Don Miguel's house, the palace of Epila, and it was no doubt as a sign of gratitude that on 5 December of the same year the emperor made him 'Duque de Xérica' (Dormer, 1697, p. 582). Don Miguel was not only a renowned soldier, but also, like his father, an amateur poet, and the author of a treatise entitled *Instrucción política cristiana* (*Canc.*, ed. Villar, p. ix). It was to Don Miguel that Don Pedro Manuel addressed his *Sepoltura de amor*, an enigmatic poem in which the poet has a vision of his own death, and in which he alludes, under a veil of allegory, to the feud with the Counts of Ribagorza. Don Miguel's wife was Doña Aldonza, the daughter of the Duke of Cardona, the richest of the Aragonese nobles. To her the poet addressed a very fine sacro-profane panegyric (fol. xiᵛ; p. 95). The poet's mistress was Leonor. Her name is mentioned or spelt out in acrostics in at least six poems, and she is twice referred to as a 'dama real'.¹⁰ There are at least nine women called Leonor in the *Disparates* cited above, but the most likely candidate is a lady of the royal court, Leonor de Mur:

> Dixo más: doña Leonor
> de Mur con toda su gala,
> por tenerte, rey, amor,
> con tu liçençia, señor,
> te diré una nueba zala. . . .
> (*Canc. Ixar*, p. 788)

(He added: Leonor de Mur with all her finery; as she loves you, oh king, with your permission Sir, I shall utter another salaam. . . .)

The *afrenta* which Urrea receives from Leonor's eyes and the *yerro* for which he suffers exile are deliberately ambivalent; in addition to being his adversary in the war of love, Leonor belonged to the enemy camp. Antonio de Mur, it should be noted, was the messenger whom the Archbishop of Saragossa sent to the Count of Ribagorza on 20 June 1487, when he sought the latter's collaboration.

Despite his professed adherence to the troubadour doctrine of *fin'amors*, which (most critics would agree) was essentially extra-conjugal, Urrea dedicated several poems to his wife, Doña María de Sesé. These include a poem in praise of marriage, which extols Doña María's honesty, prudence and good sense (fols xiv–xv; pp. 110–22), and a gloss on Garci Sánchez de Badajoz's *canción* 'Lo que queda es lo seguro' (That which remains is what is secure) (Urrea substituted 'está' for 'es lo') (Gallagher, 1968, p. 72, crit. analysis p. 262). The Sesés were a family of court officials: Dona María's mother, Doña Blanca de Agramonte, was Lady-in-Waiting to Queen Isabella; her father, Don Manuel, was a royal chamberlain who had by 1533 attained the post of Chief Bailiff of Aragon and Knight of the Order of Santiago (Dormer, 1697, p. 396). To judge by the following lines from the *Disparates* the Sesés were of Jewish extraction:

> Doña Blanca de Sessé
> y doña Angela Torrellas
> y ell abad de Santa Fee;
> después que el dilubio fue,
> nunca vieron las estrellas.
> (*Canc. Ixar*, p. 793)

(Blanca de Sesé and Angela Torrellas and the Abbot of Santa Fe never saw the stars after the flood.)

Appendix 3

Eugenio Asensio conjectures, in his introduction to *Eglogas dramáticas y poesías desconocidas de Pedro Manuel de Urrea*, that Urrea himself was of Jewish descent:

> In his allegorical prose works he deals with the subject of the Jews and their effort to create division in the Roman Catholic world. In the *Batalla de amores* he emphasises the social and economic symbiosis of Christian Spain and the Hebrew people. Perhaps the Arandas themselves were of Jewish stock, if we are to believe the calumnies of the Aragonese *Libro verde*. (p. xliii)

The hermit in the *Batalla de amores* declares that intermarriage between Jews and Christians is an undeniable fact of life, an opinion which was expressed by Francisco Mendoza y Bobadilla, Bishop of Burgos, in a work entitled *El tizón de la nobleza*. However, the policy of peaceful coexistence between Judaism, Christianity and Islam, which Urrea propounded in his *Rueda de peregrinación*, reflects a spirit of religious tolerance which was extremely rare in the early years of the sixteenth century.

It is difficult to ascertain where Urrea could have acquired his liberal ideas and his classical education. The Italian humanist, Marineus Siculus, lamented the deplorable state of Spanish schools in 1513, and described his protector, Alonso de Aragón, the Archbishop of Saragossa, as 'the only hope of learned men'.[11] The archbishop was, however, no friend of the Urreas. Although circumstances were unfavourable, Pedro Manuel de Urrea was a precocious child, displaying an aptitude for Latin which was comparatively rare in court circles (as can be inferred from the large number of translations which were made from Latin into Spanish): 'yo siempre, de muy pequeño, he sido codicioso dela lengua latina' (fol. iv; p. 6) (I have always, ever since I was very small, been keen on the Latin tongue). As soon as the poet graduated to the status of a squire at the age of fourteen most of his time must have been taken up with military exercises.

The period from 1510 to 1513 is well documented, since, quite apart from the testimony of Urrea's verse, two separate accounts exist of the feud with the Counts of Ribagorza. Fray Atilano de la Espina is strongly biased against the Urrea brothers, because the monastery of Veruela, to which he was attached, had become involved in a dispute with them over irrigation rights,[12] whereas Zurita favours them, and omits any reference to Fray Atilano's allegation that Pedro Manuel de Urrea's men had entered the village of Litago and had killed a man called Juan Jaime, an incident which apparently so incensed the monks of Veruela that they sang a psalm of malediction against the poet: 'Through God we shall do valiantly: for he it is that shall tread down our enemies' (Psalm 108, v. 13). The poet was then asked by the Archbishop of Saragossa to give his word of honour not to repeat what he had done, and the feud subsided, at least temporarily. The poet was banished, for almost a year, to his country estate at

Trasmoz. For the sake of his mother, wife and children, he was obliged to obey the archbishop's orders, even though he was bored by the solitude and the lack of refinement of village life.[13] Pedro Manuel's exile was broken in December 1511, when he and his brother, the Count of Aranda, were invited by the city of Saragossa to assist in the arrest of Don Francisco de Luna, after the latter had refused to allow the municipal authorities to enter his estates in connection with another dispute over irrigation rights. Francisco de Luna eventually took his revenge on Pedro Manuel by burning down the village of Luçena in July 1512. The poet, as he was returning home with an army of 2,000 footsoldiers and 250 horsemen, passed Pedrola, a village belonging to the Count of Ribagorza, where his men cut down two pine trees 'as a sign that they could do more' (*Canc.*, ed. Villar, p. xiii). In July 1512 the Count of Ribagorza, who was under house arrest, left his estates on the pretext that he had to attend the Cortes at Monzón. The poet received a letter from the count challenging him to battle on 4 July. Taken by surprise, the poet's troops were vanquished. Catalonia as well as Aragon rose up in arms, and the king himself attempted to bring about a reconciliation. Having failed to unite the families through intermarriage (through the mediation of Fray Juan de Estúniga and then Luis de Lizerago), he declared, in Buengrado on 6 October 1513, that the Count of Ribagorza should be sent into exile for having broken the pact, and, moreover, that he should pay damages.

Pedro Manuel de Urrea's later life, after the publication of his *Cancionero* in 1513, is more conjectural. He was present at the Cortes of Saragossa on 27 July 1518, when the Emperor Charles V swore to abide by the laws and privileges of Aragon. It is possible that he, like the emperor, witnessed the theatrical representation of the Day of Judgment which was performed in the market place of Saragossa on 6 June as part of the Corpus Christi celebrations (Dormer, 1697, p. 90). He was absent from the Cortes held in January 1519. Since he is known to have published, in 1523, a work entitled *Peregrinación de Jerusalem, Roma, y Santiago* (which is no longer extant), he probably left Spain in 1518. This pilgrimage was presumably the same expedition about which Juan del Encina wrote. Encina was commissioned by the leader of the pilgrimage, the Marquis of Ribera, to compose a diary in verse.[14] Fernando Colón's description of the contents of Urrea's work suggests that, both literally and metaphorically, he was following in Encina's footsteps. Don Fadrique left Andalusia on 24 November 1518, travelling overland as far as Venice, and thence by ship to the Holy Land; he did not arrive home until October 1520.

There is no mention of Urrea's name in the chronicles after 1518. The religious commitment expressed in his later dramatic eclogues tends to support the hypothesis that, after his return from Jerusalem, he entered the church. A decision to take holy orders might explain why, in March 1528, when the chancellor, Mercurio de Gattinaria, called a meeting of the deputies of Aragon, the poet's eldest son, Don Lope, held the title 'Señor de Trasmoz' (Dormer,

1697, p. 339). On the other hand, in March 1528, the poet may have already died. Martín Villar asserts that, according to 'la común opinión', Urrea died between 1528 and 1530, but he fails to substantiate this statement (*Canc.*, ed. Villar, p. viii). He must have died before 17 November 1536, when Doña María de Sesé made out a will in which she describes herself as the widow of Don Pedro Manuel Ximénez de Urrea. On 29 July 1533 the poet's brother, nephew and children are represented by a deputy (Pedro Miguel de Ycis), which suggests that the poet was no longer living (Dormer, 1697, p. 534). There is unfortunately insufficient evidence in the chronicles to establish the precise year in which Urrea died.

Urrea's literary works

1 *Petri de Vrrea. Glosa en coplas super el Credo.* Listed as no. 12436 in the 'Catálogo de algunos pliegos sueltos fechables tomados del Abecedarium B de D. Fernando Colón' in the facsimile edition of the *Cancionero general*, compiled by Hernando del Castillo, edited by Antonio Rodríguez-Moñino (Madrid, 1958), p. 125.

2 *Cancionero delas obras de dõ Pedro mãuel de Vrrea* (Logroño: Arnao Guillén de Brocar, 1513). There are forty-nine folios. Copies of this edition are to be found in the British Library, the Biblioteca Nacional, Madrid, and the Hispanic Society of America. The British Library copy of this work, which belongs to the Grenville Collection (G. 11385), originally came from the Biblioteca del Duque de Medinaceli. Martín Villar based his edition, published by the Diputación de Zaragoza in 1878, on this copy. The *villancicos* have been edited by Robert L. Hathaway in Exeter Hispanic Texts, no. 14 (Exeter, 1976).

3 *Penitencia de amor* (Burgos: Fadrique Alemán de Basilea, 1514). A copy is in the Bibliothèque Nationale, Paris. Raymond Foulché-Delbosc edited the work for the Hispanic Society of America, Bibliotheca Hispánica 10 (Barcelona, 1902). The work was translated by the Archbishop of Toledo's secretary, Gabriel de Gramond Navarre (according to Germán Bleiberg and Julián Marías, *Diccionario de literatura española* [Madrid: Revista de Occidente, 1972, 1st edn 1949], p. 496). Jacques-Charles Brunet, in his *Manuel du Libraire et de l'amateur de livres*, IV (Paris, 1863), pp. 477-8, and V (Paris, 1864), p. 1146, suggests that René Bertaut's *Penitence d'amour*, published in 1537 (at Lyons?) is a translation of Urrea's *Penitencia*, but the description in Brunet does not support this hypothesis.

4 *Cancionero de todas las obras de dõ pedro mãuel de Urrea, nueuamente añadido* (Toledo: Juan de Villaquirán, 1516). There are 106 numbered folios, in fact 104. The only known copy is in the Biblioteca Nacional, Lisbon. It once

belonged to Queen Catalina, sister of Charles V and wife of King John III of Portugal. It was amongst the books which she received in Evora on 10 July 1534, freshly bound in leather with Petrarch's *Remedios* (Seville, 1524). It passed into the hands of Tuetonio de Bragança, Archbishop of Evora, and thence to the neighbouring convent, the Cartuja de Scala Caeli. F. J. Norton refers to this *Cancionero* in *Printing in Spain, 1501–1520* (Cambridge, 1966), p. 54. Eugenio Asensio published some of its contents, with an introduction, in a limited edition of 250 copies, entitled *Eglogas dramáticas y poesías desconocidas de Pedro Manuel de Urrea*, Joyas Bibliográficas, 5 (Madrid, 1950). A copy can be found in the University Library, Cambridge; or in King's College, London. This enlarged *Cancionero* contains three prose works (all less than half the size of the *Penitencia de amor*), five dramatic eclogues and thirty poems which were not published in the 1513 *Cancionero*. The three prose works (*Batalla de amores*, *Jardín de hermosura* and *Rueda de peregrinación*) and thirteen poems, including all the longer ones, were excluded from Asensio's edition and are not easily accessible. Asensio only admits having omitted seven poems. (He in fact mentioned eight poems, but the *villancico* 'Descansada y gozosa' formed an epilogue to one of the eclogues.) It should also be noted that this *Cancionero* contains the *Penitencia de amor*.

5 *Peregrinación de Jerusalem, Roma y Santiago* (Burgos, 1523). A copy once existed in the Biblioteca Colombina, Seville. The work is no longer extant. Fernando Colón summarises the contents in his *Registrum Librorum*:

> 4074 Peregrinación de Jerusalem, Roma y Santiago, compuesta por D. Pedro Manuel de Urrea. Divídese en 3 libros, y los libros por capítulos epith., cuya tabla está al principio, 2 fol. It. otra tabla de las ciudades, villas y lugares que hay desde su casa a Jerusalem, y desde Roma a Santiago. Prologus: I. 'Donde hay caudal de entendimiento'. It. se sigue una obra suya en metro castellano entre la razón y corazón: I. '¡Oh corazón animoso!' D. 'La calabaza y bordén'. It. una oración suya: I. '¡Oh primor divino!' El primer libro: I 'Trasmos hace cien fuegos'. El tercero: D. 'Mayor cantidad de obra'. It. se siguen unas coplas y romances sobre la muerte de la condesa de Aranda: I 'Carne mía, tú que enojas'. El romance: I 'Tal precio tienes agora'. It. se sigue una tabla de las leguas y millas que hay en la obra. It. una adición de la obra: I 'En todo o lo más'. D. 'A su santo, servicio'. Al fin está una oración del autor: I 'Padre y hijo'. Es en fol., 2 col.; tiene algunas coplas y figuras. Impr. en Burgos, a 20 de Marzo de 1523, – Costó en Medina del Campo 98 maravedis, a 19 de noviembre de 1524.

See Bartolomé José Gallardo, *Ensayo de una biblioteca española de libros raros y curiosos*, Vol. II (Madrid, 1866), cols 547–9. The *Peregrinación* was placed on the Index of the Inquisition in 1559 and 1583.

Appendix 3

Poetic theory in Urrea's dedicatory epistles

Pedro Manuel Ximénez de Urrea never attempted, as Juan del Encina had done in his *Arte de poesía castellana*,[15] to synthesise his ideas on poetry into a coherent system. A wide variety of attitudes to poetry and artistic creation can, however, be gleaned from the dedicatory epistles in the *Cancionero* which he published in 1513. Many of these ideas are contradictory, not merely because they reflect the poet's mood at the time of writing but because the study of the theoretical principles of literature, as opposed to the practical application of rhetoric expounded in *artes dictaminis* and *artes poeticae*, was still in its infancy: Urrea expresses a desire for prestige and immortal fame, but he hesitates to publish for fear of slander; he considers renouncing poetry, but he is moved irresistibly to write; he respects scholarship, yet he disparages the notion of poetry as a full-time profession. Broadly speaking, four current theories about the nature of poetry can be discerned in the epistles: the courtly-devotional (poetry as a form of service or an act of homage); the ludic-therapeutic (poetry as entertainment and consolation); the moralistic-didactic (poetry as precept); and the cognitive-aesthetic (poetry as the pursuit of truth and beauty). The only notable omission is the charismatic-prophetic theory (poetry as grace or numinous inspiration), to which some earlier Spanish poets, such as Juan Alfonso de Baena and the Marquis of Santillana, seem to have subscribed (Fraker, 1966, pp. 63–90).

Poets who were the disciples of the troubadour doctrine of *fin'amors* generally adhered to the courtly-devotional theory of poetry.[16] It was this theory, based on the concept of service, which was central to Urrea's work: love service, feudal, courtly, filial or devotional, was the primary impulse behind the creative process. Most of his poetry is dedicated to relatives, lovers or friends, supplying them with advice, praise, solace or promises of constant love. Even poems to Christ and to the Virgin Mary share a similar format: eulogy, thanksgiving, a plea for mercy and an oath of allegiance. Writing was for Urrea above all a personal affair: his poems were circulated amongst his relatives and acquaintances, who were invited to judge them or suggest possible emendations; his dramatic eclogues may well have been performed at his elder brother's house, the palace of Epila, whilst his *villancicos* were undoubtedly sung to his own musical accompaniment. Some poems are *poèmes de circonstances* which pivot on a particular incident, such as the sight of Leonor at a window or the gift of a pair of gloves; others contain topical or veiled allusions which would not be apparent to the casual reader, because they are intended for a small gathering of initiates. Urrea's fear of *maldizientes* and his deprecatory attitude towards poetry as a profession must be understood within the context of this aristocratic courtly-devotional theory.

Urrea, like most *cancionero* poets, was an élitist and a dilettante. He was disconcerted by the prospect of widespread publicity offered by the invention

of the printing press, and regarded the distribution of his poetry to the masses
as a form of self-prostitution:

¿Cómo pensaré yo que mi travajo está bien empleado, viendo que por
la emprenta ande yo en bodegones y cozinas y en poder de rapazes, que
me juzguen maldizientes, y que quantos lo quisieren saber, lo sepan, y que
venga yo a ser vendido? (Letter to Doña Catalina, fol. ii^v; p. 11)

(How can I consider that my work is being put to good use when I see
myself conveyed in print to taverns and kitchens and into the hands of
scoundrels, so that slanderers may judge me and all who wish to learn of it
may do so, and I shall be sold in public?)

He prefers 'secreta enmienda' to 'público juyzio' (fol. ii^r; p. 6), and begs his
mother, who insists that he should publish his poetry, to protect his work from
the mordant tongues of slanderers:

Suplico a vuestra señora no lo dé [mi Cancionero] de manera que
anduviesse tanto que fuesse a dar en poder de algunos maldizientes, que
muerden con dientes largartinos que nunca sueltan. (Letter to the
Countess of Aranda, fol. ii^r; p. 7)

(I beseech your ladyship not to permit my song book to be too widely
distributed lest it should fall into the hands of certain slanderers who bite
with lizards' teeth that never let go.)

In view of the feud which existed between the Urrea family and the Counts of
Ribagorza, the poet must have had good cause to be apprehensive. It should,
however, be emphasised that the *maldiziente* was a stock figure in medieval
literature, particularly in the literature of courtly love. The contrast between
public acclaim and private criticism was also a conventional one, and is found
in Diego de San Pedro's introduction to his *Tractado de amores*:

suplico que la burla sea secreta y el fabor público, pues en esto la condición
de la virtud consiste. (*Obras*, I, p. 87)

(I beg that the ridicule be in private and the favour in public, since this is
what constitutes the state of virtue.)

The anonymous author of the *Questión de amor*, a *roman à clef* in which real
characters are given pseudonyms, maintains that only the vulgar and the
stupid will speak ill of his work.[17] Yet he did not succeed in convincing himself
that criticism was harmless, as his decision to remain anonymous demonstrates. The 'Carta a un su amigo', which precedes the 1501 edition of *La
Celestina*, justifies the author's choice of anonymity by referring to 'nocibles

lenguas, más aparejadas a reprehender que a saber inventar'[18] (harmful tongues, more apt to reprove than to be capable of invention), and Urrea likewise speaks of 'algunas que, quiçá con alguna razón y mucha maliçia, reprehendan lo que por ventura no sabrían hazer' (some who, perhaps with a little reason and a good deal of malice, criticise what they would probably not have been able to do themselves). The same phrase occurs in the prologue to a short allegorical prose work addressed to his mother concerning the coexistence of the three religions, entitled *Rueda de peregrinación (Canc.*, 1516, fol. lxi[r]). The fear of slander was thus very much more than a mere *topos*.

One reason for Urrea's reluctance to have his works published is related to the social status of poets and scholars in the late Middle Ages. He was an aristocrat, not a member of the middle-class lettered minority; as such, he was primarily a warrior, a landowner and a courtier. According to Baldassare Castiglione, the courtier should be well versed in all the activities befitting his condition: warfare, jousting, dancing, music and poetry, to cite but a few; it was considered improper that he should take a professional interest in any one subject.[19] Urrea believes that it is unchivalrous to be a professional writer, and even declares that the composition of poetry is difficult to reconcile with the duties of a courtier:

> que yo más devría usar de la gala del palacio que del arte de la poesía,
> pues que todo junto muy pocos usar pueden.

(I ought to be more practised in the pomp of the palace than in poetic craftsmanship, since very few men are able to combine the two.)

Elsewhere he feigns indifference to his vocation as a poet:

> yo, viendo quán poco caso se haze del trobar, ya no curo mucho dello, porque se tiene por yerro el tal exercicio, que parece estar hombre sin cuydados quando en esto entiende mucho. (Letter to María de Sesé, fol. xiv[r]; p. 109)

(Since such slight attention is given to the art of composing songs [*trobar*], I care little about it now: this occupation is considered a defect, because a man who understands it well seems to be devoid of responsibilities.)

In his prologue to the above-mentioned *Rueda de peregrinación* he writes:

> no soy tan sin conoscimiento que no vea no ser cosa de cavallero estas largas escripturas: mas crea vuestra señoría que es un vicio tan dulce. (Aun que paresce trabajoso). El escrivir que después que está tornado por descanso y passatiempo no se puede dexar.

(I am not so ignorant as to be unaware that these lengthy writings are not the business of a knight. But believe me, my lady, writing is such a sweet vice [although it seems laborious] that after it has developed into a relaxation and a pastime it cannot be abandoned.)

These passages tend to corroborate Nicholas Round's contention that in late medieval Spain there existed, especially amongst the aristocracy, a deep-seated prejudice against scholarship and the arts (Round, 1962). To what extent the duty of non-derogation was reinforced by anti-Semitism is of course debatable. Poetry which is based on the concept of love service is chiefly designed to amuse and to entertain. The poetic genres most highly favoured in palace circles were those which are brief and easily improvised: *coplas, motes, villancicos, canciones* and *romances*. Urrea knows that his *villancicos* will please his sister Beatriz, because they are written to be sung and consequently 'they bring with them more pleasure and bustle'.[20] The sound of poetry has, like music, a therapeutic effect. It enables the poet to forget the sorrow which he has experienced as a result of the lawsuit over his inheritance:

Porque la fuerça dela tristura . . . no tomasse en mí possessión antigua, he de contino travajado . . . que me olvidasse lo injusto y se acordasse lo devido . . . y con la dulce poesía alivio los amargos pensamientos que en mí moran, causados por el triste pleyto . . . en lo qual nadi deve hablar. (Letter to Don Luis de Híjar, fol. vii^v; p. 56)

(In order that the power of grief . . . might not regain its former hold over me, I have continually worked . . . that the injustice might be forgotten and the duties remembered . . . and with sweet poetry I assuage the bitter thoughts that dwell with me, produced by the sad lawsuit . . . about which no one must speak.)

Urrea indeed confesses that he owes his creativity to misfortune. For the court poet music was traditionally a means of alleviating the anguish caused by unrequited love, as well as being simply a means of serving and amusing the ladies. Boscán seems to have been one of the few poets in Spain during Urrea's lifetime who asserted that love poetry need not be an expression of anguish.[21]

It is surprising that Urrea does not defend his art by claiming that it has a moral or didactic function. According to the traditional medieval view the moral is a bitter pill which must be sugar-coated to make it digestible. Santillana's definition of poetry is well known:

un fingimiento de cosas útiles, cubiertas o veladas con muy fermosa cobertura, compuestas, distinguidas e scandidas por çierto cuento, peso o medida. (López de Mendoza, *Letter*, p. 70)

(a simulation of useful things, concealed or veiled by a very beautiful covering, composed, divided and scanned according to a certain count, stress or measure.)

Following the Horatian principle of 'dulce et utile', Santillana blends didactic with aesthetic considerations. Furthermore he assigns a special role to allegory similar to that of *trobar clus*: it repels the vulgar and entices the connoisseur, thereby ensuring that poetry remains the sole preserve of an intellectual élite capable of comprehending it. Urrea's recourse to techniques of moral indoctrination, such as his use of allegory and *exempla*, shows that he was familiar with this theory of poetry. The allegorical guesswork of the poem *Peligro del mundo*, in which the Seven Deadly Sins are conveyed by their respective attributes, requires exegesis:

> Ay siete caminos que van alo hondo . . .
> que todos sus nombres aquí los escondo.
> (fol. xii^r; p. 100)

(There are seven roads leading to the abyss . . . all their names I have here concealed.)

The typically medieval practice of listing *exempla* is employed by Urrea in praise of his mother's continence. Classical authors are cited as moral authorities, rather than as enjoyable reading or models of good taste. Seneca and Cicero, for example, furnish maxims on the fickleness of Fortune and the evils resulting from greed and self-interest.

The idea of poetry as precept is implicit in both cognitive-aesthetic and charismatic-prophetic theories. The former is anthropocentric; the latter theocentric. Urrea believes that poetry is a natural gift, and he asserts, as an Aristotelian, that intellectual curiosity is man's prime instinct:

> dize [el gran filósofo i.e. Aristotle] ser todos, de nuestras propias voluntades, inclinados y movidos para la sabiduría y çiençia. (Letter to Don Jaime de Luna, fol. xvii^v; p. 140)

(The great philosopher [Aristotle] states that we are all, by our own wills, inclined and motivated towards wisdom and knowledge.)

Quintilian's *Institutio oratoria*, to which Urrea refers, evidently encouraged the medieval tendency to regard *eloquentia, poesia, philosophia* and *sapientia* as 'different names of the same thing' (Curtius, 1953, pp. 437–8). However, a number of late medieval Spanish poets were acquainted with the ancient theory of poetry as a divine frenzy, as opposed to an instrument of rational discovery. This is a subject which deserves to be investigated more fully.

Juan Alfonso de Baena, in the prologue to the *Cancionero* which he compiled for Juan II of Castile and completed before 1445, defined poetry as a knowledge attained through grace, 'por graçia infusa del señor Dios' (ed. Azáceta, I, p. 9; cf. Fraker, 1966, pp. 69–90). Santillana, in a prefatory letter to his works, addressed to Dom Pedro, the Constable of Portugal, in 1449, defined the *gaya sçiençia* as a divinely inspired craving for perfection to which noble and perspicacious minds are particularly susceptible:

> un zelo çeleste, una affectión divina, un insaçiable çibo del ánimo; el qual, asý como la materia busca la forma e lo imperfecto la perfecçión, nunca esta sçiençia de poesía e gaya sçiençia buscaron nin se fallaron, sinon en los ánimos gentiles, claros ingenios e elevados spíritus. (*Letter of the Marquis*, p. 70)

> (a celestial zeal, a divine passion, an insatiable soaring of the soul; for, just as matter seeks form and imperfection perfection, so this science of poetry or Gay Science has never been sought or discovered except by noble souls, clear minds and elevated spirits.)

It is tempting to see in these works the influence of Florentine Neoplatonism. However, the Academy was not established until 1450. It is perhaps significant that the Consistori de la Gaya Sciència at Barcelona received money for prizes on the Day of Pentecost (according to a document signed by King Martin I on 1 May 1398) (see above, p. 135). Santillana alludes once again to the idea of poetic *furor* when he declares, at the close of his letter, that Dom Pedro has been accepted amidst the throng of the Muses who dance round the Castalian spring, a place at the foot of Mount Parnassus where pilgrims would purify themselves before visiting the Delphic oracle, the water being reputed in later times to inspire whomsoever drank of it with the gift of poetry. Juan del Encina, in his *Arte de poesía castellana*, a work which must have been known to Urrea, discusses the sacred origin of poetry, and adds that the pagans of antiquity honoured poets as bards or *vates*, singers of divine things. The *exempla* which he cites derive from Quintilian or Horace: Tyrtaeus, Orpheus and Stesichorus.[22] In a grandiloquent and mischievous comparison, Encina makes himself the rival of the gods: just as Prometheus, with the help of Minerva, stole the fire from Mount Olympus in order to bring bodies of clay to life, so he, by contemplating the excellence of his patrons, obtained a spark of their splendour with which to imbue his 'dead work' with 'vital spirits'.[23] A less exalted metaphor for literary aspiration than either the Castalian spring or the fire of Prometheus is that of the ant, a poor man's Icarus, which tries to rise above itself and is eaten by birds, an image which occurs in the prefatory acrostic verses of *La Celestina*.

Appendix 3

It is doubtful whether any of the above references to divine frenzy can be taken as indicating a genuine belief in the charismatic nature of poetry. Charles Fraker, who describes the illuminist doctrine of grace held by certain *enriqueño* poets as 'a curious amalgam of Spiritual theology and Provençal poetics' (Fraker, 1966, p. 90), maintains that it was in practice 'an apology for ignorance' (p. 88), since its exponents were vigorously opposed to the erudition of the schoolmen and needed to meet the accusation that they were not qualified to debate about obscure metaphysical problems. In Spain theological poetics was to become a conventional element in eulogies of poetry during the sixteenth and seventeenth centuries. As E. R. Curtius points out, these works generally state that the Old Testament prophets were the earliest poets, and they invariably appeal, like Santillana and Encina, to the authority of Isidore of Seville and Jerome (Curtius, 1953, pp. 546–58). It is hard to say whether the absence of such ideas in Urrea's dedicatory epistles is a sign of his fidelity to, or departure from, the troubadour tradition.

The heterogeneous character of Urrea's ideas on poetry and artistic creation can be attributed to the fact that he is a transitional medieval-renaissance figure. On the one hand, he could be considered one of the last of the European troubadours, committed to a theory of poetry here termed courtly-devotional; on the other hand, he is an author of dramatic eclogues and a fluent reader of Latin, and his works betray a characteristically Renaissance concern for aesthetic perfection, decorum, originality and immortal fame. He is reluctant to take the irrevocable decision to publish, because he is aware that nothing in life is perfect; had he not published, he would have been free to make emendations, and he would have had no cause for self-reproach. He mentions having read 'enla singular arte de gramática antoniana' that the Greek painter Apelles,[24] when singing his masterpieces, would never refer, in the past tense, to their having been completed:

el maestre que ponía nombre debaxo no dezía la hizo, sino la hazía, que mostrava poder no ser acabada. (Letter to Don Miguel, fol. xxiii^r; p. 197)

(the artist, when placing his name under his work, would not say that he made it, but that he was making it, which indicated that it could never be completed.)

Urrea did not seriously attempt to perfect his work, because not a single poem in the 1513 *Cancionero* was omitted from the enlarged *Cancionero* published in 1516, nor does he seem to have made any alterations. Menéndez y Pelayo's chief criticism of this poetry was indeed that it lacked polish: 'he writes in a diffuse and slipshod manner; he does not have an instinct for the perfect form' (*Antología*, III, p. 435). Urrea nevertheless wished to be recognised by posterity and was confident that his work would survive:

Lo que yo hasta aquí he hecho no a sido otra cosa sino una sperança de ser algo. (Letter to the Countess of Aranda, fol. ii^v; p. 6)

(What I have done up till now has been nothing other than a hope of being something.)

He assured his sister Doña Catalina that his poetry would remain 'para que después de yo muerto puedan ver que he vivido' (fol. ii^v; p. 10) (in order that after my death they may see that I have lived).

Urrea imitated his literary predecessors and contemporaries, including Petrarch, Juan de Mena and Juan del Encina. However, the problem of originality seems to have obsessed him; he attributes the highly derivative character of his work to a universal exhaustion of creative potentiality: 'nadie puede trobar syno por el estylo de otros, porque ya todo lo que es a ssido' (no one can compose poetry except in the style of others, because everything that now exists has been done before). This statement from the prologue to the *Penitencia de amor*, a dramatic prose romance strongly influenced, as Barbara Matulka has shown, by *Grisel y Mirabella* and by *La Celestina*,[25] is echoed by Encina's proverb: 'No ay cosa que no esté dicha' (There is nothing that has not been said). Urrea belonged to a generation of Spanish poets who shared Encina's conviction that Spanish culture had passed its prime and faced the prospect of an imminent decline (see Part II, n. 39). This sense of belonging to the end of an era, together with a growing reverence for the achievements of classical antiquity, seems to have acted as a serious impediment to innovation. Yet, partly as a consequence of the dissemination of Quintilian's *Instituto oratoria* (rediscovered by Poggio in 1416, and first printed in 1470), which maintains that *ingenium* (i.e. wit or inventiveness) is a desirable quality, writers were troubled as never before by the nature of their profession.[26] Urrea's dedicatory epistles thus provide a useful indication of current attitudes to poetry prior to the Golden Age of Spanish literature, illustrating the belatedness of Spanish literary theory and practice as writers and scholars gradually turned to Italy for guidance.

Notes

Introduction

1 *The Pursuit of the Millennium*, London: Secker & Warburg, 1957 (rev. edn, Paladin, 1970).
2 Jaume March (uncle of Ausias March) and Lluís d'Aversó, appointed as *defensores* or *mantenedors* of the Consistori poètic at Barcelona in 1393, both wrote theoretical works on poetry which actually antedate the establishment of the academy. The former compiled a *Libre de concordances* for Pedro IV in 1371; see March, *Diccionari*. The latter composed the *Torcimany* [*Interpreter*], a treatise of versification and rhetoric, followed by a rhyming dictionary; see Aversó, *Torcimany*. A Castilian rhyming dictionary was compiled for Alfonso Carrillo, Archbishop of Toledo, *c.* 1474-9 by Pero Guillén de Segovia (b. 1413); see Guillén de Segovia, *La gaya ciencia*, and O. J. Tallgren, *Estudios sobre la Gaya de Segovia* (Helsinki, 1907).
3 Corominas, *Diccionario crítico-etimológico de la lengua castellana* (4 vols, Madrid, 1954-7), *s.v.* 'trovar'. Cercamon used the word in a poem written *c.* 1150 (Riquer, 1975, p. 19).
4 Steunou and Knapp, 1975–, I, pp. 763-99. The authors consulted ninety *cancioneros* including manuscripts.
5 It is difficult to be more precise without further biographical information. Rodríguez-Moñino's alphabetical index lists 201 authors, but there are considerable overlaps. Roberto de Souza proposes for purposes of linguistic research the figure of 185, but adds in a footnote that the number is more probably 178 (Souza, 1964, p. 7).
6 Marcial d'Auvergne, 1731, I, no. 40, pp. 389-90. About fifteen editions of *Les Arrêts d'amours* were published between *c.* 1520 and 1597. This work, written in the late fifteenth century, was translated into Castilian by Diego Gracián in 1569. The ceremonial of Marcial's Parliament of Love is similar to that of the Floral Games in Barcelona, as described in Enrique de Villena's *Arte de trovar* (*c.* 1420).
7 *Spain. A Companion to Spanish Studies*, ed. Russell, p. 240. Cf. Round, 1962, and Russell, 1967.

Notes

8 There are: 3 dukes (Medina Sidonia, Alba, Albuquerque); 4 marquises (Santillana, Astorga, Villena, Villafranca); 10 counts (Olivia, Haro, Benavente, Ribadeo, Coruña, Castro, Feria, Ureña, Paredes, Ribagorza); 1 Admiral of Castile; 1 Governor of Murcia; 1 marshal; 3 untitled nobles of rank (Fernán Pérez de Guzmán, Gómez Manrique and Lope d'Estúñiga); and 28 persons with the prefix 'Don'. This gives 51 out of a total of 137, i.e. about 38 per cent, although this list is admittedly incomplete; see n. 5 above.

9 Giménez, 1976. This excellent article on the aristocratic ideals expressed in late medieval Spanish literature adopts an approach similar to mine. Following Suárez Fernández, he believes that the absence of a strong Castilian bourgeoisie, due in part to the monopoly of the sheep drovers' guild known as the Mesta, was a factor which made the conflict between monarchy and aristocracy more acute than in other European countries.

Part I

1 'The weakness of trade and of monetary circulation . . . reduced to insignificance the social function of wages. . . . In all grades of the hierarchy, whether it was a question of the king's making sure of the services of a great official, or of a small landlord's retaining those of an armed follower or a farm-hand, it was necessary to have recourse to a method of remuneration which was not based on the periodic payment of a sum of money. Two alternatives offered: one was to take the man into one's household, to feed and clothe him, to provide him with a "prebend", as the phrase went; the other was to grant him, in return for his services, an estate which, if exploited directly or in the form of dues levied on the cultivators of the soil, would enable him to provide for himself' (Bloch, 1965, I, p. 68).

2 *The Right Plesaunt and Goodly Histoire of the Foure Sonnes of Aymon*, ed. Octavia Richardson, EETS, extra series 44 and 45 (London, 1885), xxiii, p. 495, ll. 23–4. 'Estado, Lat. status, conditio, habitus. . . . Poner a uno en estado es darle modo de vivir' (Covarrubias, *Tesoro*, I, p. 268) (To put someone in estate is to give him a livelihood).

3 Veblen, 1973, has analysed the 'liberal' or 'civilised' values of Western culture in a tone of veiled, but sardonic, irony. Whereas Huizinga stressed the impact of aristocratic ideals on human conduct and the course of history, Veblen illustrated the relevance of economics to the study of cultural history by demonstrating that these ideals were to some extent a consequence of an economic system based on the concept of status.

4 Dumézil, 1958, pp. 7–8. Adrian G. Montoro applied Dumézil's findings to the *Cantar de Mio Cid* in 'La épica medieval española y la estructura trifuncional de los indoeuropeos', *CHA*, no. 285 (March 1974), 554–71.

5 In Aragon the *ricoshombres* and *caballeros* formed two separate juridical estates; see Chaytor, 1933, p. 113.

6 'In omni Gallia eorum hominum qui aliquo sunt numero atque honore, genera sunt duo. Nam plebes paene servorum habetur loco, quam nihil audet per se, nullo adhibetur consilio. Plerique, cum aut aere alieno aut magnitudine tributorum aut iniuria potentiorum, sese in servitutem dicant nobilibus: in hos eadem omnia sunt iura, quae dominis in servos. Sed de his duobus generibus alterum est druidum, alterum equitum' (Caesar, *The Gallic War*, VI, 13, pp. 334–5).

7 *Ibid.*, VI, 14, p. 337. Other parallels, apart from the three-caste system, can be found linking Gallic and ancient Indian society. For example, the Gauls came near to practising suttee. Dead bodies were cremated, and living creatures known to have been dear to the deceased were cast into the flames. Slaves and dependants had once been burnt alive with the bodies of their masters (VI, 19, p. 345).

8 *Doctrinal delos cavalleros*, 1477, título i [no foliation]; a passage that derives from the *Siete partidas*, II, xxi, pról.

9 'Sens mercaders les comunitats caen, los príceps tornen tirans, los jóvens se perden, los pobres se'n ploren' (*Regiment*, ed. Molins de Rei, p. 168) (Without merchants communities decline, princes become tyrants, young men are led astray, the poor implore for help). This attitude to commerce would have been unthinkable in Castile. Julio Rodríguez-Puértolas makes the same point in 'La crisis de la baja edad media catalana y la poesía de la época', *De la Edad Media*, 1972, pp. 252–65, at p. 263. In the first chapter he compares Eiximenis to another Franciscan, Fray Iñigo de Mendoza (pp. 13–54).

10 Penna, *Prosistas*, pp. 77–87, 89–116. Valera uses Aristotle's theory of distributive justice (*Ethics*, V) to support the contention that those in high office are more worthy of honour: 'en qualquier manera de justicia particular, la egualdad es de guardar segúnt cierta proporción; que si todas las cossas que se deven dar o distribuir se diesen egualmente a todos, no sería justicia, mas grande injusticia' (*Prosistas*, p. 82) (in any type of individual justice equality should be observed according to a certain proportion; for if all things that ought to be given or distributed were given equally to all men, it would not be justice, but great injustice). In Plato's words 'Equal treatment of unequals must beget inequity', which is a good example of George Orwell's 'doublethink'.

11 Sánchez de Arévalo makes no concessions to the third estate: '[Aristote] dit après que les dictes gendarmes, les conseilliers, les iuges et les gens d'églises font la vraye partie de la cité. Les marchans, les laboureurs, les méchaniques et marcenaires combien qu'ils soient riches et nécessaires à une cité. Néautmoins ils ne font pas la partie de la cité' (*Le Miroir*, fol. d5ʳ) ([Aristotle] then says that the said policemen, counsellors, judges and

clergy constitute the true component of the city. Although merchants, labourers, mechanics and mercenaries may be rich and necessary to a city, they nevertheless do not constitute part of the city).

12 The belly is 'the store-house, and the shop/Of the whole body' (Shakespeare, *Coriolanus*, I, i). This organic theory of the state is universal in Indo-European literature, and is mentioned several times in the famous book of laws commissioned by Alfonso el Sabio: 'ca así como el alma yace en el corazón del home ... así en el Rey yace la justicia, que es vida et mantenimiento del pueblo de su señorío' (*Siete part.*, II, i, 5) (for just as the soul resides in the heart of man ... so justice resides in the king, who is the life and support of the people under his dominion).

13 'De las otras personas ... así como piratos o cursarios, ladrones, robadores, violentadores, inçensores, vagabundos, vaibitas, girovagos, infieles, paganos ... non fazen estado por sí, nin son mienbros sanos del cuerpo místico universal de la espeçie humana e congregación del mundo' (Villena, *Doze trabajos*, p. 14) (As regards other persons ... such as pirates or privateers, thieves, robbers, rapists, incendiaries, vagabonds, tramps, infidels, pagans ... they do not form an estate in their own right, nor are they healthy members of the universal mystical body of the human species and world congregation).

14 See articles by Aragoneses and Beneyto Pérez in Viñas y Mey, 1949, pp. 275–423, 555–66. Fray Juan García de Castrojeriz writes: 'es bien ordenada la sociedad y la tierra cuando es ordenada como la sociedad del Cielo' (*Glosa ... a Egidio Romano*, *ibid.*, p. 303) (society on earth is well ordered when it is ordered like the society of heaven).

15 Castro, 1971, pp. 474–5, 488, 494–5. Cf. Manuel, *Lib. est.*, I, lxxvi, pp. 147–8.

16 *Sermon on the Ploughers* [preached on 18 January 1548], ed. Edward Arber, English Reprints (London: Bowes, 1868), p. 29.

17 *Five Questions on Love* in *Select English Writings*, ed. Herbert E. Winn (OUP; London: Humphrey Milford, 1929), p. 111.

18 John Gower, despite his conservatism, wrote: 'Au vois commune est acordant la vois de dieu' (*Mirour de l'omme* [c. 1378], l. 12725). The infallibility of the populace was proclaimed by Bachiller de la Palma: 'E porque la voz común e voluntad de los pueblos del rreyno e ssennoríos era seguir a sus naturales Rey e Reyna, ssennores, como la voz del pueblo sea la voz de Dios, que es la verdat que es nasçida de la tierra, que son los labradores e pueblos humilldes, los quales no podrían así ser engannados ni atraydos a seguir opinión, porque están sobre aviso de notoria verdat' (*Divina retribución*, pp. 29–30) (And because it was the common voice and will of the people and of the feudal domains to follow the king and queen, their natural lords, the voice of the people being the voice of God, which is the truth born of the soil, the labourers and people of humble origin cannot

be deceived, nor can they be drawn into giving credence to mere opinion, as they are fully aware of the plain truth).

19 '[el] Rey ... mandó que las Hermandades se tornasen a confirmar y estar fuertes para guarda e seguridad de los caminos, pues que el Maestro de Sanctiago ... y sus sequaces los estorvaban quanto podían, disciendo que los villanos e gente común se harían Señores, e presumirían de mandar sobre los hidalgos' (Blanco-González, 1962, pp. 327–8) (the king ... commanded that the Hermandades [local police organisations] should be authorised and strengthened once again for the protection and security of the highways, since the Master of Santiago ... and his henchmen obstructed them as much as they could, saying that villeins and common folk would become lords and would presume to hold sway over the *hidalgos*).

20 It was translated by Juan de Cuenca from a Portuguese version by Robert Payn, an Englishman attached to Queen Philippa's household and a canon of the city of Lisbon; see P. E. Russell, 'Robert Payn and Juan de Cuenca, translators of Gower's *Confessio amantis*', *MAe*, XXX (1961), 26–32.

21 'Sed constat quod merito virtutis nobilitantur homines virtus videlicet proprie vel maiorum' (*De monarchia*, II, iii, 3 and 4).

22 *Dante's Convivio*, ed. and trans. William Walrond Jackson (Oxford: Clarendon, 1909), p. 231; 'E dico che più volte a li malvagi che a li buoni pervegnono li retaggi, legati e caduti' (IV, xi, 9).

23 Huizinga, 1955, p. 61; 'Così fosse piaciuto a Dio che quello che addoinandò lo Provenzale fosse stato, che chi non è reda de la bontade perdesse lo retaggio de l'avere' (*Convivio*, IV, xi, 10) (Would that it had pleased God to vouchsafe what the Provençal requested, that he who is not the heir of goodness should lose the inheritance of wealth).

24 Moreno de Vargas, 1622, fol. 10. It is asserted in the *Siete partidas* that a king may confer *hidalguía*: 'puédeles dar honra de fijosdalgo a los que non fueren por linage' (II, xxvii, 6) (he can give the honour of *hidalgo* to those who are not *hidalgos* by birth).

25 Rodríguez del Padrón makes the same observation in *La cadira del honor* (*Obras*, p. 138).

26 Ruiz, *LBA*, sts 1271, 1278, 1287, 1294; pp. 344–50. The meaning of the allegory is cryptically expressed by Love: 'El tablero, la tabla, la dança, la carrera,/ son quatro temporadas del año del espera;/los omnes son los meses, cosa es verdadera;/andan e non se alcançan, atiéndense en ribera' (st. 1300, p. 353) (The table, the board [i.e. for chess or gambling?], the dance and the road are the four seasons of the year of the celestial sphere; the men are the months, this is the truth; they advance but they do not overtake each other, they await each other at their borders). These lines and the metaphors employed to denote the distance separating the figures in each social group suggest that the knights are poor and are prepared to gamble; the *hidalgos*

are dedicated to love and eat well; the *ricoshombres* engage in warfare and dance; the labourers walk and labour.

27 *Confessio*, viii, l. 2387; *Complete Works*, III, p. 463. These words are written in the margin at the point where the poet, having been offered a mirror by Venus, gazes at himself, at his wrinkled face, white hair and sad eyes, and recalls his youth. This vision rids him of his worldly attachments and frees him from the charms of Venus.

28 *Anales de Aragón*, ed. Ángel Canellas López, III, xxxix, p. 543.

29 Since the reign of Alfonso XI Castilian kings had assumed the right to appoint *regidores* to govern the chief towns in the kingdom, which resulted in closed urban oligarchies dominated by *hidalgos*; see Suárez Fernández, 1959, pp. 12–13.

30 Corominas, *Diccionario crítico-etimológico*, II, *s.v.* 'hidalgo'. Other etymological explanations have been proposed. It has been derived from *fidalgot*, meaning 'son of Goth': 'Sed certe probabilius est. *Fijo dalgo*. Gothi filium significare nam ex Gothorum sanguine descendentes apud nos nobilissimi reputantur' (Baeza, 1570, 46, fol. 114^v) (But it is certainly probable that *hidalgo* means 'son of Goth', since those decended by blood from the Goths are reputed in this country to be very noble). R. B. Merriman suspected a derivation from *adalingi*, 'which meant "nobles" among the Visigoths and Lombards' (Merriman, 1918–34, I, p. 169).

31 'Fijos dalgo devan ser escogidos que vengan de derecho linaje de padre et de avuelo fasta en el quarto grado a que llama bisavuelos' (*Siete part.*, II, xxi, 2) (*Hidalgos* should be selected whose nobility can be traced directly from the father and grandfather as far as the fourth degree, namely from the great-grandparents).

32 Castro, 1971, p. 263. He argues that *vergüenza* translates the Arabic concept of '*ār*, an obligation with respect to someone, implying 'a conditional curse: if you do not do what I desire, you may die, or something very bad may happen to you'. This theory seems unnecessary to explain the fear of betraying one's obligations which was central to feudal and courtly ethics.

33 *Siete part.*, III, xxi, 14; Barber, 1974, pp. 38–41. Barber erroneously states that Llull knew nothing of the *colée* or *paumée*. The blow, which had a mnemonic function, was an important part of the ritual: 'L'escuder davant l'altar se deu agenoylar, e que leu sos uyls corporals e spirituals, e ses mans a Déu; e lo Cavayler li deu senyir l'espasa, a significar castedat e justicia; e en significança de caritat deu besar L'escuder, e donar-li quexade, per so que promet, e del gran càrrech a que[o]s oblique, e de le gran honor que pren per L'orde de Cavayleria' (*Lib. cav.*, IV, xi, p. 45) (The squire must kneel before the altar and raise his corporal and spiritual eyes and his hands to God; and the knight must then gird on his sword to symbolise chastity and justice; and, as a symbol of charity, he must kiss the squire, and he must

give him a blow, on account of his oath and on account of the great responsibility which he has taken upon himself and the great honour which he derives from the order of chivalry). Professor Round suggests that the *paumée* may have originated in the ancient Roman slap of manumission, the blow received by a slave in the ceremony that freed him from bondage and gave him the status of a client or *cliens* (see p. 54).

34 Froissart, *Œuvres*, I, part I, p. 209; cf. Geoffroi de Charny, *Le livre de chevalerie*, *ibid.*, I, parts 2 and 3, p. 469. These words were spoken when Jacques left home at the age of sixteen to become a squire in the household of the Duke of Clèves.

35 'Dic michi nunc aliud: quid honoris victor habebit,/Si mulieris amor vincere possit eum?. . ./Nil nisi stulticiam pariet sibi finis habendam,/Cui Venus inceptam ducit ad arma viam?' (*Vox clamantis*, ll. 19–20; 25–6) (Now tell me something else: what glory will a conqueror have, if a woman's love can overcome him?. . . The end will produce nothing but folly for the man whom Venus leads to take up the way of arms).

36 Sempere, 1788, II, p. 161. Oliver, in *The Foure Sonnes of Aymon*, praising Renaud's generosity to indigent knights, says: 'And yf he be yll appoynted/ he shall anone araye hym after his astate' (EETS, extra series 14 and 15, p. 295, l. 2).

37 Sempere, 1788, I, p. 112. The son of an Aragonese knight was forbidden to sit at table with his father until he had been knighted (a custom inherited from ancient Gaul); Catalan knights were treated as commoners if they had not been knighted by the age of thirty (Madramany, 1788, p. 164).

38 Álvaro is accompanied in a joust by two knights in black (Carrillo de Huete, *Crónica*, p. 156).

39 Huizinga, 1955, notes this change of meaning and speaks of the late medieval 'tendency to identify all serious occupation of the mind with sadness' (p. 33).

40 *Siete part.*, II, xxi, 24; *Fuero viejo*, II, iv, 2; Otalora, 1553, fols 17 and 344; Baeza, 1570, fols 125–8.

41 Fernández de Béthencourt, 1897–1920, I, p. 25; Colmeiro, 1873, p. 395; *Fuero viejo*, I, iii, 4.

42 *Siete part.*, V, vi, 1; *Libro de los fueros de Castiella* [*c.* 1250], ed. Galo Sánchez (Barcelona: Universidad de Barcelona, Facultad de Derecho, 1924), tít. 175, p. 92.

43 'The sterile vanity of *hidalguía* gave us a propensity for the idle life, impoverished the nation and, by diminishing individual initiative, retarded our industrial education, which is always so favourable to the development of the free spirit' (Colmeiro, 1873, p. 402). It is of course questionable whether industrialisation brings liberty, but it is undeniable that the medieval idea of what was appropriate to the noble estate was a hindrance to economic growth.

44 *New Catholic Encyclopedia*, XX (1967), *s.v.* 'Prelate'.
45 The expansion of the ecclesiastical domains resulted in a decline of the Crown's tax revenue. For this reason Alfonso X granted tax immunity to ecclesiastical estates which had been acquired from the king, but not to those which the church had bought from taxpayers (*Siete part.*, I, vi, 55). A law was passed in 1447 which stipulated that property could not be sold to the church unless a fifth of its value was levied in the form of tax (Colmeiro, 1873, p. 450).
46 Clergy holding lands from the king or possessing honours entailing service were obliged to heed the call to arms (*Siete part.*, I, vi, 64). Prelates even took an active part in Spain's civil wars.
47 Pero López de Ayala, *El rimado de palacio*, cited in Stéfano, 1966, p. 131.
48 'Folwyng upon off intent ful cleene,/Laboreris, as ye han herd devised,/Shal this bodi bern up and susteene/As feet and leggis, which may nat be despised' (John Lydgate, *Fall of Princes*, ed. Henry Bergen, EETS, extra series 121 [London, 1924], part I, bk 2, ll. 890–3, p. 224).
49 *The Art of Courtly Love*, p. 149. 'Dicimus enim vix contingere posse, quod agricolae in amoris inveniantur curia militare, sed naturaliter sicut equus et mulus ad Veneris opera promoventur, quemadmodum impetus eis naturae demonstrat. Sufficit ergo agricultori labor assiduus et vomeris ligonisque continua sine intermissione solatia . . . in amoris doctrina non expedit erudire' (*De amore*, ed. Trojel, bk I, xi, p. 235).
50 Edmund Dudley, *Tree of Common Wealth* (*c.* 1509), cited in Mohl, 1933, pp. 152–3.
51 *The Encyclopaedia Britannica*, 11th edn, XX (1911), pp. 935–6.
52 *Sharī'a* 'comprises as an infallible doctrine of ethics the whole religious, political, social, domestic and private life of those who profess Islām' (*The Encyclopaedia of Islām*, IV [1934], *s.v. sharī'a*).
53 *Epístola exhortatoria a las letras*, in Paz y Melia, *Opúsculos*, p. 216.
54 Francesco Guicciardini, 'Relación de su viaje', in García Mercadal, *Viajes*, I, p. 620.
55 This is a subject which has been studied by some social anthropologists. See Julian Pitt-Rivers, 'Ritual kinship in Spain', *Transactions of the New York Academy of Sciences*, 2nd series, XX, no. 5, 424–31.
56 M.E.C. Walcott, *Sacred Archaeology: a Popular Dictionary of Ecclesiastical Art and Institutions, from Primitive to Modern Times* (London, 1868), *s.v.* 'patron saint'.
57 The Romance of 'Antar, said to have been written by al-Asma'ī at the court of Baghdad and completed in 1080, is in the *Kitāb al-Aghānī* (*The Encyclopaedia of Islām*, new series, I [1960], *s.v.* 'Antar).
58 Castro, 1954, p. 149; 'Los moros llaman Mafómat, e los cristianos Sancti Yagü[e]' (Díaz de Vivar, *Cid*, p. 60, l. 731) (The Moors call on Muhammad and the Christians on St James).

59 R. P. Benoist, *Histoire des Albigeois et des Vaudois* (Paris, 1691), I, fol. 235; cited in Nelli, 1952, p. 86.
60 Ed. F. J. Furnivall, EETS 32 (London, 1868); see Mohl, 1933, p. 131.
61 Martin Le Franc, dedication in *Champion des dames*, addressed to Philippe le Bon, Duke of Burgundy, cited in Moore, 1913, p. 379. Cf. Holzknecht, 1966.
62 'Creativity: social aspects', in David L. Sills (ed.), *International Encyclopaedia of the Social Sciences* (USA: Macmillan and Free Press, 1968), III, pp. 442–55, at p. 452.

Part II

1 'Bourgeois' in this context is an objective, not a derogatory, term.
2 Ruiz, *LBA*, sts 491 and 500, pp. 137–9. This passage expresses a common theme in goliardic verse and contains verbal parallels with some lines in the *Carmina Burana* (cf. Lecoy, 1974, pp. 237–43). It is none the less significant that Juan Ruiz should have picked on this particular theme for development.
3 Roth, 1964, p. 25. Vicens Vives gives the more conservative figure of 130,000 (Vicens Vives, 1969, p. 292).
4 Whether 'it is permissible and reasonable to suspect that the new and strange procedures of the Spanish Inquisition were a survival of procedures customary in the *aljamas*', as Américo Castro believes, is open to doubt (cf. Baer, 1961–6, II, Appendix). It is nevertheless true that 'numerous Jews ... in the fifteenth century became bishops, monks, and even members of the Supreme Council of the Inquisition' (Castro, 1954, p. 534). Some converts from Judaism vainly hoped to escape victimisation by collaborating with the persecutors of their former co-religionists. One such was Pedro de la Caballería, a member of an influential Jewish family, who *c*. 1476 dedicated an anti-Semitic treatise to Alonso de Aragón, Duke of Villahermosa, an illegitimate son of Juan II of Aragon, entitled *Tractatus zelus Christi contra Judaeos, Sarracenos et Infideles* (Venice: Barezzi, 1592). The paradoxical tendency of the persecuted to become persecutors is discussed by Léon Poliakov in *The History of Anti-Semitism* (3 vols, London: RKP, 1974), II, p. ix.
5 The king's mother, Juana Enríquez, daughter of Admiral Fadrique Enríquez, was of Jewish ancestry.
6 Some would say this is an exaggeration. According to Vicens Vives, the nobility comprised 2 per cent of the population of Aragon and Castile, and consisted of about 5,000 magnates, 60,000 knights and *hidalgos*, and 60,000 'aristocrats of the cities', in short a total of 125,000 individuals (Vicens Vives, 1969, p. 293). In a census made in 1590 the estimated proportion of *hidalgos* to the total number of *pecheros* or taxpayers in the various provinces ranged from one quarter in Valladolid to one fourteenth in Murcia and

Segovia (González, 1829, pp. 25 and 368). Judging from figures for military recruitment the population of Spain in 1496 was about 7,200,000 (Girard, 1928, p. 435). It has been estimated that before the Black Death the population of Spain was about 9.5 million and that between 1450 and 1550 it averaged 8.3 million (J. C. Russell, 1958, p. 113).

7 'Que por mengua de caudal/mis casas e mis lagares/sson tornados muladares/ a manera de ospital' (*Canc. Baena*, ed. Azáceta, no. 200, II, p. 366) (For want of funds my houses and wine-presses are transformed into dungheaps like a hospital).

8 *El Cancionero de Baena*, ed. P. J. Pidal (Madrid, 1851), p. 648 n.

9 'Ordenacions fetes per lo molt alt senyor en Pere terç rey Daragó sobra lo regiment de tots los officials de la sua cort', in Bofarull y Mascaró, *Colección*, V, pp. 7–321. Other works include the following: a treatise on chivalry, 'Obra de Mossen Sent Jordi e de cavalleria', *ibid.*, VI, pp. 21–65, and P. Bohigas Balaguer (ed.), *Tractats de cavalleria*, Els Nostres Clàssics 57 (Barcelona, 1947); *Chronique catalane de Pierre IV d'Aragon, III de Catalogne, dit le Cérémonieux ou del Punyalet*, ed. Amédée Pagès, Bibliothèque Méridionale, 2nd series, 31 (Toulouse and Paris, 1941); *Las tablas astronómicas del rey don Pedro el Ceremonioso. Edición crítica de los textos hebraico, catalán y latino* ed. by José M. Millás Vallicrosa (Madrid and Barcelona: CSIC, Instituto 'Arias Montano', 1962).

10 Próspero de Bofarull y Mascaró, 'Generación de Juan I de Aragón. Apéndice documentado a los condes de Barcelona vindicados', in *Memorias de la Real Academia de Buenas Letras*, VI (Barcelona, 1898), pp. 289–366, at p. 304. Yolande de Bar gave birth to at least seven children. All died prematurely save Yolande.

11 The work was completed in Atienza in 1446, and has a preface by Juan de Mena.

12 The contents of this lost collection were first described by Rafael Floranes in *Memorias históricas de la vida y acciones del rey D. Alonso [VIII] et Noble*, ed. Francisco Cerdá y Rico (Madrid: Antonio de Sancha, 1783), Appendix XVI; cf. Severin, 1976, and Benito Ruano, 1964.

13 He was an illegitimate son of Fadrique, Pedro I's half-brother. His mother was Jewish. His grand-daughter was mother of Ferdinand the Catholic.

14 Seneca was extolled by Juan de Mena as one of 'los sabios de Córdoba', and his letters were translated for Juan II; see Segundo Serrano Poncela, 'Séneca entre españoles', in Hornik, 1965, pp. 383–96.

15 Benito Ruano, discussing the Battle of Ponza and Santillana's treatment of the subject, observes that never, except perhaps during the Romantic era, have life and art been so closely interlinked ('Ponza: batalla y comedieta', in Aldea, 1967, p. 123). Cf. Riquer, 1967.

16 Penna, *Prosistas*, 'Estudio preliminar'; Valera, *Tratado delos rieptos*, c. 1500, fol. d7^r.

17 Salazar de Mendoza, 1608, fol. 140ᵛ. A still unpublished biography of
Ruy López Dávalos, prepared for publication in 1642, exists in the British
Library: Juan Dávalos de Ayala, *Vida, hechos ilustres sucesiones gloriosas de
Don Rui López Dávalos el bueno, III Condestable de Castilla, Conde de Ribadeo,
Adelantado mayor del Reyno de Murcia. Dos Libros*, dedicated to Pedro López
de Ayala, VI Conde de Fuensalida (MS. Add. 10,239; Gayangos, *Cat.*,
p. 587).
18 Marcelino Menéndez y Pelayo, *Antología de poetas líricos españoles* (10 vols,
Madrid, 1890–1908), V, p. 278.
19 Miller, 1972, p. 130. There is no justification for the abuse heaped on the
Prince of Viana by this historian. The populace craved for a messiah and his
air of saintliness made him eligible for the role. In 1515 the Archbishop of
Tarragona was instructed to investigate his life and the miracles attributed
to him, and his cult still flourished in the seventeenth century.
20 Yangüas y Miranda, 1840, I, pp. 186–92. The letter was not actually dispatched until after his death by his secretary Fernando Bolea y Galloz in
1480.
21 MS. of the prince's correspondence in the Library of the Counts of Trigona
in Valencia; list of contents in Amador de los Ríos, 1861–5, VII, p. 19. The
same dilemma is debated by Antón de Montoro in *Cancionero de Montoro*
(ed. Cotarelo y Mori [Madrid, 1900], nos 44 and 45). See Massó Torrents,
1922, and Cummins, 1965.
22 BAE, 36 (Madrid, 1907), pp. 337–402; J. P. Wickersham Crawford, 'The
seven liberal arts in the *Visión delectable* of Alfonso de la Torre', *RR*,
IV (1913), 58–75, and 'The *Visión delectable* of Alfonso de la Torre, and
Maimonides's *Guide of the Perplexed*', *PMLA*, XXVIII (1913), 188–212;
Curtius, 1953, pp. 542–3. Crawford shows that Alfonso de la Torre's chief
sources were Al-Ghazālī, Isidore and Maimonides.
23 Ed. Carolina Michaëlis de Vasconcelos (2nd edn, Coimbra, 1922).
24 Anthón Durrea dedicated Dom Pedro's *Coplas* to Alonso de Aragón,
Archbishop of Saragossa, in 1478; see Bibliography. The poem 'sobre o
menospreço das cousas do mundo' is also in the *Cancioneiro geral*, fol. 75ʳ ff.,
although Dom Pedro is here described as 'fylho del rrey dom joan',
i.e. confused with his father.
25 'The queen is especially fond of this monastery which she calls her paradise'
(García Mercadal, *Viajes*, p. 296). So wrote Hieronymus Münzer, who
visited Castile in 1494–5. The queen built a royal hostel at the monastery in
1485.
26 'Peticiones originales hechas al señor Rey D. Enrique IV por diferentes
Arzobispos, Obispos, Caballeros y Grandes de estos reinos, Cigales 5 de
diciembre de 1464' (*CODOIN*, XXV, p. 371) (Original petitions submitted
to Henry IV by various archbishops, bishops, knights and grandees of these
realms. Cigales 5 December 1464).

Notes

27 Rožmitála a Blatné, *Travels*, pp. 91–2. According to Palencia, Enrique IV hated all Christian cults and was 'fond of the Mohammedan sect' (*Crónica*, I, pp. 86 and 176).

28 'The significance of the reign of Isabella the Catholic, according to her contemporaries', in Highfield, 1972, pp. 380–404, at p. 388.

29 Penna, *Prosistas*, p. 15. Valera recommends devaluing the coinage, making it a capital offence to export money, and relating the value of currency to the price of gold and silver.

30 Cited by Menéndez Pidal in Highfield, 1972, p. 390.

31 Cited by Keith Whinnom in his edition of San Pedro's *Obras*, II, p. 32.

32 Letter from Diego de Valera to Isabella, probably written in 1479, in Penna, *Prosistas*, p. 17.

33 García Mercadal, *Viajes*, p. 406. It seems that the queen was influenced by the Joachimist ideas of the Aragonese knight Diego Ruiz (Reeves, 1969, p. 222 n.).

34 'Un breve tratado que fizo Gómez Manrrique a mandamiento dela muy yllustre señora ynfanta Isabel, para unos momos que su excelencia fizo con los fados siguientes' (Foulché-Delbosc, *Cancionero castellano*, II, no. 391, pp. 101–2) (A brief treatise which Gómez Manrique composed by order of the very illustrious lady Princess Isabella for some mummings [*momos*] which were given by Her Excellency, with the following fates [or prophetic voices]).

35 *Libro de vida beata*, in Paz y Melia, *Opúsculos*, pp. 105–217, at pp. 126 and 166; Castro, 1971, p. 158.

36 *Epístola exhortatoria a las letras* in Paz y Melia, *Opúsculos*, pp. 209–17, at p. 216.

37 *Cancionero de Llavia*, fol. 39ᵛ; Rodríguez Valencia, 1970, III, p. 407.

38 Von Poppelau, in García Mercadal, *Viajes*, p. 319. An example of Isabella's anti-Semitism is reported by Rafael Floranes, 'Estudio de la profesión genealógica', *CODOIN*, XXV, pp. 217–18 n.

39 Encina maintains that Antonio Nebrija wrote his *Gramática* because he believed that, as regards purity of diction, 'más se podía temer el decendimiento que la subida', and he continues, 'assí yo por esta misma razón, creyendo nunca aver estado tan puesta en la cumbre nuestra poesía y manera de trobar, pareció me ser cosa provechosa poner la en arte y encerrarla debaxo de ciertas leyes y reglas porque ninguna antigüedad de tiempos le pueda traer olvido' (Temprano, 1973, pp. 326–7) (a decline was more to be feared than an ascent . . . therefore, for this same reason, believing that our poetry and style of versifying has never before reached such a summit, it seemed to me a profitable thing to set it down as an art and to define it under certain rules and regulations, so that no lapse of time may cast it into oblivion).

Part III

1 This was the year of Charles VI's coronation. The embassy must therefore have had a diplomatic function.

2 The king's choice of Pentecost could be taken to imply that he believed that poetry was an oracular gift, that it was a knowledge which, in the words of Juan Alfonso de Baena, was attained 'por gracia infusa del señor Dios' (*Canc. Baena*, I, p. 9; cf. Fraker, 1966, pp. 63–90).

3 These were guilds or fraternities, all of them originally religious in character, which existed at Valenciennes, Arras, Rouen, Caen, Amiens, Abbeville, Dieppe, Cambray, Evreu, Lille, Béthune and London. Their foundation was usually attributed to clerks who had had miraculous visions of the Virgin Mary. The 'confrérie de Notre-Dame des Ardents' at Arras was instituted to commemorate the Virgin's donation of a healing candle to two minstrels during a plague epidemic in 1105. The president of the society was called 'Prince', and the envoys of poems were frequently addressed to him. The influence of these popular institutions on the 'Court d'amours' obviously deserves to be studied in more detail. The term 'puy' derives from the Latin *podium*, an 'elevation', 'mountain' or 'platform'. It has been conjectured that the fame of the Virgin of Le Puy in the Midi may have caused religious societies named after her to spring up in northern France, or that a literary society actually existed at Le Puy which was a model for similar societies in the north. The term may be connected with the primitive notion that the Muses reside on the summit of a mountain, or, more simply, that it denotes the platform on which the poets recited their verses. See Cohen, 1915, pp. 39–44.

4 From P. V. Chalvet, *Poésies de Charles d'Orléans* (Grenoble, 1802), quoted in Potvin, 1886, p. 199.

5 Monthly song contests were held by the French 'Court d'amours', but are not mentioned in the Aragonese royal documents cited above.

6 From the sense one can infer that the text should read 'nuestras flechas', not 'nuestros fechos'.

7 The editor has inadvertently omitted one line of the manuscript: 'viles, en las variables assegurar, ni trabar' (fol. 17^r).

Part IV

1 Martín Villar and Eugenio Asensio are apparently the only scholars who have carried out research on the poet's life and works. P. M. X. de Urrea is sometimes mistakenly identified with the ambassador Pedro de Urrea, the poet's first cousin once removed. George Tickner made this error in his *History of Spanish Literature*, I (London, 1863), p. 433. This Pedro de Urrea

was a nephew of the poet's grandfather, Don Lope Ximénez de Urrea, the Viceroy of Sicily. See Bartolomé Leonardo y Argensola, *Primera parte de los Anales de Aragón* . . . *desde el año 1516 hasta el de 1620* (Logroño, 1630), I, p. 13. King Ferdinand sent him as an envoy to the pope and to the Emperor Maximilian I during the Italian wars from 1510 to 1513, and he fulfilled the role of mediator in an ecclesiastical dispute between Don Felipe Urríes and the Bishop of Huesca (a bastard son of Prince Charles of Viana), which lasted from 1516 until the latter's death in 1526. See Diego Josef Dormer, 1697, ch. xx, p. 257. His diplomatic correspondence was edited by Baron de Terratecy, *Política en Italia del Rey Católica 1507–16; correspondencia inédita con el embajador Vich*, Bibl. Reyes Católicos, Estudios, 12 (Madrid, 1963). The ambassador's father, also called Pedro de Urrea, corresponded with the poet Torrellas (cf. Asensio, *Eglogas dramáticas*, p. xv).

2 Atienza, 1954, p. 800; cf. Cadenas y Vicent, 1956, p. 55. Atienza erroneously states that the title of count was first conferred on 19 January 1508, to Don Lope. This was possibly the date when the poet's elder brother inherited the the title. The *Índice* affirms that the title was granted by King Ferdinand to 'López Ximénez de Urrea' in 1488.

3 *Diccionario de historia de España*, ed. German Bleiberg (3 vols, Madrid: Revista de Occidente, 1968–9), I, p. 187; II, p. 577.

4 *Cancionero*, ed. Villar, p. 115; *Cancionero* (Logroño, 1513), fol. xiv^{v}. Quotations are from the 1513 edition, with folio number in parentheses, followed by the page number in Villar. Félix de Latassa y Ortín, *Biblioteca nueva de los escritores aragoneses que florecieron desde 1500 hasta 1599* (Pamplona, 1798–1802), states that P. M. X. de Urrea married Doña María de Sesé on 8 February 1493. It is possible that he was referring to the date of the poet's betrothal.

5 Zurita, 1579–80, bk X, ch. lxxx.

6 Asensio speaks of Don Lope's imprisonment in the introduction to *Eglogas* (p. xliii) without disclosing the source of his information.

7 'Estava deposada con doña Catalina de Urrea, hija de don Lope Ximénez de Urrea . . . no tenía veynte y un años y era . . . muy favorecido del Rey y amado de toda la corte' (Zurita, 1579–80, bk XX, ch. lxxii).

8 Zurita, 1579–80, bk X, ch. xl. Urrea's only explicitly martial poem celebrates victory over the French in 1512: 'Con gran vitoria quedamos;/ muy gran mengua an recebido/los franceses, que an huydo' (fol. xlix^{v}; p. 481).

9 Zurita, 1579–80, bk XX, ch. xli. For details on the poet Juan Fernández de Heredia, see *Obras*, ed. Ferreres, pp. xi–xvii.

10 Fol. x, pp. 84–5; fol. xi, pp. 86–8; fol. xii, pp. 97–8; fol. xxviii, pp. 251–4; *Eglogas*, ed. Asensio, p. 91; *ibid.*, pp. 92–3. Other women in the *Cancionero* are Violante Voscana, Francisca Climente, Doña Aldura de Torres and Moragas, a Moorish girl.

11 *De rebus Hispaniae memoralibus* (Alcalá de Henares, 1533), Ep. VII, 16, pp. 92–3.

12 Fray Atilano de la Espina, 'Testamentos y sepulcro de los Excmos. Duques de Villahermosa', a chapter in *Registro universal de todas las escrituras que se hallan en el archivo de este santo y real monasterio de Veruela* (MS. of the year 1671), fol. 587 ff.; cf. *Canc.*, ed. Villar, p. x.

13 In the poem *Estando triste porque yva a una aldea* the poet expresses his frustration at being confined in Trasmoz as though he were a hermit or a fox on the run. His chief amusements are to hunt hares and rabbits, and to shoot thrushes in the orchard with his bow and arrow (fol. xi; p. 89).

14 'Narración de viaje', in Fadrique Enríquez de Rivera, *Este libro es de el viaje q̃ hize a Jerusalem . . . 24 de Noviembre de 1518 hasta 20 de Otubre de 1520* (Seville, 1606).

15 Prologue to Prince Juan in *Cancionero de las obras de Juan del enzina* (1496), fols iiʳ–vᵛ; Temprano, 1973. The structure of Urrea's *Cancionero*, based on a hierarchy of genres ranging from devotional and moralistic works to dramatic eclogues, seems to have been borrowed from Encina.

16 Urrea refers to *fino amor*: 'El amor qu'es fino amor/ningún galardón procura' (*Canc.*, fol. 40ʳ). Like Diego de San Pedro, Rodríguez del Padrón and others he later composed a palinode: 'Yo me arrepiento de verme fundado/en coplas tan vanas de amor de este mundo' (*Eglogas*, ed. Asensio, pp. 86–7).

17 Ed. Marcelino Menéndez y Pelayo, *Orígenes de la novela* (Madrid, 1905–15), II, p. 41.

18 Fernando de Rojas, *La Celestina*, ed. J. Cejador y Frauca (2 vols, Madrid: CC, 1913; repr. 1963), I, p. 6. It would seem that many of the writers who express a fear of *maldizientes* were New Christians. In an age when purity of faith was identified with purity of lineage such men lived under the tyranny of public opinion. Urrea's wife came from a family of *conversos*, and his attitude to Judaism and Islam is remarkably tolerant (see above p. 170).

19 *Il cortegiano* [written 1514–18], trans. Juan Boscán, *El cortesano* (Barcelona, 1534), introd. M. Menéndez y Pelayo, *RFE* Anejo, 25 (Madrid, 1942).

20 According to Graeco-Arabic medical treatises, music could dispel love-melancholy or *amor hereos*. In Juan de Lucena's *Vida beata* (Zamora, 1483) the following words are spoken by Santillana: 'La música, sçiēçia enamorada, despierta el sp̃u [spíritu], y la persona recrea; no es cosa tan suave como oyr diversidad de bozes señoras, entonadas sin discordia . . . segũd los mathemáticos, huyē della los malos sp̃us: no pueden sofrir los demonios el armonía' (fol. xiiᵛ).

21 *Obras poéticas*, ed. M. de Riquer et al. (Barcelona, 1957), Soneto CXVII (vol. I, p. 225). Boscán writes: 'sé que'n Amor no es término forçado/sólo scrivir aquel que dolor siente'.

22 Temprano, 1973, pp. 328–9. Stesichorus (*c.* 640–*c.* 555 BC), 'the reputed inventor of the choral heroic hymn,' was said to have been struck with blindness for having censured Helen. He is mentioned by Horace (Od., IV, ix, 8) and praised by Quintilian; see *Oxford Companion to Classical Literature*, ed. Paul Harvey (Oxford, 1937), pp. 406–7.

23 This metaphor inspired the title of J. Richard Andrews' *Juan del Encina: Prometheus in Search of Prestige*, UCPMP, 53 (Berkeley, 1959).

24 Apelles exemplifies for Castiglione the virtue of *desprecio* or *sprezzatura*, the capacity to display an air of graceful improvisation: 'Apeles reprehendió a Prothógenas, porque cuando pintaba, de nunca satisfacerse, jamás sabía quitar la mano de la tabla' (*El cortesano*, p. 62).

25 *The Novels of Juan de Flores and their European Diffusion* (New York, 1931), p. 14. The influence of Diego de San Pedro's *Cárcel de Amor* is also strong.

26 For a discussion of *ingenium* see Edward Glaser, 'Se a tanto me ajudar o engenho e arte: the poetics of the proem to *Os Lusíades*', in *Homenaje a Rodríguez-Moñino* (Madrid, 1966), I, pp. 197–204.

Select Bibliography

ABBOU, I. D. (1953), *Musulmans andalous et judéo-espagnols*. Casablanca: Antar.

ALDEA, QUINTÍN, et al. (1967), *El tránsito de la Edad Media al Renacimiento en la historia de España* (Cuadernos de Historia, 1). Madrid: CSIC, Instituto 'Jerónimo Zurita'.

ALFONSO X, *Las siete partidas del rey don Alfonso el Sabio cotejadas con varios códices antiguos por la Real Academia de la Historia*. 3 vols, Madrid, 1807 (facsimile repr. Ediciones Atlas, 1972).

ALLEN, DON CAMERON (1938), 'The degeneration of man and Renaissance pessimism', *SP*, XXXV, 202–27.

AMADOR DE LOS RÍOS, JOSÉ (1861–5), *Historia crítica de la literatura española*. 7 vols, Madrid: printed by J. Muñoz.

AMETLLER Y VIÑAS, JOSÉ (1903–23), *Alfonso V de Aragón en Italia y la crisis religiosa del siglo XV*. 3 vols, Gerona: Octavio Vader.

ANDREAS CAPELLANUS, *De amore libri tres*. Ed. E. Trojel. Copenhagen: Libraria Gadiana, 1892.

ANDREAS CAPELLANUS, *The Art of Courtly Love [De amore]*. Trans. J. J. Parry. New York: Columbia University Press, 1941.

ARAGONESES, MANUEL JORGE (1949), 'Los movimientos y luchas sociales en la baja edad media', in Viñas y Mey, 1949, pp. 275–423.

ARISTOTLE, *The Politics*. Trans. Ernest Barker. Oxford: Clarendon Press, 1948.

ASENSIO, EUGENIO (1957), *Poética y realidad en al cancionero peninsular de la edad media* (Biblioteca románica hispánica II, Estudios y ensayos, 34). Madrid: Gredos.

ATIENZA, JULIO DE (1954), *Nobiliario español: diccionario de apellidos españoles y de títulos nobiliarios*. Madrid: Aguilar.

AUBRUN, CHARLES V. (1948), 'Un traité de l'amour attribué à Juan de Mena', *BH*, L, 333–44.

AVERSÓ, LLUÍS D', *Torcimany*. Ed. J. M. Casas Homs. 2 vols, Barcelona: CSIC, 1956.

Select Bibliography

BAER, YITZHAK (1961–6), *A History of the Jews in Christian Spain*. Trans. from the Hebrew by Louis Schoffman. 2 vols, Philadelphia: Jewish Publication Society of America.

BAEZA, GASPAR DE (1570), *Prima pars tractatus de inope debitore ex castellana consuetudine creditoribus addicendo*. Granada: Apud Hugonem Menam.

BARBER, RICHARD (1974), *The Knight and Chivalry*. London: Sphere Books.

BECCADELLI, ANTONIO [Panormita] (1552), *Libro de los dictos y echos elegantes y graciosos del sabio Rey don Alonso de Aragón*. Trans. Joan de Molina. Saragossa: Miguel de Çapilla.

BENEYTO PÉREZ, JUAN (1949), 'La concepción jerárquica de la sociedad medieval en el pensamiento político español', in Viñas y Mey (1949), pp. 555–66.

BENITO RUANO, ELOY (1964), 'Fortuna literaria del Infante D. Enrique de Aragón', *Archivum* (Oviedo), XIV, 161–9.

BENITO RUANO, ELOY (1968), 'Lope de Stúñiga. Vida y cancionero', *RFE*, LI, 17–109.

BEZZOLA, RETO (1944–63), *Les Origines et la formation de la littérature courtoise en Occident (500–1200)*. 3 vols, Paris: Champion.

BLANCO-GONZÁLEZ, BERNARDO (1962), *Del cortesano al discreto: examen de una 'decadencia'*. Madrid: Gredos.

BLOCH, MARC (1965), *Feudal Society*. Trans. L. A. Manyon. 2nd edn, 2 vols, London: RKP.

BOASE, ROGER (1977), *The Origin and Meaning of Courtly Love. A Critical Study of European Scholarship*. Manchester: MUP.

BOFARULL Y MASCARÓ, PRÓSPERO DE, *Colección de documentos inéditos del Archivo General de la Corona de Aragón* (41 vols, 1847–1910). Vols V and VI, Barcelona, 1850.

BOHIGAS Y BALAGUER, PERE (1920–2), 'Profecies catalanes dels segles XIV i XV', *BBCat*, VI, 24–49.

BRADDY, HALDEEN (1947), *Chaucer and the French Poet Graunson*. Baton Rouge: Louisiana State University Press.

BULLOCK, I. (ed.), *Villena, Lebrija, Encina*. Cambridge: CUP, 1926.

BURCKHARDT, JACOB (1960), *The Civilization of the Renaissance in Italy*. Ed. Irene Gordon. New York: Mentor Books (based on 2nd German edn of 1868).

BURKE, PETER (1974), *Tradition and Innovation in Renaissance Italy. A Sociological Approach*. London: Collins.

CADENAS Y VICENT, VICENTE, et al. (1956), *Índice nobiliario español*. Madrid: Ediciones Hidalguía.

CAESAR, JULIUS, *The Gallic War* (LCL). Trans. H. J. Edwards. London: Heinemann, 1917.

CANCIONERO, *Cancionero de Baena*. Ed. José M. Azáceta. 3 vols, Madrid: CH, 1966.

Select Bibliography

CANCIONERO, 'Der spanische *Cancionero der Brit. Museums* (Ms.add.10431)', *RF*, X (1895–99), 1–176.

CANCIONERO, *El Cancionero catalán de la universidad de Zaragoza*. Ed. Mariano Baselga y Ramírez. Saragossa: Cecilio Gasca, 1896.

CANCIONERO, *Cancionero de Fernández de Ixar*. Ed. J. M. Azáceta. 2 vols, Madrid: CSIC, 1956.

CANCIONERO, *Cancionero general* [facsimile of 1511 edition]. Ed. Antonio Rodríguez-Moñino. Madrid: RAE, 1958.

CANCIONERO, *Suplemento del Cancionero general* [editions from 1514 to 1557]. Ed. A. Rodríguez-Moñino. Valencia: Castalia, 1959.

CANCIONERO, *Cancioneiro geral* [compiled by Garcia de Resende]. Lisbon, 1516; facsimile repr. New York: Hispanic Society of America, 1904.

CANCIONERO, *Le Chansonnier espagnol d'Herberay des Essarts* (BEHEH, fasc. 25). Ed. C. V. Aubrun. Bordeaux, 1951.

CANCIONERO, *El 'Cancionero de Palacio' (manuscrito no. 594)*. Ed. Francisca Vendrell de Millás. Barcelona: CSIC, Instituto 'Antonio de Nebrija', 1945.

CARAVAGGI, GIOVANNI (1969), 'Villasandino et les derniers troubadours de Castille', in *Mélanges offerts à Rita Lejeune*. Gembloux: Ducolet, I, pp. 395–421.

CARLOS, PRINCE OF VIANA (trans.) (1509), *La philosophía moral de Aristótel: es a saber Éthicas: Políthicas: y Económicas: En Romance*. Saragossa: Gorge Coci Alemán.

CARMEN CARLÉ, MARÍA DE (1961), 'Infanzones e hidalgos', *CHE*, XXXIII–XXXIV, 56–100.

CARRILLO DE HUETE, PEDRO, *Crónica del halconero de Juan II*. Ed. Juan de Mata Carriazo (Col. Crón. Esp., 8). Madrid, 1946.

CARTAGENA, ALFONSO DE (1477), *Este libro se llama doctrinal delos cavalleros. En que están copilados ciertas leyes E ordenanças que están enlos fueros E partidas delos rreynos de castilla E de León tocantes alos cavalleros.*

CARTELLIERI, OTTO (1929), *The Court of Burgundy. Studies in the History of Civilization*. London: Kegan Paul, Trench, Trubner & Co.

CASTRO, AMÉRICO (1954), *The Structure of Spanish History*. Trans. Edmund L. King. Princeton University Press.

CASTRO, AMÉRICO (1971), *The Spaniards. An Introduction to their History*. Trans. Willard F. King and Selma Margaretten. Berkeley, Los Angeles and London: University of California Press.

CHAUCER, GEOFFREY, *The Works*. Ed. F. N. Robinson. London and Oxford. OUP, 1974.

CHAYTOR, H. J. (1933), *A History of Aragon and Catalonia*. London: Methuen.

CHEYETTE, FREDRIC L. (ed.) (1968), *Lordship and Community in Medieval Europe. Selected Readings*. New York: Holt, Rinehart & Winston.

CHEYNEY, EDWARD P. (1936), *The Dawn of a New Era, 1250–1453*. New York and London: Harper & Brothers.

CHRÉTIEN DE TROYES, *Les Romans* (CFMA). Ed. Alexandre Micha. Vol. II, Paris: H. Champion, 1957.

COHEN, HELEN LOUISE (1915), *The Ballade*. New York: Columbia University Press.

COLMEIRO, MANUEL (1873), *Curso de derecho político según la historia de León y Castilla*. Madrid: F. Martínez García.

COLMEIRO, MANUEL (ed.), *Cortes de los antiguos reinos de León y de Castilla*. 6 vols, Madrid: RAH, 1883–1903.

COVARRUBIAS HOROZCO, SEBASTIÁN, *Tesoro de la lengua castellana*. 2 vols, Madrid: Melchor Sánchez, 1673–74.

CROCE, BENEDETTO (1894), *La Corte spagnuola di Alfonso d'Aragona a Napoli*. *Memoria* (Atti dell' Accademia Pontaniana, 24). Naples.

CUMMINS, JOHN G. (1963), 'Methods and conventions in the 15th-century poetic debate', *HR*, XXXI, 307–23.

CUMMINS, JOHN G. (1965), 'The survival in the Spanish *Cancioneros* of the form and themes of Provençal and Old French poetic debates', *BHS*, XLII, 9–17.

CURTIUS, ERNST ROBERT (1953), *European Literature and the Latin Middle Ages*. Trans. W. R. Trask. London: RKP.

DESDEVISES DU DÉZERT, G. (1889), *Don Carlos d'Aragon, Prince de Viana. Étude sur l'Espagne du nord au XVe siècle*. Paris: Armand Colin.

DÍAZ DE VIVAR, RODRIGO, *The Poem of the Cid*. Ed. Ian Michael; trans. Rita Hamilton and Janet Perry. Manchester: MUP; New York: Barnes & Noble, 1975.

DI CAMILLO, OTTAVIO (1976), *El humanismo castellano del siglo XV*. Valencia: Fernando Torres.

DÍEZ DE GAMES, GUTIERRE, *El Victorial. Crónica de don Pero Niño, conde de Buelna* (Col. Crón. Esp., 1). Ed. Juan de Mata Carriazo. Madrid: Espasa Calpe, 1940.

DORMER, DIEGO JOSEF (1697), *Anales de Aragón desde el año M.D. XXV ... hasta el de M.D. XL*. Saragossa.

DUMÉZIL, GEORGES (1958), *L'Idéologie tripartie des Indo-Européens* (Collection Latomus, 31). Brussels.

EIXIMENIS, FRANCESC, *Doctrina compendionsa* (Els Nostres Clàssics, 24). Ed. P. Martí. Barcelona: Editorial Barcino, 1929.

EIXIMENIS, FRANCESC, *Regiment de la cosa pública* [completed 1384; 1st edn Valencia: Cristòfal Cofman, 1499] (Els Nostres Clàssics, 13). Ed. P. Daniel de Molins de Rei. Barcelona: Editorial Barcino, 1927.

ENRÍQUEZ DEL CASTILLO, DIEGO, *Crónica del Rey don Enrique el Cuarto* (BAE, 70). Madrid, 1878.

FERGUSON, ARTHUR B. (1960), *The Indian Summer of English Chivalry. Studies in the Decline and Transformation of Chivalric Idealism.* Durham, North Carolina: Duke University Press.

FERNÁNDEZ DE BÉTHENCOURT, F. (1897–1920), *Historia genealógica heráldica de la monarquía española, casa real, y grandes de España.* 10 vols, Madrid: Enrique Teodoro.

FERNÁNDEZ DE HEREDIA, JUAN, *Obras.* Ed. Rafael Ferreres. Madrid: CC, 1955.

FERNÁNDEZ DE OVIEDO, GONZALO, *Libro de la cámara real del príncipe Don Juan e offiçios de su casa e serviçio ordinario* (SBE[7]). Madrid, 1870.

FLORANES, RAFAEL DE (1851–2), 'Estado de la profesión genealógica en tiempo de nuestro Canciller [Pedro López de Ayala]. Progresos de esta ciencia desde que él la restableció', *CODOIN*, XIX, 205–19.

FOULCHÉ-DELBOSC, R. (ed.), *Cancionero castellano del siglo XV* (NBAE, 19 and 22). Madrid, 1912–15.

FRAKER, CHARLES F. (1966), *Studies on the 'Cancionero de Baena'* (UNCSRLL, 61). Chapel Hill.

FRANK, ISTVÁN (1953–7), *Répertoire métrique de la poésie des troubadours* (Bibliothèque de l'École des Hautes Études, fasc. 302). 2 vols, Paris: Champion.

FROISSART, *Œuvres.* Ed. Kervyn de Lettenhove. 25 vols, Brussels: Victor Devaux, 1867–77.

GALLAGHER, PATRICK (1968), *The Life and Works of Garci Sánchez de Badajoz.* London: Tamesis.

GARCÍA MERCADAL, J. (ed. and trans.), *Viajes de extranjeros por España y Portugal.* Vol. I, Madrid: Aguilar, 1952.

GAYANGOS, PASCUAL DE (1875–81), *Catalogue of the Manuscripts in the Spanish Language in the British Museum* [ed. F. A. Bond]. 3 vols, London: the Trustees.

GERBET, MARIE-CLAUDE (1972), 'Les guerres et l'accès à la noblesse en Espagne de 1465 à 1592', *Mélanges de la casa de Velázquez*, VIII, 295–326.

GIMÉNEZ, ANTONIO (1976), 'Cortesanía e ideal aristocrático en *El Victorial*', *BBMP*, LII, 3–20.

GIMENO CASALDUERO, JOAQUÍN (1972), *La imagen del monarca en la Castilla del siglo XIV.* Madrid: Revista de Occidente.

GIRARD, ALBERT (1928), 'Le chiffre de la population de l'Espagne dans les temps modernes', *RHM*, III, 420–36.

GOMBRICH, E. H. (1974), 'The logic of vanity fair', in Paul A. Schilpp (ed.), *The Philosophy of Karl Popper.* La Salle, Illinois: Open Court Publishing, 1974, pp. 925–57.

GONZÁLEZ, TOMÁS (1829), *Censo de la población de las provincias y partidos de la Corona de Castilla en el siglo XVI.* Madrid: n.p.

GOWER, JOHN, *The Complete Works.* Ed. G. C. Macaulay. 4 vols, Oxford: Clarendon, 1899–1902.

GOWER, JOHN, *Confisión del amante por Joan Goer* [Escorial MS. G II 19]. Trans. Juan de Cuenca [*c.* 1415]; ed. Hermann Knust and Adolf Birch-Hirschfeld. Leipzig: D. Seele, 1909.

GREEN, V. H. H. (1971), *Medieval Civilization in Western Europe*. London: Arnold.

GUILLÉN DE SEGOVIA, PERO, *La gaya ciencia*. Ed. J. M. Casas Homs and O. J. Tuulio. 2 vols, Madrid: CH, 1962.

HEER, FRIEDRICH (1974), *The Medieval World: Europe from 1100 to 1350*. Trans. Janet Sondheimer. London: Sphere Books.

HIGHFIELD, J. R. L. (1965), 'The Catholic kings and titled nobility of Castile', in *Europe in the Late Middle Ages*, ed. J. R. Hale, J. R. L. Highfield and B. Smalley. London: Faber & Faber, pp. 358–85.

HIGHFIELD, ROGER (ed.) (1972), *Spain in the Fifteenth Century 1369–1516*. London and Basingstoke: Macmillan.

HOLZKNECHT, KARL JULIUS (1966 repr.), *Literary Patronage in the Middle Ages*. Philadelphia, 1923; repr. London: Frank Cass.

HORNIK, M. P. (ed.) (1965), *Collected Studies in Honour of Américo Castro's Eightieth Year*. Oxford: Lincombe Lodge.

HUIZINGA, JOHAN (1955 edn), *The Waning of the Middle Ages*. Trans. F. Hopman. Harmondsworth: Penguin [1st edn 1924].

JONES, R. O. (1962), 'Isabel la Católica y el amor cortés', *RLit*, XXI, 55–64.

KELSO, RUTH (1929), *The Doctrine of the English Gentleman in the Sixteenth Century* (UISLL, 14). Urbana.

KENDALL, PAUL MURRAY (1974), *Louis XI*. London: Sphere Books.

KNUST, HERMANN (ed.) (1878), *Castigos y dotrinas que un sabio dava a sus hijas*, in *Dos obras didácticas y dos leyendas sacadas de manuscritos de la Biblioteca del Escorial* (SBE, 6). Madrid, pp. 249–93.

KÖHLER, ERICH (1964), 'Observations historiques et sociologiques sur la poésie des troubadours', *CCMe*, VII, 27–51.

LA TOUR LANDRY, CHEVALIER DE, *The Book of the Knight of the Tower*. Trans. and printed by William Caxton; ed. M.Y. Offord (EETS, supplementary series 2). London, New York and Toronto: OUP, 1971.

LECOY, FÉLIX (1974), *Recherches sur 'Le Libro de Buen Amor'*. Ed. A. D. Deyermond. 2nd edn. Farnborough, Hants: Gregg International.

LE MEINGRE, JEAN [Boucicaut] (1620), *Histoire de Mre Iean de Boucicaut, Maréschal de France, Gouverneur de Gennes, et de ses mémorables faicts en France, Italie, et autres lieux, du Règne des Roys Charles V et Charles VI iusques l'an 1408*. Ed. Théodore Godefroy. Paris: Abraham Pacard.

LIDA, MARÍA ROSA (1946), 'La hipérbole sagrada en la poesía castellana del siglo XV', *RFH*, VIII, 121–30.

LLULL, RAMON, *The Book of the Ordre of Chivalry*. Trans. and printed by William Caxton from the French version. Ed. Alfred T. P. Byles (EETS, original series 168). London: OUP, 1926.

LLULL, RAMON, *Libre de l'orde de cavayleria* [*c.* 1275]. Ed. José Ramón de Luanco. Barcelona: Real Academia de Buenas Letras de Barcelona, 1901.

LÓPEZ DE MENDOZA, IÑIGO, Marquis of Santillana, *Letter of the Marquis of Santillana to Don Peter, Constable of Portugal*. Ed. Antonio R. Pastor and Edgar Prestage. Oxford: Clarendon, 1927.

LOYSEAU, CHARLES (1610), *Traité des ordres et simples dignitez*. Châteaudun: Abel l'Angelier.

LUNA, ÁLVARO DE, *Libro de las claras e virtuosas mugeres*. Ed. Don Manuel Castillo. Madrid and Toledo: Tip. de R. G. Menor, 1908.

MACKAY, ANGUS (1976), 'The ballad and the frontier in late medieval Spain', *BHS*, LIII, 15–33.

MACKAY, ANGUS (1977), *Spain in the Middle Ages. From Frontier to Empire, 1000–1500*. London and Basingstoke: Macmillan.

MADRAMANY Y CALATAYUD, MARIANO (1788), *Tratado de la nobleza de la Corona de Aragón*. Valencia: J. & T. de Orga.

MANN, JILL (1973), *Chaucer and Medieval Estates Satire: the Literature of Social Classes and the 'General Prologue' to the 'Canterbury Tales'*. Cambridge: CUP.

MANUEL, DON JUAN, *Libro de los estados*. Ed. R. B. Tate and I. R. Macpherson. Oxford: Clarendon, 1974.

MANUEL, DON JUAN, *Libro infinido y tractado de la asunçión* (Colección Filológica, 2). Granada, 1952.

MARAVALL, JOSÉ ANTONIO (1972 edn), *El mundo social de 'La Celestina'* (Biblioteca Románica Hispánica II, Estudios y Ensayos, 80). Rev. edn, Madrid: Gredos.

MARAVALL, JOSÉ ANTONIO (1972a), *Estado moderno y mentalidad social. Siglos XV a XVII*. 2 vols, Madrid: Ediciones de la Revista de Occidente.

·RCH, JAUME, *Diccionari de rims* (Biblioteca Filológica, 8). Ed. A. Griera. Barcelona, 1921.

MARCIAL D'AUVERGNE (1731), *Les Arrêts d'Amours avec l'Amant rendu Cordelier à l'Observance d'Amour.... Accompagnez des Commentaires juridiques & joyeux de Benoît de Cour, jurisconsulte*. 2 vols. Vol. I, Paris: Pierre Gandouin; vol. II, Amsterdam: François Changuion.

MÁRMOL CARVAJAL, LUIS DE (1573), *Descripción general de Áffrica con todos los successos de guerras que a avido entre los infieles y el pueblo Christiano, y entre ellos mesmos desde Mahoma hasta nuestros tiempos*. 11 bks, Granada: René Rabut.

Select Bibliography

Massó Torrents, Jaime (1922), *L'antiga escola poètica de Barcelona*. Barcelona: Caritat.

Massó Torrents, Jaime (1923), *La cançó provençal en la literatura catalana*. Barcelona: Institut d'Estùdis Catalans.

Massó Torrents, Jaime (1927), *El princep de Viana i les seves relacions literaries; discurs en la sessió inaugural del curs acadèmic de 1926-27, celebrada el 4 de desembre 1926*. Barcelona.

Mata Carriazo, Juan de (ed.), *Crónica de Álvaro de Luna* [attributed to Gonzalo Chacón] (Col. Crón. Esp., 2). Madrid, 1940.

Mata Carriazo, Juan de (ed.), *Hechos del condestable Don Miguel Lucas de Iranzo* [attributed to Pedro de Escavias] (Col. Crón. Esp., 3). Madrid, 1940.

Mathew, Gervase (1968), *The Court of Richard II*. London: John Murray.

Menéndez y Pelayo, Marcelino, *Antología de poetas líricos españoles*. Edicion nacional. 10 vols, Madrid: CSIC, 1944-45.

Menéndez y Pelayo, Marcelino (1946), *Poetas de la corte de Don Juan II* [extract from *Antología*]. Buenos Aires: Austral.

Menéndez Pidal, Ramón (1914), '*Elena y María* (Disputa del clérigo y el caballero). Poesía leonesa inédita del siglo XIII', *RFE*, I, 52-96.

Merriman, R. B. (1918-34), *The Rise of the Spanish Empire*. 2 vols, New York: Macmillan.

Milán, Luis (1561), *Libro intitulado el Cortesano. . . . Donde se verá lo que deve tener por regla y prática*. Valencia: Ioan de Arcos.

Miller, Townsend (1972), *Henry IV of Castile 1425-1474*. London: Victor Gollancz.

Mitré Fernández, E. (1968), *Evolución de la nobleza en Castilla bajo Enrique III (1396-1406)*. Valladolid: Universidad de Valladolid.

Mohl, Ruth (1933), *The Three Estates in Medieval and Renaissance Literature*. New York: Columbia University Press.

Moller, Herbert (1958-9), 'The social causation of the courtly love complex', *CSSH*, I, 137-63.

Moncada, Sancho de (1619), *Restauración política de España*. Toledo: Luis Sánchez.

Monte, Alberto del (1958), 'La *Disertación sobre el amor* attribuita a J. de Mena', in *Civiltà e poesia romanze*. Bari: Adriatica Editrice, pp. 148-69.

Moore, Samuel (1913), 'General aspects of literary patronage in the Middle Ages', *Library*, IV, 369-92.

Moreno de Vargas, Bernabé (1622), *Discursos de la nobleza de España*. Madrid: A. Martín.

Mousnier, Roland (1969). *Les Hiérarchies sociales de 1450 à nos jours*. Paris: PUF.

Moxó, Salvador de (1970), 'La nobleza castellano-leonesa en la Edad Media. Problemática que suscita su estudio en el marco de una historia social', *His*, XXX, no. 114, 5-68.

NAVAGIERO, ANDREA (1563), *Il Viaggio fatto in Spagna et in Francia*. Venice: Domenico Farri.

NELLI, RENÉ (1952), *L'Amour et les mythes du cœur*. Paris: Hachette.

NELLI, RENÉ, and LAVAUD, RENÉ (1966), *Les Troubadours: le trésor poétique de l'occitanie*. 2 vols, Paris: Desclée de Brouwer.

OTALORA, JUAN ARCE DE (1553), *De nobilitatis, et immunitatis hispaniae causis (quas hidalguía appellunt) deque Regalium tributorum (quos pechos dicunt) iure, ordine, iudico, et excusatione summa, seu tractatus*. Granada [Sancho de Lebrija].

PALENCIA, ALONSO DE, *Crónica de Enrique IV*. Trans. A. Paz y Melia. 5 vols, Madrid: Tip. de la Revista de archivos, 1904–9.

PALMA [Alonso de la?], EL BACHILLER, *Divina retribución sobre la caída de España en el tiempo del noble rey Don Juan el Primero [c. 1479]*. Ed. J. M. Escudero de la Peña (SBE [18]). Madrid, 1879.

PAZ Y MELIA, A. (ed.), *Opúsculos literarios de los siglos XIV a XVI* (SBE, 9). Madrid, 1892.

PEDRO, DOM, Constable of Portugal, *Coplas fechas por el muy illustre Señor infante don Pedro de portugal: en los quales ay Mil versos con sus glosas contenientes del menosprecio: e contempto delas cosas fermosas del mundo: e demostrando la su vana e feble beldad* [Lisbon, c. 1499].

PENNA, MARIO (ed.), *Prosistas castellanos del siglo XV* (BAE, 116). Madrid, 1959.

PÉREZ DE GUZMÁN, FERNÁN, *Generaciones y semblanzas*. Ed. R. B. Tate. London: Tamesis, 1965.

PESCADOR, CARMELA (1961), 'La caballería popular en León y Castilla', *CHE*, XXXIII–XXXIV, 101–238.

PICCOLOMINI, AENEAS SYLVIUS [Pius II], *Memoirs of a Renaissance Pope: the Commentaries of Pius II. An Abridgement*. Trans. Florence A. Gragg; ed. Leona C. Gabel. New York: G. P. Putnam's, 1959.

POPPER, K. R. (1966), *The Open Society and its Enemies*. 2 vols, London: RKP [first edn 1945].

POTVIN, C. (1886), 'La Charte de la Cour d'Amour de l'année 1401', *BARB*, 3rd series, XII, 191–220.

PRESCOTT, WILLIAM H. (1841), *History of the Reign of Ferdinand and Isabella the Catholic*. 2 vols, rev. edn, London: George Routledge.

PRÉVITÉ-ORTON, C. W. (1936), 'Epilogue', in *The Cambridge Medieval History*. Vol. VIII, Cambridge: CUP.

PULGAR, FERNANDO DEL, *Claros varones de Castilla*. Ed. R. B. Tate. Oxford: Clarendon, 1971.

PUYMAIGRE, T. J. BOUDET DE (1873), *La Cour littéraire de Juan II, roi de Castille*. 2 vols, Paris: Lib. A. Franck.

RAHNER, HUGO (1965), *Man at Play, or did You ever Practise Eutropelia?* Trans. Brian Battershaw and Edward Quinn. London: Burns & Oates.

Select Bibliography

REEVES, MARJORIE (1969), *The Influence of Prophecy in the Later Middle Ages. A Study in Joachimism*. Oxford: Clarendon.

REY, EUSEBIO (1958), 'La polémica suscitada por Américo Castro en torno a la interpretación histórica de España', *Razón y Fe*, CLVII, 343–62.

RICCIO, MICHELE (1543), *De re di Francia, libri III, De re d'Ispagna, libri III.*... Trans. from Latin by Giovanni Tatti. Venice: Vincenzo Vaugris al segno d'Erasmo.

RICKETTS, PETER T. (1972), 'The hispanic tradition of the *Breviari d'amor* by Matfre Ermengaud of Béziers', *Hispanic Studies in Honour of Joseph Manson*. Ed. Dorothy M. Atkinson and Anthony H. Clarke. Oxford: Dolphin Book Co., pp. 227–53.

RIQUER, MARTÍN DE (1967), *Caballeros andantes españoles*. Madrid: Austral.

RIQUER, MARTÍN DE (1964), *Història de la literatura catalana*. 4 vols, Barcelona: Edicions Ariel.

RIQUER, MARTÍN DE (1975), *Los trovadores. Historia literaria y textos*. 3 vols, Barcelona: Planeta.

RODRÍGUEZ DE LENA, PERO, *Libro del passo honroso*. Ed. M. de Riquer. Madrid: Espasa-Calpe, 1970. Facsimile edn by F. Arroyo Ilero (Textos Medievales, 38). Valencia, 1970.

RODRÍGUEZ DEL PADRÓN, JUAN, *Obras* (SBE, 22). Ed. Antonio Paz y Melia. Madrid, 1884.

RODRÍGUEZ-PUÉRTOLAS, JULIO (1972), *De la Edad Media a la edad conflictiva: estudios de literatura española*. Madrid: Gredos.

RODRÍGUEZ VALENCIA, VICENTE (1970), *Isabel la Católica en la opinión de españoles y extranjeros. Siglos XV al XX*. 3 vols, Valladolid: Instituto 'Isabel la Católica' de Historia Eclesiástica.

ROMERO, J. L. (1944), 'Sobre la biografía española del siglo XV y los ideales de vida', *CHE*, I–II, 115–38.

ROTH, CECIL (1964), *The Spanish Inquisition*. New York: W. W. Norton.

ROUND, NICHOLAS G. (1962), 'Renaissance culture and its opponents in fifteenth-century Castile', *MLR*, LVII, 204–15.

ROUND, NICHOLAS G. (1970), 'Garci Sánchez de Badajoz and the revaluation of *cancionero* poetry', *FMLS*, VI, 178–87.

ROŽMITÁLA A BLATNÉ, Baron J. L. z., *The Travels of Leo of Rozmital through Germany, Flanders, England, Spain, Portugal and Italy 1465–1467* (Hakluyt Society, 2nd series, 108). Translated from German and Latin by Malcolm Letts. Cambridge: CUP, 1957.

RUBIÓ Y BALAGUER, J. (1943), *Vida española en la época gótica*. Barcelona: Editorial Alberto Martín.

RUBIÓ Y LLUCH, ANTONIO, *Documents per l'història de la cultura catalana mig-eval*. 2 vols, Barcelona: Institut d'Estùdis Catalans, 1908–21.

RUIZ, JUAN, *Libro de Buen Amor*. Ed. and trans. Raymond S. Willis. Princeton University Press, 1972.

RUSSELL, J. C. (1958), 'Late ancient and medieval population', *Transactions of the American Philosophical Society*, XLVIII, no. 3, 1–152.

RUSSELL, P. E. (1955), *The English Intervention in Spain and Portugal in the Time of Edward III and Richard II.* Oxford: Clarendon.

RUSSELL, P. E. (1967), 'Arms versus letters: towards a definition of Spanish fifteenth-century humanism', in *Aspects of the Renaissance. A Symposium.* Ed. A. R. Lewis. Austin and London: University of Texas Press, pp. 47–58.

RUSSELL, P. E. (ed.) (1975), *Spain. A Companion to Spanish Studies.* London: Methuen.

RYDER, ALAN (1976), *The Kingdom of Naples under Alfonso the Magnanimous. The Making of a Modern State.* Oxford: Clarendon.

SALAZAR Y CASTRO, LUIS (1688), *Advertencias históricas sobre las obras de algunos doctos escritores modernos.* Madrid: M. de Llanos y Guzmán.

SALAZAR DE MENDOZA, PEDRO (1608), *Origen de las dignidades seglares de Castilla y León.* Toledo.

SÁNCHEZ DE ARÉVALO, RODRIGO, *Cy commence le livre intitulé le miroir de vie humaine fait par rodorique hispaignol évesque de zamorensis . . . translaté de latin en françois par frère iulien [Macho] docteur en théologie.* Lyon: Bartholomieu Buyer, 1477.

SÁNCHEZ DE ARÉVALO, RODRIGO, *[Speculum vitae humanae] [S]Anctiss[i]mo ac clementissimo in christo parti domino: domino Paulo secundo . . . pontifici maximo.* Rome: Petri de Maximo, 1468 [ed. A. Morel Fatio (Gesellschaft für Romanische Literatur, 10). Dresden, 1906].

SÁNCHEZ DE ARÉVALO, RODRIGO, *Suma de la política.* Ed. Juan Beneyto Pérez (Publicaciones del Seminario de las Doctrinas Políticas, 2). Madrid: CSIC, 1944.

SÁNCHEZ CANTÓN, F. J. (1919), 'El *Arte de trovar* de Don Enrique de Villena', *RFE*, VI, 158–80.

SANCHIS I SIVERA, JOSEP (ed.), *Dietari del capellá d'Anfos el Magnànim* [attributed to Melchor Miralles]. Valencia: Acción Bibliográfica Valenciana, 1932.

SAN PEDRO, DIEGO DE, *Obras completas.* Ed. Keith Whinnom. 2 vols, Madrid: Castalia, 1971–3.

SANPERE Y MIQUEL, SALVADOR (1878), *Las costumbres catalanas en tiempo de Juan I.* Gerona: Vicente Dorca.

SANTOTÍS, CRISTÓBAL (1591), *Vita Pauli Burgensis.* Burgos: Felipe de Junta.

SCHOLBERG, KENNETH R. (1965), *Spanish Life in the Late Middle Ages* (UNCSRLL, 57). Chapel Hill.

SEMPERE Y GUARIÑOS, JUAN (1788), *Historia del luxo.* 2 vols, Madrid. Repr. Ediciones Atlas, 1973.

SERRANO, LUCIANO (1942), *Los conversos. Don Pablo de Santa María y Don Alfonso de Cartagena, obispos de Burgos, gobernantes, diplomáticos y escritores.* Madrid: CSIC, Instituto 'Arias Montano'.

Select Bibliography

SERVAIS, VICTOR (1865–7), *Annales historiques du Barrois de 1352 à 1411, ou histoire politique, civile, militaire et ecclésiastique du Duché de Bar sous le règne de Robert, duc de Bar.* 2 vols, Bar-le-Duc: Contant-Laguerre.

SEVERIN, DOROTHY SHERMAN (1976), *The 'Cancionero de Martínez de Burgos'. A Description of its Contents, with an Edition of the Prose and Poetry of Juan Martínez de Burgos* (EHT, 12). Exeter University.

SIMÓN DÍAZ, JOSÉ (1963–5), *Bibliografía de la literatura hispánica.* Vol. III. 2nd edn, 2 parts, Madrid.

SORIA, ANDRÉS (1956), *Los humanistas de la corte de Alfonso el Magnánimo (según los epistolarios).* Granada: Universidad de Granada.

SOUTHERN, R. W. (1970), *Western Society and the Church in the Middle Ages.* Harmondsworth: Penguin.

SOUZA, ROBERTO DE (1964), 'Desinencias verbales correspondientes a la persona *vos/vosotros* en el *Cancionero general* (Valencia, 1511)', *Fi*, X, 1–95.

STÉFANO, LUCIANA DE (1966), *La sociedad estamental de la baja Edad Media española a la luz de la literatura de la época.* Caracas: Universidad Central de Venezuela.

STEUNOU, JACQUELINE, and KNAPP, LOTHAR (1975–), *Bibliografía de los cancioneros castellanos del siglo XV y repertorio de sus géneros poéticos* (Documents, études et répertoires, 22). 3 vols, Paris: Centre National de la Recherche Scientifique.

STONE, LAWRENCE (1965), *The Crisis of the Aristocracy 1558–1641.* Oxford: Clarendon.

SUÁREZ FERNÁNDEZ, LUIS (1959), *Nobleza y monarquía: puntos de vista sobre la historia castellana del siglo XV* (CHM, 15). University of Valladolid.

TAFUR, PERO, *Andanças e viajes.* Ed. José María Ramos. Madrid, 1954.

TATE, ROBERT B. (1970), *Ensayos sobre la historiografía peninsular del siglo XV.* Madrid: Gredos.

TAWNEY, R. H. (1926), *Religion and the Rise of Capitalism.* London: J. Murray.

TEMPRANO, JUAN CARLOS (1973), 'El *Arte de poesía castellano* de Juan del Encina (edición y notas)', *BRAE*, LIII, 321–50.

THIBAULT, MARCEL (1903), *Isabeau de Bavière, reine de France. La jeunesse 1370–1405.* Paris: Didier.

TORRES AMAT, FÉLIX (1836), *Memorias para ayudar a formar un diccionario crítico de los escritores catalanes.* Barcelona: Impr. de J. Verdaguer.

TOYNBEE, ARNOLD (1935–54), *A Study of History.* 10 vols, London: OUP.

TUCOO-CHALA, PIERRE (1959), *Gaston Fébus et la vicomté de Béarn 1343–1391.* Bordeaux: Impr. Bièvre.

VALDEAVELLANO, LUIS A. G. DE (1968), *Curso de historia de las instituciones españolas de los orígenes al final de la edad media.* Madrid: Revista de Occidente (rev. edn 1970).

VALERA, DIEGO DE, *Espejo de verdadera nobleza,* in Penna, *Prosistas,* pp. 89–116.

Select Bibliography

VALERA, DIEGO DE, Tratado delos rieptos e desafíos que entre cavalleros e hijos dalgo se acostumbran hazer según las costumbres de españa, francia e ynglaterra [dedicated to Afonso V of Portugal; printed c. 1500].

VALERA, DIEGO DE, Tratado en defensa de virtuosas mugeres (BAE, 116). Madrid, 1959.

VEBLEN, THORSTEIN (1973 repr.), The Theory of the Leisure Class. An Economic Study in the Evolution of Institutions. Boston: Houghton Mifflin [1st edn 1899].

VENDRELL DE MILLÁS, FRANCISCA (1933), La corte literaria deA lfonso V y tres poetas de la misma [Juan de Dueñas, Pedro de Santa Fe and Juan de Tapia]. Madrid: Tipografía de Archivos.

VICENS VIVES, JAIME (1953), Juan II de Aragón, 1398-1479. Monarquía y revolución en la España del siglo XV. Barcelona: Editorial Teide.

VICENS VIVES, JAIME (1967), Approaches to the History of Spain. Trans. Joan Connelly Ullman. Berkeley and Los Angeles: University of California Press.

VICENS VIVES, JAIME (1969), An Economic History of Spain. Princeton University Press.

VILLENA, ENRIQUE DE, Los doze trabajos de Hércules [completed 1417]. Ed. Margherita Morreale. Madrid: RAE, 1958.

VIÑAS Y MEY, CARMELO (ed.) (1949), Estudios de historia social de España. Madrid: CSIC.

WEBER, MAX (1948), Essays in Sociology. Trans. and ed. H. H. Gerth and C. Wright Mills. London and Boston: RKP.

XIMÉNEZ DE URREA, PEDRO MANUEL (1513), Cancionero. Logroño: Arnao Guillén de Brocar.

YANGÜAS Y MIRANDA, JOSÉ (1840), Diccionario de antigüedades del reino de Navarra. 2 vols, Pamplona.

ZURITA, GERÓNIMO, Anales de la Corona de Aragón. 6 vols, Saragossa: Lorenço de Robles, 1610-21 [first edition 1562-8].

ZURITA, GERÓNIMO, Indices rerum ab Aragoniae regibus gestarum ab initiis regni ad annum MCDX. Saragossa: Dominica Portonariis de Ursinis, 1578.

ZURITA, GERÓNIMO (1579-80), Segunda parte de los Anales de la Corona de Aragón, 4 vols. Saragossa.

Index

213